I Guess I'll Just Keep on Walking

Continuing the Search for Meaning

Noel Braun

ABOUT THE AUTHOR

Noel Braun commenced his working career as a country school teacher, then moved into a corporate career, which took him from Melbourne to Perth and Sydney. He has had a lifelong passion for writing and wrote the first words of his novels nearly forty years ago. After a busy career and raising a family of four, he has found the time in retirement to fulfil his long-held ambition and see his work in print.

Noel has published two novels: *Friend and Philosopher* and *Whistler Street*. He has also published a memoir, *No Way to Behave at a Funeral*, which describes his journey following the death by suicide of his wife Maris, and *The Day Was Made for Walking*, his first exploration of Le Chemin de Saint-Jacques-de-Compostelle and El Camino de Santiago de Compostela. He is working on other manuscripts and on developing a new career in writing.

Noel lives in the Snowy Mountains. He is a keen walker and enjoys getting out in the national parks surrounding his home.

Published in Australia by Sid Harta Publishers Pty Ltd,
ABN: 46 119 415 842
23 Stirling Crescent, Glen Waverley, Victoria
3150 Australia
Telephone: +61 3 9560 9920, Facsimile: +61 3 9545 1742
E-mail: author@sidharta.com.au

First published in Australia 2017
This edition published 2017
Copyright © Noel Braun 2017
Cover design, typesetting: WorkingType Studio

The right of Noel Braun to be identified as the Author of the Work has been asserted in accordance with the Copyright, Designs and Patents Act 1988.

Braun, Noel
I Guess I'll Just Keep on Walking
ISBN: 978-1-921030-68-0
pp280

Dedicated to the memory of my cherished wife, Maris,
whose support, confidence and quiet encouragement
inspired me, and continues to do so

CONTENTS

Preamble

Another Day for Walking

1

Nul ne peut atteindre l'aube sans passer par le chemin de la nuit
(No one can reach the dawn without passing through the night)
Khalil Gibran

Here we go again! The plane's ready for take-off. Monday, 22nd July 2013. The day has arrived, so quickly after all the work preparing my body. My French guide book describes this Camino route as solitary and much less travelled. Much of it is in forests, its terrains are diverse, the hills are serious, with soaring altitudes even before climbing the Pyrenees. Therefore:

'Le marcheur doit s'y préparer et être en bonne condition physique.'
(The walker should prepare himself well and be
in good physical shape).

Every Camino route requires a decent level of fitness. This one sounded far more arduous. I attended the gym every other day and toiled with Jenni, my gym trainer. She put a lot of work into preparing me for my earlier walks; she was equally enthusiastic, bossy and caring. I was her oldest client (eighty years of age) but she worked me hard and took no prisoners. Really, she was proud of me and told everyone what her Noel was up to. With her encouragement, I attended gym classes in yoga, Pilates and stretching, often the lone male in a class of older biddies or young leotard clad dolls. I went for long walks with a fully loaded pack in the National Park adjacent to my home.

I was hurting in the left leg, knee and hip. Some days they

ached separately, other days they joined together in a painful chorus. I didn't want to look too closely into the cause. They weren't going to stop me. I visited my chiropractor, Steven, one of my scouts back in the eighties. I had sessions with the gym physio, Gary. He could see that staying at home wasn't an option, so he prepared a sheet of stick figures with exercises after each day's walking. I had a check-up with my cardiologist. He had inserted a stent into my left anterior artery back in May 2007. He did a stress test and had me walking on the treadmill at 7 km per hour up an incline level of 17. No wonder I was exhausted. He said he detected 'something' and had me return for a sound echo test with one of his colleagues. He had me doing more stress testing. He wanted to see my heart during exercise and at rest. This second cardiologist said: *'You can pack your bags. I can detect a difference but it's very subtle.'* My cardiologist didn't actually say *'Don't go!'* but he stressed that men of my age usually don't go in for long distance walking in difficult terrain. No, of course not, they go on cruises and sit around in deck chairs drinking beer and putting on weight.

A distraction was seeing my latest book through to publication. I was hoping to see the final galley print before going overseas. I began writing as soon as I returned from Spain and France in October 2011. My aim was to check the copies, make any final corrections and give the approval for the commercial run. The book would be ready for release by the time I returned, I hoped. In frustration, I checked the letter box every day up to the last. I was annoyed because checking the galleys would be delayed by another three months and the book would not be available until 2014. I gave the publisher an address in Montpellier, France. The galley print of my first book chased me across the world back in 2005 and eventually found me in

Oregon, USA. I read the print on internal flights and finished it late at night in a hostel in Washington DC.

I should have known what to pack, having already walked the Camino twice. On my first trip, I set out with a backpack of eighteen kilos. By the end of the second trip I had reduced the weight to ten. I travelled with the essentials. Yet I was tempted to take this and that item just in case... I should know by now.

I recalled the lessons learned from my two earlier pilgrimages.

- Travel lightly — that applies to life as well.
- Stay with the moment. Don't go fretting about what might happen. What I worry about never happens.
- I'm far more resourceful than I think. I may have thought that I'd struggle with the languages or be hopeless with directions, or be awkward with new people, or couldn't cope with a crisis. But I was thrown into the deep end, and not only survived, but thrived.
- Never think that you are in control or that your plans will work out. It's a bonus if they do. Recognise that you can never be dead sure about anything. Life is full of uncertainties, ambiguities and contradictions. Leave it to God. Things work out in the end. Recall the words of Descartes: *'Except for our thoughts, there is nothing absolutely in our power.'*

I was about to travel to France and set out on the Way of St James, or in French Le Chemin de Saint-Jacques de Compostelle, or in Spanish, El Camino de Santiago de Compostela. It's a series of long distance footpaths across Europe comprising the great routes of pilgrimage towards Santiago de Compostela in Western Galicia, Spain. For over a thousand years, pilgrims have been following these routes, their destination being the supposed burial place of Saint James the Apostle. The practice of pilgrimage has been resurrected in modern times and today's pilgrims still follow much the same paths taken by the medieval pilgrims. They climb the same mountains, cross the same rivers and pass the same villages, churches, chapels and cathedrals.

I had already traversed two of these routes. In 2010, I walked the route known as La Via Podensis in France from Le Puy-en-Velay to Saint-Jean-Pied-de-Port at the foot of the Pyrenees. In 2011, I returned to Saint-Jean-Pied-de-Port, crossed the Pyrenees and followed the route known as the Camino Francés through Spain to Santiago de Compostela.

I was about to tackle a third route. I dedicated my walking to the memory of my wife Maris. She died eight and a half years previously by suicide after years of suffering from depression. Her image will never vanish into the mists of memory. I have eight photographs of her at various stages of our lives together on display throughout my home. In my bedroom, there are two photos of Maris and me, taken a few months before her death by my daughter Angela. *'Act like you're sixteen'* was her instruction. One shows us cuddling together, which appears on the dedication page of this book. A smile masked her torment. The other photo has us kissing. A drawing of my *'My Gran'* by her six-year-old granddaughter, Tessa, hangs by my bed. Overlooking my dining table are four photographs taken at various stages of Maris' life. One is when I met her. She was twenty-two. The next photo was taken on our wedding day. She was twenty-five. Then I have a photo of the family — Angela, Jacinta, Stephen and Tim, Maris and I. She was due to go into hospital for a lung operation — removal of fungus from her lung. She decided in her matter-of-fact manner a photo session with a professional was needed, in case she didn't survive. We had never sat for a formal photo of the family. She was thirty-nine. The fourth was taken a few months before her death. She was sixty-six. Her face shows the strain of years of struggle against her insidious oppressor. On a bookcase stands a photo of us signing the register at our wedding. It exudes beauty and the joy of anticipation of our life together. We were married for forty-two years.

In front of these photos are candles. I light one regularly, perhaps when some trigger ignites the ever-present hollow in my heart. Maris is always with me. I talk to her and sometimes I sense her talking to me, chastising me or telling me what to do. (Whenever she said 'Noël!' with an emphasis on the two syllables, I knew I was in trouble.) She travelled with me every painful and joyful step of the way across France and Spain. I lit candles for her in chapels and churches. Maris continues to be with me, albeit in another form. She lives in my heart and my soul. She walks with me, every painful and enlightening step of the way.

There are many reasons why people undertake the Camino. For some, it's a long-distance walk, a holiday, a break from the routine of their daily lives. Others are there for the adventure of travelling in another country. Others are curious: What's this Camino about? Many enjoy the cultural aspects; history surrounds the pilgrims along the way like passing through an outdoor museum. For many, motivations are spiritual. They remove themselves from the bustle and, in silence and solitude, seek meaning in their lives. They may be processing bereavement, a major crisis, a significant transition such as retirement. Those who have religious yearning may have a desire for intense prayer or may feel they will find God on the way. The daily grind can numb awareness of the possibility of spiritual and emotional insights in our everyday life.

The physical pilgrimage is a metaphor for an inner spiritual journey. It's like travelling through two parallel landscapes.

The physical journey is interwoven and in dialogue with the inner spiritual journey. Enduring deprivation and hardship is an important part of the experience. I was continuing a journey of self-discovery that would involve many dark passages before reaching the light. Undertaking another Camino route was a compulsion as strong as any addiction. My left leg was a new factor. How would it stand up to another 700 km? How would I go? I thought of some French graffiti:

> 'Il faut marcher doucement and lentement.'
> (One must walk gently and slowly).

I was determined not to rush. I had given myself plenty of time. I would savour every step of the way. I was thankful for the health, fitness, confidence and enthusiasm to undertake such an arduous challenge at my age.

When I told my friends, many just shook their heads. Out of awe or envy? Everyone wished me well. I felt the pressure of their expectations. Now that I had committed myself, I knew I had to complete the task. Jo, one of my Lifeline friends, walked the Camino Francés with her daughter. Often on those days when they were almost done, they used to say to each other, 'If Noel can do it, so can we.'

Earlier that year I was guest speaker at a Probus club meeting. I spoke about the Camino, its history and the distances involved. One of the members asked if I had actually walked it. His tone suggested that any reasonable person wouldn't hear of it. When I replied that I had walked 1500 km, first through France and then across Spain I sensed his disbelief. Most of my listeners had that same look of scepticism. I kid you not; one smart Alec asked if self-flagellation was my next project. I sensed that the travellers in this audience went in for cruises where every comfort was taken care of and their sense of adventure was expressed in trying a few new drinks from the cocktail list. (Do I hear my Maris saying: *'Noël! Don't be so dismissive.'*)

I was an eighty-year-old adventurer. This was no Sunday arvo stroll in the park but I was desperate to undertake this walk. I wanted it with a determination that threatened to burst out of my skin and join the forces of creation. I'd set myself a task likely to make people decades younger blanch at the mere thought. I wanted to be ready for anything — well, not exactly anything — I wanted to see this Camino through.

My sense of adventure was about to be tested.

2. Today is a gift

My daughter, Angela, drove me to the airport. She'd had a gut-full of managing three demanding children and balancing family life with full-time work. She wished she could leave her family behind and escape with me. Her final words: '*Go for it, Dad!*' The plane was about a third full, a contrast to my earlier overseas flights when every seat was taken. I sat in the window seat and watched Australia pass beneath me in the early afternoon; another contrast to earlier flights which left in the darkness of night. The plane passed through a blue sky into grey cloud masses edged with white lumps and emerged in a blaze of sunlight. I was already a pilgrim, passing through an inaccessible timeless and mysterious world. Outback Australia on a fine day! Red sand hills rippling like waves stretched across the vast landscape. Aboriginal tribes probably called this home for thousands of years and just as likely it was still home. Did any live below in this empty land? There were no signs of modern living, no houses, no tracks across this pristine and undisturbed terrain. The ancient Aboriginal people roamed this land long before Europeans. In its silence and solitude, they knew its secrets, secrets that I and other non-indigenous people will never know. It was part of their creation just as the beautiful French and Spanish countryside and mountains were part of me in my earlier Camino walks.

We left behind the Australian land mass and below there was nothing to look at or admire. I ignored the inflight entertainment and reflected. What I had learned from my two previous pilgrimages is that I am the judge and jury of what my limits are and what I am capable of. As I look forward to this next pilgrimage, I am armed with the knowledge that age had not limited me. I'd like to think my aging has stopped here. My world has widened rather than narrowed, which seems to be the fate of many people my age. I remember my C's and S's, the formula I developed shortly after Maris' death at Fairfield in the snow blanketed prairies of Idaho. Meet my challenges with C's — that's courage, conviction, confidence and compassion and don't be too worried about the S's — that's concern for social approval, security and safely. Don't be afraid to go beyond my boundaries.

The ancient pilgrim had to pass through unknown sometimes dangerous countries on his way to Santiago. My first stop was Singapore, not that dangerous, but not without its hazards, to call on my great nephew James who had taken up a new job in January. I was the first family member to visit. My niece, his mother Anne, was keen to know how her younger son was faring on his first overseas jaunt. My sister Maria, the doting grandmother, was anxious for a first-hand report.

I encountered my first hazard at immigration. The young official wouldn't accept that I didn't know James' address. He wouldn't let me loose on Singapore until I had filled out where I was staying. I rang James. Actually, he could see me from the other side of the immigration enclosure. We waved to each other. James willingly gave his address not before suggesting I buy him some duty-free vodka. James was his usual enthusiastic fast-talking self. His time in Singapore hadn't dimmed his exuberance for life. Singapore suited him. Hustle and bustle and boundless striving has transformed a tropical island into one of the world's richest countries. Crowds of well-dressed men and women march into gleaming new skyscrapers and colonial buildings. Buses, cars and taxis steam past. The steamy air is full of honking horns, engine sounds, chirps and trills from pedestrian crossings.

He took me home in West Coast Gardens to a complex of high rise buildings around three swimming pools and gave me, his eighty-year great uncle, a mattress to sleep on the living room floor of his 18th floor unit. He shared with two other employees of the company he worked for — Waterworld at Universal Studios. James pointed out the other units in the complex where the company housed their staff.

Next day James took me to Universal Studios. It's a twenty hectares fun park located within Resorts World Sentosa on Sentosa Island. It consists of seven themed zones based on a blockbuster movie or television shows such as Battlestar Galactica, Shrek and Monster Rock. Waterworld is inspired by the 1995 American post-apocalyptic science fiction film starring Kevin Costner and directed by Kevin Reynolds. James is one of three actors who played the role of the Deacon, the arch villain of the show. James got this job on the basis of his experience at Movieworld on the Gold Coast where he played characters such as Shrek and Scooby Doo. He's an aspiring actor.

Waterworld is one of the biggest spectacles in the theme park. The action *'comes surging to life in a tidal wave of death-defying stunts, along with thrills and spills from real explosions of fire and water.'* James was on duty that day so I saw him in action in three shows. I certainly enjoyed the spectacle, a complex combination of stunts, jet skis, gun shots, explosions, flames, pyrotechnics, and a seaplane to add to the action — the whole shebang.

This pilgrim, along with the audience, had to face their own hazards. The performers were intent on getting their spectators as wet as possible. The 'warm up' for the show involved throwing buckets of water over the people. The jet skiers sent great sprays of water over their audience. Just as well

Singapore has a hot climate, the people who seemed to love their drenching dried in minutes. I loved James' performance. The role gave him a wicked opportunity to ham up and his evil laugh added to his villainy. I could see that he loved his job and enjoyed strutting his stuff. The Deacon meets his fate by falling in flames from a great height and by the third show I could spot where the stuntman took over. After the show, spectators vied with each other to have their photos taken with the cast. If you don't mind getting soaked, it's a great spectacle.

After the shows, James showed me his Singapore. We enjoyed a couple of beers at the Hard Rock Café after a tiring day in the heat. He took me for a meal to the Ayer Rajah Hawker Centre and Food Hall. Before we made our selections, we worked our way around the many food stalls. Everyone wanted us to taste. I enjoyed the Centre, a little piece of authentic Asia, in contrast to the imported world of Universal Studies, Hard Rock Café, Starbucks and McDonalds.

The Centre was close to James' unit so we walked home and on the way encountered our next hazard. We witnessed domestic violence. A group of Indians were gathered in a park, some in the light but many in the shadows. A man was beating up a woman. She cringed from his blows, crying and shrieking. James wanted to intervene. I felt for that woman, too. I'm glad he didn't. He, an impulsive youth, could have crossed a cultural line into unknown territory. What was the story behind this scene? Why was she being punished? If he had tried to stop the man, what would the others have done? I had visions of an Indian mob emerging from the dark, descending on us and dispensing retribution for our interference. Concern for my own skin overcame my sense of injustice, I'm afraid.

Next day we took the commune bus to the MRT station at

Clementi. We travelled by train a few stations to visit some Chinese and Japanese gardens. Strange to see open space in such a bustling, noisy crowded city. Here was Singapore in a more contemplative light. In the peace of the Japanese gardens we sat on a stone bridge over a small stream, the water flowing gently below, and talked.

James believed that he had done a lot of growing up in Singapore. He was a party animal when he arrived. The others in his unit were the same so the company separated them. His mind was darting in all directions, full of ideas and only limited by money of which he had little. It's perfectly okay for young people like James to cherish dreams that may seem almost too big, I replied. If they start out with no expectations, they'll end up accomplishing nothing. He hoped his time in Singapore would be an opportunity to save, although by the mind-blowing costs of drinks at the Hard Rock Café, I knew he would need some determination to achieve that objective. He felt that coming to Singapore was an opportunity for him to mature, to get himself out of a rut. James was searching for an identity, not an unusual quest for a young man. To me, James who liked to be now known as Jimmy, was still the person I had always known from a little boy — a dreamer, full of exuberance and enthusiasm for the world.

I felt a close bond with James. Both of us are searching. He is a pilgrim starting on his life's journey. I, too, am a pilgrim seeking answers to unanswerable questions and a new identity after my Maris' suicide overturned all my assumptions about life. I was thankful that he gave me an opportunity to view Singapore from a perspective that the tourist who stays in one of the multitude of hotels never sees.

One is supposed to shop in Singapore. Apart from drinks I didn't buy a thing although I visited a Stone Art stall in

Clementi supermarket and was intrigued by some of the inscriptions — fitting messages for any pilgrim.

Yesterday was history
Tomorrow's a mystery
Today is a gift.

Don't walk behind me
Don't walk ahead of me
Walk beside me and be my friend.

3

Que cette bougie soit un peu de moi-même
(May this candle be a little of myself)

My second stop was France. I arrived in Paris early on a warm Thursday morning, feeling zonked after a sleepless night of travelling, too weary to appreciate the beauty of the city of light. Wishing to avoid the phenomenal cost of their hotels that set hip pocket nerves jangling, I arranged accommodation through airbnb. I gave the centre of Paris a pass and went for Issy-les-Moulineaux on the outskirts in the Ile de France. As this was my fifth visit, I knew my way around the Metro and soon arrived at Mairie d'Issy at the terminus of Line 12. I rang my host Georges and he arrived on his scooter. A young man about thirty looking very French with his short beard, dark hair and complexion, he grabbed my pilgrim backpack and insisted on wearing it for me as we walked up the hill for about 15 minutes to his apartment building. Feeling tired after the twelve-hour flight, I slept for two hours. No one was home as I let myself out of the 3rd floor apartment and went exploring. I found the supermarket Monoprix, bought a few items for breakfast and a sandwich which I ate in the park, a tree covered oasis in the midst of modern commercial buildings, an ideal spot for the office workers to take a break from their desks and computers. While I was admiring the garden beds and thinking of nothing in particular, a young man on an adjacent seat asked me for a light. He was not unlike George with his goatee beard and dark features. I replied that I didn't smoke. My accent intrigued him. It was obvious I was not a native

French speaker. He asked me where I was from. *'Amerique?' 'Non!'* *'Angleterre (England)?' 'Non! Australie!'* I replied. He was impressed. Things are bad in France, he said, there are no jobs. Australia is a paradise to many young French. He apologised and said he had to get back to work. I was relieved that he had a job. He seemed a decent bloke and I did not want him to be one of the unemployed. (*les chomeurs*)

I got lost trying to find my way back. Bizarre! Only in France for a few hours! I hadn't even started the Camino. What should have taken me fifteen minutes took about 90, wandering in a circle until I found my way back to the metro. Lesson One. Always note a landmark or two in unfamiliar ground. Perhaps I had been too busy puffing up the hill to notice. After another sleep of four hours I went out again to look for dinner, this time noting buildings, a white one with a green roof on a corner being the most important. After buying a not-very-Gallic chicken burger and fries, I returned safely to the apartment. I met Georges' partner, David. who was as fair in complexion as Georges was dark. I was ready for a chat but he didn't have much to say, except that Georges and he were chefs and worked odd hours. I retired to my room for some much-needed sleep. I heard Georges come home. I fell into deep sleep to the sounds of their discussion and to the movement of furniture.

I woke at 7 am, refreshed and rested. The place was quiet. I ate my breakfast in silence and solitude apart from Georges' fluffy white cat. Its usual spot was on top of the cupboard but it came down to inspect me. Georges' apartment was quaint. The building was modern, white and light, recently built but the furniture was incongruous, of a dark heavy old style as if inherited from an elderly relative. Lots of unpacked banana boxes overflowing with kitchen utensils suggested a recent move. I couldn't find a decent sharp knife in the drawers but there was quite a selection in one of the boxes. Last night there were two refrigerators in the kitchen but one had been moved out to the balcony. I paused to admire the Eiffel Tower, prominent on the horizon.

The day was Friday 26th July — Maris' birthday. A good day to visit Chartres Cathedral because Friday is the day they move the chairs which cover the labyrinth. I took the train from Montparnasse, familiar from the number of times I had visited Chartres. In the hour's train ride my eyes rested on the farms and forests of the passing French countryside but my mind was on Maris. She would have been seventy-seven. What would our life have been if she had survived her suicide attempt?

I walked up the familiar hill to the cathedral. The facade was covered with scaffolding. I paused at the entrance. The beggar, hand outstretched, was familiar, too, the same chap, I'm sure, who kept vigil last time. If you visit Chartres cathedral as a tourist you will find an excellent model of aesthetic achievement, but, if you arrive as a pilgrim, you will enter a wonderful instrument of spiritual action, of a faith expressed in stone that generates its own energy. On previous visits, I gave myself to appreciating its beauty and absorbing its harmony. It was difficult not to be inspired as your eyes become accustomed to the light and soar to the ceiling as if searching for heaven.

As expected, the chairs had been removed and people were walking the labyrinth, installed on the floor of the nave. Its single path design represents the journey of the spirit. It's a path of prayer and reflection, walked for spiritual insight and healing. It's not a maze. A maze is designed to lose your way, whereas a labyrinth is designed to find your way. It's a metaphor for your own spiritual journey, the same as the Camino.

The labyrinth was my spiritual preamble. I joined the people and walked barefooted along the cold gritty stones worn smooth by millions of feet. People of faith have been walking the labyrinth for generations. I was joining a brotherhood, in much the same way that the Camino admits you to a similar brotherhood stretching back a thousand years. I could almost hear the prayers of pilgrims long gone to God. I felt small and humble, just one of a vast multitude.

I gave myself over to the feelings of excitement and apprehension about the impending Camino. I focused on nothing but the present moment and repeated the mantra I picked up in Singapore: *'Yesterday was history, tomorrow's a mystery, today is a gift'*. I walked the labyrinth once more. I seemed to hear my Maris saying *'I'm with you.'* I strolled around the cathedral and paused before the Black Madonna for a few prayers. I gazed upwards at the beautiful stained glass windows which were dismantled, I'm told, piece by piece, during the war. On the way back to the station, my trepidations had vanished, my self-confidence and faith in self was restored. I heard the voice of Albert Camus: *'In the depth of winter I finally learned that within me lay an invincible summer.'* I experienced a sense of peace and contentment.

In contrast to the trip out of Paris the return train was crowded. People going to Paris for the weekend! Montparnasse station was an extraordinary bedlam like an anthill gone berserk with crowds of wide-eyed travellers hurrying this way and that, dragging their cases behind them. Everyone leaving Paris ran almost headlong into the people arriving. Back at Mairie d'Issy I bought a microwave dinner at Monoprix. After dinner, I went to sleep watching television. Someone came in, probably David, and disappeared into their room. The place felt spooky with unseen people. The apartment was nice enough but the boys weren't outgoing nor communicative. I won't ask if I can stay again at the end of my trip when I'll have a few more days in Paris.

I had one more day before departing south. On a warm Saturday, I bought lunch and sat in the local park with the pigeons and the blossom. The office workers were enjoying their weekend but opposite was the Mairie and a number of wedding parties took a short-cut across the lawns. The men looked uncomfortable in their suits and the children were wearing hats but I could sense the joy of their day. I left them to their celebrations because I wanted to use the afternoon to visit one of my sacred places. I took the metro into the 5th arrondissement, walked up Rue des Carmes to the church of St Etienne du Mont, my favourite Parisian church. On two previous trips, I had rented an apartment in Rue des Carmes and visited daily. I recall in particular my presence at Easter celebrations in 2005. Just at the back of the Panthéon, it houses the shrine of St Geneviève, the patron saint of Paris. Most impressive is the wood pulpit supported by Sampson, a jaw bone in one hand and a lion under his feet. Equally impressive is the rood screen of elaborate and intricate design in stone which stretches across the nave with spiral cases on either side, which somehow managed to survive the French Revolution. Over the years, I had lit many candles for Maris in this beautiful church and spent time in contemplation. I was just about to light a candle when they kicked out the visitors because of a wedding which they said was private.

Back at Georges' I had another microwave dinner. The boys came home early; they were planning to leave next morning for a trip into the country to visit Georges' mother. They had left by the time I was ready so I let myself out. On the way to the metro I visited the local church St Etienne and lit the candle I missed out on at the other St. Etienne. I hoped this would be the first of many. Above the candles was a short prayer:

'Je ne peux rester dans cette église qu'un moment. Que cette bougie soit un peu de moi-même. Fais que mes rencontres et mon travail d'aujourd'hui soient le prolongement de ma prière.'
(I can only stay a moment in this church. May this candle be a little of myself. Would that my meetings and my work today be a continuation of my prayer.)

4. When am I just going to enjoy the moment?

Gare de Lyon is such a chaotic place. Thousands of people, taking up every available seat, the rest sitting on cases or backpacks, all heads craned to the boards watching the dancing train information; the food and drink stalls in constant demand; the rush of passengers in search of their train once their number is announced; the arrival of thousands of others; the roar of conversation and announcements; the slow pacing soldiers with guns at the ready strolling in threes through the crowds, putting on their meanest, don't-mess-with-me look, their eyes constantly on the alert.

This Sunday morning, I waited like everyone else. I was to spend three weeks in Montpellier, enrolled in a refresher French language school. My plan was to commence walking either at Arles or Montpellier along La via Tolosana to Puente la Reina in Spain. I found the TGV (*train de grande vitesse*), the high-speed train with no fuss. I prefer to travel by train. You'll arrive quickly in an aeroplane, but getting to the airport can take longer than the plane trip. On a train you meet people, walk around, stretch yourself, buy a drink or food at the bar or watch the world go past your window. This time I talked to no one. The other passengers seemed happy to snooze the four-hour journey away and I was content to join them to the soporific rhythm of the train.

The peace and quiet was shattered once I was confronted by the chaos of the *gare de Montpellier*. Thousands were arriving, leaving or just hanging around. To add to the confusion, the station was in the process of being rebuilt. Most of it seemed to be barricaded off and everyone fought for survival in the confined space. People struggled through the melée, dragging their cases behind them, in danger of tripping the unwary or being tripped themselves. In such conditions backpacks come into their own. You feel far less encumbered and your hands are free. The school had told me my home-stay host would meet me. On the second time around the two levels of the building, I spotted a middle-aged woman with greying hair holding a placard with my name (*Monsieur Braun*). I introduced myself. Michèle beckoned me to follow and we hurried out into the busy street to the tram stop. We took a blue tram (Ligne No 1) on a ten-minute journey, standing all the way, to the suburb of Antigone. Montpellier was a blur. The day was hot. Lots of people were about. This was summer and the middle of the tourist season.

We alighted outside a large indoor swimming pool complex (*Piscine Olympique d'Antigone*) of glass and steel, looking something like a Spanish architect's dream. Free of the confines of the train, Michèle explained the pool is a paradise for lovers of swimming. One pool, nicknamed Venus, is of Olympic proportions. The other, nicknamed Aphrodite, is warmer and includes whirlpools and slides. The French national swimming championships were held here and the complex hosts about 400,000 a year.

The humble residential building which was Michèle's home was in sharp contrast. A grey cement building on a corner, it was only about 100 metres distant. We climbed the stairs to the fourth floor into a small apartment. My room was on the corner, overlooking the tram lines. I had a great view of the swimming complex and of the tram stop outside. I watched the blue trams swinging around the corner, slowing at the cross roads and halting at the stop. The buildings of Montpellier surrounded me. I would explore the next day.

I met the other students at dinner — a boy from Columbia and two young girls from Switzerland. The idea of staying with a family is to experience a total immersion. We were supposed to speak in French. Students are discouraged from using their own language, but there was no conversation around this table, squeezed into a small dining room dominated by an enormous TV. The girls were ultra-shy and the boy seemed switched off. All I found out about him was that he called himself Fred and he was Columbian. The girls whispered their names. I didn't bother to ask to repeat a second time. The only conversation was a monologue. Michèle nattered the whole meal about nothing.

I was not sure how this would work out. The Amboise experience had spoilt me. I couldn't help but compare. There I stayed with Danièle and Michèle in a spacious two-storey house on the edge of town. The other students were Maya and Marie. We were a wonderful family. Danièle and Michèle were prepared to spend up to two hours every evening sitting over dinner, encouraging us to speak and were patient with their listening. Danièle was a retired chef and every meal was a work of art. In contrast, Michèle was an ordinary cook. We were crammed into a tiny apartment. Somehow there were four bedrooms — one for Michèle, one for Fred, one for the two girls and one for me. At least, my room was furnished with a desk and was opposite the bathroom. This will be a different experience but I suppose I will get used to it. I thought, however, I will inquire about changing to self-accommodation. Back in Chambéry in 2006, I spend three months learning French and enjoyed staying in my own studio apartment. I cooked for myself and loved shopping in the markets.

We were up early for the first day. Michèle came into town with me on the blue tram to ensure I got to the school by 8.00

am for the induction. We alighted at the sprawling Place de la Comédie in the old city. The school was on the first floor of a building which was elegant in its day but had been turned into a warren of classrooms and corridors. A large number of students were milling around. In the induction class, we were given the ropes. Talking to some other students who had taken the self-accommodation option, I got the impression that the facilities offered were rather inadequate. Staying with a host family wasn't such a bad choice after all. After the induction, we were allocated to our classes based on a test we had taken by internet before our arrival in France. My teacher was Mèlanie.

Class finished at 1 pm so I spent time looking for lunch and exploring the city. Montpellier is a city of contrasts. It's the capital of the Languedoc-Roussillon of south France, about 10 km inland from the Mediterranean Sea. The medieval city thrives with its narrow winding alleyways. Yet, as well as the swimming complex, there are many stylish modern buildings which must have been an architect's dream to design. It's a bustling city packed with tourists. The main means of transport are the trams. There are four main routes and each route has a different colour. My tram was blue.

I strolled through the old city along a warren of pedestrian streets past limestone building, cafes, take-aways, churches, civic monuments, boutique shops and down-at-heel bars. I found St Roch's, an important pilgrim church. Born in Montpellier, St Roch is a special pilgrim saint. Although from a rich and powerful family, he gave away his wealth and became a pilgrim in Italy but stopped on the way to care for victims of the plague. I had some successful interactions in French with shop assistants; they understood me and I understood them. I was feeling old and out of my comfort zone, a fish out of water. I was tired and pleased to get to the apartment to rest before dinner.

Next day I felt better, as if my body had adjusted to the time zone. It can get used to anything. My spirit was more comfortable and even though it was hot, I was not tired. After class I took the blue tram through the suburbs to the outskirts of Montpellier, to Mosson, the terminus. I visited the shops. This was an area where many Algerians had settled. The supermarket was Algerian and Arabic was spoken. The signs were in Arabic. The goods were in heaps, spread out untidily, in sharp contrast to the orderly Monoprix supermarket where attention to detail was paramount, as if the owner had once run a stall in the untidy markets of Algiers and hadn't shaken off old habits. He ignored me as he engaged in loud conservation with customers on the other side of his shop and only stopped to take my money for a soft drink with scarcely veiled hostility.

Riding back in the tram I reflected on the circumstances of the families I had stayed for my total language immersion experience. I learned French with Danièle and Michèle in Amboise, and Spanish with Jacinto and Loli at Pamplona. Here I was learning French with Michèle. While the others were middle class families and probably didn't need the additional income, Michèle was in the business of taking students for the money and was making maximum use of her small apartment. My dinner table companions were not so silent this evening. The girls were looking forward to returning home to Switzerland. They spoke German mostly at home and were doing the immersion thing to improve their French grades. Fred was hoping to study in a French university. I mentioned one of my fellow students at Chambéry was Juan-Carmelo. He was Columbian and had the same aspirations. Fred said there were lots of Columbian students in France. Michèle mentioned her grandson whom she minded one day a week. My comment about seeing so many Algerians that day launched her into a tirade about the problems of immigration in France. I was pleased that we had relaxed enough to talk to each other. The conversation was stilted, but a promising start.

I arrived at school in time to read the notices in reception. There was a list of names for each class. The classrooms were scattered across Montpellier so there was more than one 'campus.' There were roughly 400 names. Mèlanie confirmed the numbers. She told me there were 40 teachers at the moment and each class had about ten students. Such a large number made things impersonal, a contrast to the other language schools which were small and one had a chance to get to know the students beyond one's class. There were common areas for the students to gather, socialise and gossip. Here there was none. The students had to gather in the street below along with the shoppers and tourists. The only facilities seemed to be a room full of computers for the students and computers and screen in each classroom. I was able to use a computer to send and receive emails. No library that one could borrow from. In fact, our classroom was supposed to be the library. The positives? Mèlanie had a warm personable helpful manner. She was a good teacher and encouraged class involvement. The reception area was manned by two girls who helped the students with their queries.

Nevertheless, such a contrast to, say, Amboise! My brother-in-law Joe, died back in Australia while I was studying French there. I received great support from Danièle and Michèle. My two fellow students Marie and Maya told the other students and I had their support. I felt humbled by the compassion and care of these young people. I even had a session with the principal who made it her business to know every student.

Having explored the old city by foot, I took to the trams to explore the new town as it spread out into the suburbs. I took the tram to Odysseum, a grand shopping complex boasting one of the largest hypermarkets ever; I found a cinema complex with eighteen theatres. The sales (*les soldes*) were on and I bought a shirt and an Opinel pocket knife. I enjoyed my interactions with the shop assistants, speaking to them in French, sometimes not understanding their replies but I muddled through. I bought a newspaper *La Gazette* and was intrigued by the extraordinary number of things going on. I was surprised by the beggars. As well as homeless old men, there were children some quite young. I mentioned their presence to Michèle over dinner and she voiced her theory that the Romani children were sent out to beg during the school holidays.

Saturday the school had organised an excursion to Arles. This was an opportunity to see the town as a potential starting point for my walk. The Via Tolosana starts at Arles. I would be backtracking because Montpellier is on the way. About 50-60 students took the excursion. First, we went to an olive mill (*Moulin á huile*) at Mas de Barnes where we inspected the mill and were given a talk on the milling process. Extensive olive groves covered the gentle sloping hills, the family had been in the game for generations, and some of the buildings looked as if they were built by the founding father.

We travelled through rocky ridges and crests to Maussane-les-Alpilles. I loved the piece of hyperbole from the *Office de Tourisme*: 'When God created the sun, the earth, the mountains and the water and put them in place, he took a little of each to make paradise and thus Provence was born. A Provençal proverb making sense once in Maussane-les-Alpilles.'

It's a medieval village complete with castle, fully restored and catering to the tourists with its myriads of shops. I wandered through its narrow streets, markets, fine art and craft shops and didn't buy anything, except for a toy cicada which sounded like one when you touched it. The view across the valley to the surrounding craggy hills would have inspired many an artist.

We moved on to Arles. The bus parked by the river Rhône where a number of cruise ships were moored. We saw one depart. Arles is intent on its Roman past and the amphitheatre is its major tourist attraction. Built in the first century A.D., it provided entertainment in the form of chariot racing and bloody hand-to-hand fighting. After the fall of the Roman Empire, it became a fortress, towers were added and houses were built over the arena. In the 18th century, it was restored and today is used for bull fighting and concerts. Van Gogh's 1888 painting *Les Arènes* depicts the crowd attending a bullfight.

This was my opportunity for some interaction with the other students. There were some older people but as usual I was the granddaddy. I actually spoke with Fred and discovered he was fluent in English. The students came from many countries. I heard two boys sitting behind me speaking in English. I thought they were Americans but actually one was Dutch and the other Italian. These two boys were truly European and used English as a common language. I am always intrigued by the number of languages Europeans speak and how they can change from one to another.

That evening we lingered over dinner. Michèle was eager for company so after helping her to clean up we watched television. The Swiss girls went to bed early because they were departing very early the following morning. Fred was out. We watched a programme entitled *Echappées Belles* (Beautiful escapes) It focused on various places around France that were great get-aways. Among them was Nogaro in Gens. I had passed through Nogaro in 2010 while walking the Camino. I recognised the town. Michèle offered me a nightcap of an Armagnac (eau-de-vie). She spoke about her life — her ex-husband, her struggle to make ends meet, her dependence on the school for an income.

Sunday morning, I dreamed I had started walking and was fretting because I couldn't find a bed. All my life, pre-dawn has always been an anxious time as negative thoughts thrive in a mind emerging from sleep. I tried not to panic and reassure myself that things were in God's hand. I always found a bed on my two previous Caminos. This one would be no different. There was always a light, sometimes within, sometimes in the form of a timely intervention.

I found a church just up the road and attended 11.15 am Mass. Still feeling the pre-dawn anxiety, I lit a candle for Maris and as a prayer that I'd get through and handle whatever came my way. I devoted the rest of Sunday to being a tourist. I walked into town, found a seat in the park which I shared with two young Mormons, dressed in dark suits, white shirts and wearing their name tags, the ubiquitous Mormon uniform. They were carrying their jackets; it was another 30-degree day. They addressed me in French but soon changed to their American English. I told them I was intrigued to find Mormons in France. They assured me there was quite a Mormon presence. They were caring young men. Robert was a little older and the veteran. He'd been in France for a year. Garth had just arrived from Utah and was learning the game. I told them about my intention to walk the Camino and some of my anxieties. They were reassuring. It was as if God had sent them. Often a chance encounter seems meant to have happened. Synchronicity the scientists call it. I was grateful they spent time with me, an old bloke, when their real target was the youth. After a brief prayer together and a blessing, they left to proselytise at McDonalds. What two institutions better represent American culture and influence than McDonalds and Mormons! At opposite ends of the spiritual continuum!

Back at Michèle's (*chez Michèle*) I found a new student installing herself in the adjacent room. Ella was English. She was young, had no French so our conversation was in English. She asked many questions about the school, and I, the veteran of one week, did my best to answer them.

Monday morning saw five new students join the class, nine in all. I had a busy afternoon. I bought a cheap phone from Orange to use in France. I tried to organise a bed for the first few days. I noticed people walking across the square wearing backpacks. They looked like hot, tired pilgrims. I said *Bon Chemin* and one of them thanked me. I found the gîte at the back of St Roch, (*Gîte St Roch*) but it did not open until 5 pm. I walked back to Michèle's and beyond to the Place de l'Europe and found the Australian Bar. It was covered, inside and out with aboriginal designs — lots of dots, kangaroos, goannas, decorated oil drums, while a tattered Australian flag fluttered in the light afternoon breeze. This quaint touch of Australiana was a left over, perhaps, from the Rugby World Cup of 2007 when the Australian team was billeted and trained in Montpellier. I would have bought a drink but the bar did not open until 6.

The Australian Bar, Michèle said at dinner, was a popular rendezvous for the young people (*les jeunes*). Our conversation over dinner was mostly in English. Ella talked about her first day and Fred was trying to help her. Fred was chatty, a contrast to the previous week when he hardly said a word. The Swiss girls were a damper; they were hard work, uncommunicative, inclined to whisper and giggle to each other. Ella was warm, outgoing and talkative. She encouraged communication and brought Fred out of his shell.

The Australian Bar was only a short distance, literally just around the corner, so after dinner I returned to find only a few patrons, too early for *les jeunes*. The barman was a New Zealander, a big man whose presence filled the bar. Phil had lived in Montpellier for a year. I conversed with Tom from Melbourne. He seemed well travelled and had been everywhere in Europe. I didn't ask him his occupation. Rob was an Irishman who lived in Paris. He was a consultant to Oz Café, a chain of 'Australian' bars across France. Both were intrigued by my plans to leave Montpellier by foot and walk to Toulouse and beyond into Spain. By 10 pm the bar had filled up with *les jeunes*, so it was time to leave.

The next day was lethargic. I was half way through my Montpellier experience and it was not as I had hoped. In the afternoon, I called at the refuge for pilgrims behind St Roch church. The *Gîte St Roch* opened at 5 pm and I found five pilgrims settling in for the night. They had started at Arles. There weren't many walkers on the road, they said. That reassured me — less competition for beds. One pilgrim told me he had been walking for a year, but was stopping that day. His body had had enough. I inquired of one of the volunteers, a grey-haired lady who was gently bossing her pilgrims, about a *credencial*. She sold me one. The *credencial* is a passport. It gives you access to the infrastructure of the Camino. You get it stamped along the way and is the evidence that you have done the walk when you arrive at Santiago.

Meeting these pilgrims made me impatient to quit Montpellier and start walking. I felt I was just hanging around and worrying. My original plan was to spend three weeks at the school and depart on Saturday 17th. However, Thursday 15th

August, the Assumption, was a public holiday and the school would be closed. I decided I would start walking on the public holiday and not bother returning to school for just one day.

After class the next day I sent an email to Luke. Luke was the designer and organised the galley prints. I had hoped that the galley print of my new book would be ready before I left Australia. I had arranged with Luke to post me a copy addressed to me at the school. Every day I inquired if it had arrived and every day I was told no.

The guide book had mentioned taking the tram out to the stadium and to begin walking from there. That's what I did as a preamble. I walked about three kilometres along the route which followed the river on a fine day that beckoned action. I appreciated this activity. My rigorous training was long past, I'd been inactive in France. My left leg was a worry. I was still apprehensive whether it would withstand the Camino's rigours. The more exercise it got, I thought, the better.

The stadium is another architect's dream, a modern structure surrounded by girders painted blue and orange, Montpellier's signature colours. They were getting ready for a big game Montpellier versus Paris on the weekend. I tried to buy a ticket but the match was sold out. Rugby union is popular with this region.

Saturday was hot and windy. I was a tourist for the weekend. I did not mind missing out on the school's excursion to Carcassonne. Avignon was only an hour's train ride. Avignon has always intrigued me as the seat of the papacy 1309 to 1377. At that time the pope was fearful of the Roman mob so decided it was time to move house. Nîmes was on the way, so I broke the journey. I was also interested in seeing its famous arena. The trains were crammed full. It was definitely holiday time. Even the President of France was on holidays. At Nîmes I had an hour for the next train to Avignon, so I inquired if I had time to walk to its famous arena. Too far! The station staff told me. It wasn't. I left the station for a stroll along the promenade flanked with gardens, trees, fountains and canals, and there it was. It's amazing. Just walking up to it left me in awe. It's the best-preserved amphitheatre of the Roman era, built in the 1st century A.D. under Emperor Augustus, two stories of superimposed arches. It has a perfect symmetry, oval shaped, a lovely example of the degree of perfection the Romans could achieve. I regretted not giving myself more time to inspect its galleries, terraces and sculptures. I contented myself by walking around the statue of a French matador, Christian Montcouquiol, known as 'Nimeño 11'. The arena is used for bullfighting. I left myself just enough time to hurry back to the station for the next train to Avignon.

I was not surprised to learn that the Papal palace (*Palais des Papes*) was among the ten most visited attractions in France, judging by the throng of tourists I joined walking from the station. Now a museum, the Papal palace was the largest Gothic building of the Middle Ages. It became obsolete when the papacy returned to Rome. As I wandered from one sparsely furnished room to another, I was impressed by the sense of simplicity, beauty and grandeur and even immortality. The ambience, however, was sad, tinged with a longing for its lost glory. French poets down the centuries sensed this, too, and have referred to it as a *'work of destruction.'*

After lunch in the extensive plaza outside the palace, watching some of the buskers and entertainers in medieval costume, I walked through the town to the famous bridge. The *Pont Saint-Bénézet*, also known as the *Pont d'Avignon*, is a landmark for the city. It was originally 22 stone arches across the river Rhône but flood after flood reduced it to four arches and it was eventually abandoned. It lives on in the heart in the 15th century French song 'Sur le pont d'Avignon'.

> 'Sur le pont d'Avignon On y dance, On y dance.
> Sur le pont d'Avignon On y dance tous en rond.'

Sunday, I attended Mass. I found myself praying for a lady who had with her an intellectually handicapped teenage girl whom I assumed was her daughter. The girl had no speech but made a lot of noise. The mother managed to take her to the altar rails for communion. I admired that woman for her courage and expressed thanks that my children and grandchildren back home in Australia were sound and healthy.

The last three days passed quickly, tidying up the details. Monday morning, I inquired at reception whether my galley print had arrived. No! I guessed it wouldn't now. Who knows what had happened to it! As a contingency, I had arranged for my daughter Angela to receive a copy. I received an email from her stating she liked the book very much. I hoped and trusted that she had found all the errors. I spent the afternoon sending emails seeking accommodation for the first few days of my walk. The knockbacks raised my anxiety. I was wondering just how difficult it would be to find a bed. Accommodation was scarcer than on previous routes. I sent emails back home. I visited Monoprix for corn pads. I bought a box at the Post Office to send back stuff to Australia and at Michèle's I sorted out my stuff into what I needed for the walk and what I would send home. I thought about taking my cicada with me as a novelty and conversation starter, but I threw it into the box.

At dinner Michèle showed some curiosity about me for the first time. She asked me about my background, what was my profession. She asked about the Camino. She did not know much about it, which surprised me as Montpellier was a main point on the route. After dinner, I visited the Australian Bar where Monday Madness was in swing. Big Phil, the barman from New Zealand recognised me. I saw a few faces from the school, including Fred and Ella. I was pleased that they seemed to be getting on well. Perhaps, a romance was blossoming.

Back at the school I read a number of encouraging emails. *'Go for it, Dad'* was Angela's message. *'Show persistence and passion'* came from Patti, a long-time friend who gave Maris massages. I rang my grandson Brody for his birthday. From the background noise, he and Jacinta could have been in a pub.

The last day at the school arrived. Mèlanie gave me a critique of my verbal skills. The 'r' was a problem as with many English speakers. I arranged with reception to get my certificate. I was asked to complete a critique. I wrote about a lack of genuine interest in their students. The school was too large. There was no common area apart from the street outside for students to gather. Would I recommend the school to others? No!

At the market in the Place de la Comédie I bought fans for the ladies in the family, packed them in the box which I took to the post office. Back at Michèle's, I reckoned I still had too much to carry. I spent the last night a worry wart, anxious, keen to get going, yet apprehensive about getting on the road, distracting myself by thinking about what I'd do when I get home, which was two months away.

When am I just going to enjoy the moment?

Act Three
France and Spain

La Via Tolosana
Chemin d'Arles
Camino Aragonés

Arles — Toulouse — Col du Somport — Puente La Reina

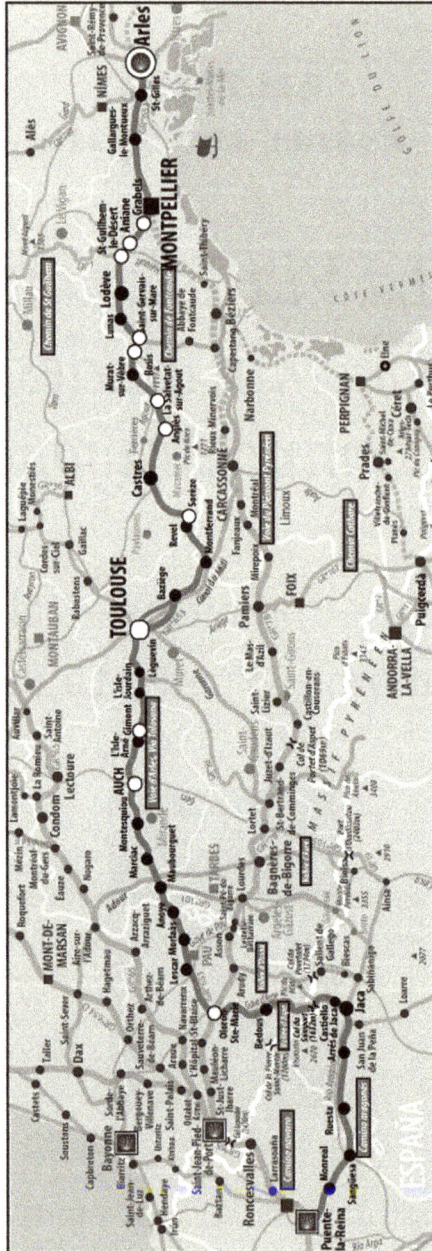

5

Si loin que vous alliez, si haut que vous montiez,
il vous faut commencer par un simple pas.
(If you go far, if you climb high,
you must begin with a single step)
—François Cheng

Pre-dawn anxieties prevailed. As I surfaced, rising through the various layers of sleep, feelings oscillated from fear to excitement, from a desire to stay safely and securely at home to stepping out of my comfort zone. I remembered my C's and S's. Meet my challenges with confidence, consistency, and compassion. From a recess in the back of my mind came the advice that Mathew, the young American backpacker, offered as he left me at Chambéry back in 2006: 'Noel, *don't be afraid to step out of your boundaries.*'

I rose early and left a fan and card on the table for Michèle. Outside the streets were quiet. I was down to the nitty gritty. I took the first step of my Chemin by catching the blue tram. As I watched the town glide by, it flashed through my mind that in both 2010 and 2011, I walked every metre of the way. At Le-Puy-en-Velay, I began at the cathedral and at Saint-Jean-Pied-de-Port at the pilgrim office. Today I was using public transport as a kick-off, I was on my third act, about to walk the route that commences at Arles, known variously as La Voie d'Arles, Camino Aragonés, La Via Tolosana. I felt a touch of guilt that I had not gone back to Arles, about 70 kilometres. The feeling was not strong and easy enough to dismiss. I would be walking about 800 kilometres anyway, quite a jaunt for anyone, let alone an eighty-year-old.

I was taking the tram because my guidebook said so. If I were to maintain the 'pure' pilgrim spirit I should have started with my back to the Cathedral and walked for more than two hours through the suburbs, taking the risk of getting lost along a poorly signed way. My guidebook suggested two alternatives: (1) Take the tram (Line No 1) to the stop at Mosson just by the stadium and start walking. (2) Take the same tram, descend at Euromédecine and take the bus to Grabels. I chose the former as there were no early buses on that public holiday. I left my tram at Mosson, walked past the stadium and then across the park to a track that followed the river along a valley. The day was hot but cool in the valley. I wasn't sure where I was headed and I was keen not to get lost on my first day of walking as I had done three years previously at Le Puy. There was no other way to go than to walk along the banks of the river lined with trees dipping into the water. The houses on the ridges on either side reminded me I was still in the suburbs. I passed through conservation parks inviting me to look, touch, listen, feel (*regardez, touchez, écoutez, sentez*) the beautiful river just as the fauna do. Eventually I arrived at a low cement footbridge and there was the familiar red and white GR marking on the end. I crossed and continued to follow the markings. I left the town behind and moved into open country which seemed to be dedicated to horse stables. I was making for Montarnaud, 19 kilometres away.

I enjoyed walking through a large corn field. I had left the town behind and felt as if I had just let myself out of prison. It was a joy to escape the confines and to hear the wind swaying the tall stalks and to feel the sun, the source of all light, on my back. The freedom inspired me. For the next five weeks on the road, I was to lead a life shining with the all-pervasive light of the sun, the source of all power, a life of victory in overcoming obstacles both physical and mental, free of regrets and full of triumphs, great and small, fuelled by the determination to win in the end. At the end of my walk I would feel deeply that I have done something creative because I have thrown myself wholeheartedly into the task and wrestled with it through to its conclusion.

As I rounded the track I noticed a bald-headed stocky man sitting under a tree. His pack was beside him so I assumed he was not a local sitting in the shade. He noticed me first and greeted me in French. I replied in French but he spoke in English saying he was fluent in that language. His name was Godfreid, he told me; he was Belgian and was fluent in Dutch, Flemish, German, French and English. Wow! I was impressed. We discussed the Camino. I told him I had just begun walking that morning from Montpellier. He had started at Arles but had found the way boring. It pleased me to hear that. I had missed nothing.

Godfreid passed me as I was eating my lunch, some sandwiches prepared by Michèle. I met no other pilgrims that afternoon which, apart from a few gentle hills, was uneventful. I was content to be alone. I enjoyed listening to the cicadas, their carefree song good company in the heat of the day. I arrived mid-afternoon in the centre of Montarnaud. There were barricades and lots of noise in the village centre with a number of young people milling around the local hamburger shop where I bought a coke. I asked the locals where the gîte for the pilgrims was but they knew nothing. I found the church which is usually the reference point, and used my French Orange phone to contact the gîte. I was given directions but it took an hour of mucking around to find the *Chambre d'hôtes*

— dortoir le Temps d'une Pause, a good kilometre out of town. I was warmly welcomed by the dogs and the Mme Cathie Frogé who led me to her veranda and gave me a beer for which I was very grateful. I was pleased my first day was over and I'd made it. I worried that my left leg might cause trouble but it was okay, whereas a corn on my right little toe wasn't. If all I felt was a sore toe I was doing well. No blisters in my new boots! I shared a dormitory with Godfreid and two other men. I had arrived early enough to do my washing and have a siesta on that warm afternoon.

Godfreid and I walked into town for dinner. The village was in festive mood celebrating the Assumption with a carnival and running of the bulls. It beats me that, despite France's claim to be a secular state, it still takes such a religious feast as the Assumption of the Blessed Virgin as a national holiday. Other walkers whom Godfreid knew joined us briefly but we had the opportunity for a good chat. He lived in Paris and had taken off two weeks to walk to Toulouse. He was seriously into Zen, Buddhism and meditation. We continued our chat as we walked back in the night to our beds. I was pleased to lie down. My first night on the Camino d'Arles. When I first began walking in 2010, I was obsessed with security, hiding my passport and wallet under my pillow, etc. but after a while I realised that the world in the form of other pilgrims wasn't out to get me. I was never robbed. I hoped and trusted that I would bring home everything this time. The most important item, my passport was at the bottom of my pack. I doubted if anyone would bother to steal my heavy pack.

In the morning, I felt more fatigued than I wished. I had hoped that a good dinner with company, a few red wines and a good sleep would revive me, but I was sluggish. I put on a brave front in front of my new friend and we walked out of the gîte together but, as he was the faster walker, I invited him to forge ahead. A few minutes later, I passed a notice inviting me *'to plunge into the heart of a Mediterranean landscape and all the sensations that go with it (plongez au coeur d'un pays méditerranéen et de son flat de sensations) and I will see a landscape of vineyards stretching over the hills as far as the eye can see, drink clear water from the village fountains, smell the fragrance of native plants, hear the songs of birds and the rustle of the wind in the trees.'*

Our destination was Saint Guilhem-le-Désert, a distance of 20 kilometres. I missed the markings and took a wrong turn. Be vigilant was the lesson I was learning. Pay attention to the details, especially the red and white markers. I was annoyed for covering unnecessary kilometres. By the time I reached La Boissière which was only 5 kilometres from Montarnaud I felt exhausted. I panicked. I was facing a reality check that I was no spring chicken. Where was my lofty resolve? How was I going to cope with the day? I visited the boulangerie to buy some bread for my lunch and as I walked back to the road feeling drained of energy and morale, weighed down both by my pack and a heavy heart, a car pulled up. An older couple spoke in English. They offered me a lift.

I was surprised. My first instinct was to politely decline. I wanted to walk the whole of this Camino. I wanted to be a hard-core pilgrim walking all the way and carrying everything on my back. Then a voice reminded me: *'Noel, you've already compromised this image by taking the tram in Montpellier and not starting at Arles.'* Perhaps my feeling of exhaustion so early in the day showed in my gait and posture. The same voice seemed to say: *'Noel, be sensible. Accept help when you need it.'* So, I thanked the couple and climbed into the back seat. They were German and owned a house in the village. They regularly saw the passing pilgrims whom they admired for their courage and determination. They were intrigued that I was Australian and had walked other routes of the Camino. I told them I was aiming for Saint Guilhem-le-Désert that day. They wanted to take me all the way but I insisted there was no need. They took me as far as Le Pont Du Diable (the devil's bridge), a distance of 11 kilometres, then turned the car, waved vigorously and drove back across the bridge the way they came. What took about ten minutes would have taken me hours. How grateful I was for that couple's generosity! Providence! God was looking after me. The Camino was looking after me, teaching me the true meaning of gratitude. The scientists call it synchronicity: *'the simultaneous occurrence of events which appear significantly related but have no discernible relation.* Whatever way, their good turn was a stroke of fortune which gave me the impetus to continue. I could not give up on my second day.

I paused by the bridge to watch the canoeists and swimmers in the river below. I had already covered 16 kilometres before midday so I took my time to cover the last four kilometres. Because the village is situated in a ravine by the river, parking is a problem. The Herault tourist board has established a tourist centre with parking by the bridge and a shuttle bus runs to Saint-Guilhem-le-Désert. I could have taken the bus but decided such an action would have really been chickening out. I have chickened out enough already.

I strolled along the busy road skirting the river with frequent stops to gaze into the ravine at the canoes darting about through the tumbled rocks. The day was becoming hotter and more heat was reflected off the surrounding rocks. I continued walking, the shuttle bus passing regularly, sustained by the idea that once I arrived I would comb my backpack for the non-essentials with the hope of lightening my load by at least a couple of kilograms, find the post office and send the stuff back to Australia.

Saint-Guilhem-le-Désert is a beautifully restored medieval village, one of the *plus beaux villages de France*. Founded by Saint Guilhem as a desert place for a monastery, the village's narrow streets teem with tourists in summer. The day was no exception. I found the *Gîte de la Tour* where I shared a room with Godfreid and three others. He was pleased to see that I had arrived in good time as he had arrived just before. I did not mention that I had not walked all the way. One of the ladies in the room looked exhausted. The heat had affected her, she said. I felt sorry for her and was grateful for my good fortune. I went through my backpack and put what I could do without into a bundle. These included my sleeping bag, a pair of town shoes and a pair of trousers. I went searching for the Post Office and found it shut. It opened only in the morning. The day being Friday, it would remain closed until Monday morning. I did not want to carry extra weight any longer. I was desperate to travel lightly so I dumped my bundle in a rubbish bin. An extravagant waste but they were replaceable and I hoped an unencumbered pack would keep me going. I should have known by now the oldest lesson of the Camino: Travel lightly. Sometimes a lesson has to be repeated to sink in.

Over dinner, Godfreid and I discussed our backgrounds. I mentioned my four children and my seven grandchildren one of whom had just arrived. Godfreid told he was aged fifty. He had had two relationships with women who had children but he had no children of his own. I felt his yearning. The last woman had just finished their relationship abruptly without explanation which had left him floundering. I felt for his sense of loss. When I mentioned Maris, her suicide and those of her sisters, he confided his sister had taken her own life. We had a lot in common. Both of us knew the grief of bereavement by suicide. Both of us were in our own ways searching for meaning, he in his Zen and Buddhism, and me in my writing and Camino walks. I was impressed with his fluency in a number of languages. He told me his job was teaching English and was also involved in translation. He frequently asked me for explanation when I used an expression, probably an Australian idiom, which he did not understand.

The next day I awoke refreshed. A good night's sleep, plus a meal and good conversation with Godfreid revitalised me for what lay ahead. I felt like a phoenix rising from the ashes. I was hopeful. My pack was lighter, my body was adapting to this journey out of its comfort zone. I knew I was in for a tough day. I left early. Saint-Guilhem was coming to life. On the square, the restaurants were setting out their tables and chairs under the branches of a huge plane tree with a circumference of about 6 or 7 metres. The shops were shut and the tourists were still in bed. It gave me an opportunity to appreciate the medieval atmosphere of the narrow streets. As I left the village I walked towards impressive limestone cliffs outlined against the blue sky along a small river winding between the olive and fig trees. To the south what appeared to be layered terraces lay abandoned. Behind me I heard the tap-tap of the walkers' stick and soon Godfreid was beside me, wishing me a good day — 'Bon Chemin', 'Buen Camino' and 'A ce soir (See you tonight).'

Looking back on that day Saturday 17th August I would have to say it was the toughest day I have endured on the Camino. Nestled in the valley of the Gellone river, Saint-Guilhem is surrounded by mountains. After a kilometre of flat walking I was confronted by the Roc de la Bissonne and the Cirque de l'Infernet, a gigantic natural wall rising above the pines and oaks. My destination was Saint-Jean-de-la-Blaquière, 25 kilometres away.

So began the steep climb. The rough narrow track zig-zagged

its way up the slope. There was no end to its twists and turns. The top was no nearer and seemed to move away. I wanted to stop, to give the whole caper away, to return to Saint-Guilhem, to Montpellier and catch the train to Paris. Sheer brute will-power kept me going. My frequent breathers allowed me to admire the exhilarating view emerging out of the mountains. The higher I climbed the more fantastic the scene. Below, the valley was tiny and the roads and fields a distant patchwork. My pack was two kilograms lighter, but it got heavier with every step of the climb. Thank God, I had lightened it. I had visions of rolling back down the slope right to the bottom. In addition, loose pebbles forced me to concentrate on every foothold. What was demoralising was the sight of younger walkers who passed me, rocketing up the slope like antelopes.

It took me over two hours to reach the top, willing myself all the way and thinking of nothing more than placing one foot in front of the other. Before I left Australia, I read in my guide book that this route was difficult and was for the fit and healthy. What was I doing here, an eighty-year-old, gasping up slopes, steep enough to make a mountain goat weep! But then as I regained my breath, I gaped at the immensity of the view, the mountaintops extending around me, the valley from which I had emerged far below, ahead, a rolling plateau. I felt on top of the world, like a soaring eagle, a master of the land, in close communion with creation and the Creator. I had succeeded. I had striven with an invincible spirit and finally triumphed over the immediate hardship. I felt new heights of joy and my eyes were opened not only to the magnificent views but to vistas of brilliant victories ahead of me as I faced the next challenge.

Enough of this lofty sentiment! Back on earth, I found myself walking along roads down a very gradual descent but then I was faced with another killer climb and an ugly descent before I reached Saint-Jean-de-la-Blaquière. The 25 kilometres took me eleven hours and an exhausted Noel arrived about 6 pm, too late for washing clothes or a siesta.

I shared a room with five others at the *Gîte St. Jacques, the Gîte municipal au Presbytère* — Godfreid, a French couple and the two girls whom I had seen earlier in the day. The French couple were intriguing because he pulled a cart on which he put both their packs. I liked the village of Saint-Jean-de-la-Blaquière. It had a nice feel about it. All the buildings faced a large square. Everything was so close. The buildings exuded welcome. Godfreid and I had dinner together in an outdoor restaurant just off the main square. Under the canopy of a huge tree we shared more of our lives. My prattling on about my family prompted Godfreid to express regret that he had no children. He had hoped to start a family with his last girlfriend but she wasn't interested and now she had dumped him. He had taken the Camino to spend time reflecting on where he might go from here.

We talked late over a second bottle of wine. It continued to amaze me how a good meal and a generous share of red wine revived me. We walked the short distance back to the gîte and the lady managing the gîte was sitting on her balcony next door. She invited us to join her. We met her husband and their neighbour who lived in a house once owned by an Australian. They were having a quiet drink and we were invited to share. I admired Godfreid's fluency in French. We spoke in English together. I wished I could have been as flexible. Although the French seemed to think I spoke their language fluently I was always conscious of what I was saying and how I was saying it. I had hoped for an early night but our hosts continued to offer us more of their locally brewed drink, to share the stories and gossip of this tiny village and to enjoy their Saturday night.

No one was in a hurry next morning. We lingered over our coffees and I did not leave until 9.00 am. I did not feel the pressure to depart as our destination Lodève was only 13 kilometres. Although shorter, the walk was surprisingly difficult. A long extensive climb was a challenge and much of the walking was over wild rocky gullies, which threatened to throw me off balance. I took my time picking my way through these hazards. After walking through pine and evergreen oak forests with some spectacular views to the south I paused at the *Prieuré Saint-Michel-de-Grandmont*, an abbey founded in the 11th century by the Grandmontaine Order now defunct. They left behind this abbey which is the only one of the Grandmontaine's to have survived. Today it's maintained by *Les Amis du Prieuré de Grandmont* and is classified as an historic monument and opened to the public. I wandered through the group of buildings — a church, a Romanesque cloister, chapter house and cellar — Apart from a lady in the gift shop there was no one else around and in the silence, I absorbed some of the spirit of the place. I thought of those monks long gone to God. They were known to be one of the strictest and austere orders of the Middle Ages. They walked with bare feet, ate no meat, fasted regularly, just worked and prayed, begged for food and lived in perpetual silence. Hard to believe in our noise-filled world!

I was disappointed not to arrive at the *Gîte La Mégisserie*, Lodève until 5 pm as I wanted time for washing and a siesta. I still had yesterdays dirties and no cleans. Still I had five hours of daylight left, time for the clothes to dry so I washed. The day was hot and the evening warm. The same six who had stayed at *Gîte St Jacques* the night before stayed at *Gîte La Mégisserie*. Was anyone else walking the Camino? The six of us dined together at another outdoor restaurant under the umbrella of a large tree. The two French girls were Pauline and Edwitz. They had been walking five days and this Sunday night was their last on the road. Pauline was a theatre teacher and everyone enjoyed her explaining what was involved. The French couple were Elias and Agnes. Elias was enthusiastic about the Camino but Agnes had never done much walking. At a concession, he agreed to bring the cart to carry her pack when she was tired. In addition, she had unspecified ailments which were being tested. We were a Camino family, like other Camino families I had joined in 2010 and 2011, temporary affairs but while we were together, the camaraderie and sharing was strong.

I was planning to walk about 23 kilometres to Joncels the following day so I was up early. I was apprehensive about the day's difficulties but it turned out to be not too bad. The steep ascent was gradual and I was rewarded with some magnificent grand views the higher I climbed. The wind was strong and I was walking into it. I had seen images of the ancient pilgrims battling against the elements, their cloak flowing behind them, the brim of their hats blown back over their heads as they learnt into the wind holding their staff (*bourdon*) tight to steady themselves. Except that I had no staff. I had to lean into the wind, too, and the brim of my hat, too, was blown back, my hat tied securely under my chin. On the heights, the land was exposed and bare. I met no other walkers. In fact, I had met few in my four days. In the distance, I saw two figures approaching. The two young men stopped to chat. Vincent and Guy had been walking from Carcassonne and were making for Montpellier. They were not actually following the Camino, just walking, but were interested in my journey. They were intrigued by my age. I imagined them telling their mates (*copains*) about meeting an eighty-year-old Australian in the middle of a wind-blown nowhere.

I met two others walking against me. They said they had spoken to Godfreid, Pauline and Edwitz. After the steep heights, a long gradual descent led me to Joncels about 4 pm. I had heard that the aubergue at Joncels, a recommended establishment, was closed, but the guide book mentioned a gîte and camping area at Joncelets, a hamlet about 2.5 kilometres from Joncels. Like many of the establishments off the Camino route, the owners were prepared to come looking for walkers and bring them in. So, feeling tired, I rang. The owner arrived shortly after. An enthusiastic young man, Fred said Godfreid had already arrived and had mentioned that I would be arriving, too, and being an older person I would be tired. I must admit I was grateful to be carried on this last stage, even though a short distance and downhill.

The *Trois Granges* was picturesque. A collection of ancient buildings, some in use, others were in a state of restoration with scaffoldings surrounding them. Below was an open area by the river dotted with a few tents. I shared a room in a cabin with Godfreid. Elias and Agnes shared the evening meal along with another couple who were friends of Fred. They had a crazy dog which dodged around the edge of the group. We sat around a large ancient table outside while through the window we watched Fred preparing the meal. He went to a great deal of trouble. The four-course meal was delicious and I was not surprised to hear that he had been a chef in a top Paris restaurant. He came here with his girlfriend about three years previously. They had worked at restoring the buildings but there was still a lot of work to be done. His girlfriend left as there were not enough 'bright lights' in Joncelets and returned to Paris. Now Fred was 'stuck'. He was short on money and the place was for sale. The group discussed many topics. The gossip included stories about walkers, including one about a couple who set out on the Camino and he broke a leg on the first day. There is a lot of interest now in France in learning English. Godfreid gave his views. English was becoming the lingua franca of the European Union. The French needed to be less parochial about their language and embrace English or else they would be left behind.

6

Blessed are you, pilgrim, if your backpack is emptying
of things and your heart does not know where to
hang so many feelings and emotions.
(The Beatitudes of the Pilgrim)

Godfreid wanted to push on and reach Toulouse before his limited time ran out. It was sad to say goodbye. He was a fellow pilgrim, lost at the moment and searching. We were supporting each other. We exchanged phone numbers and he insisted that I contact him when I returned to Paris.

I had plenty of time and wanted an easy day. Fred did not offer to return me to Joncels so I walked up the gentle slope and dawdled through Joncels where the abbey (*abbaye Saint-Pierre-aux-Liens*) is one of the oldest in the regions. I strolled along the calm and peaceful vallée du Sourian between Joncels and Lunas. In the forest, I came across Elias and Agnes eating lunch and I paused for a while with them. Agnes looked tired as usual and I noticed her pack was on the cart. I asked Elias how he negotiated the rough tracks, he replied with difficulty and sometimes he had to carry the cart, too. I felt a little sorry for him for his burden (two backpacks and a *chariot*) as there were many rough sections on this route.

I was walking in high country, in the high valley of the Orb, in the mountains of the Haut Languedoc to the village of Le Bousquet d'Orb in a very picturesque setting among the forest clad hills. The village was once known for coal mining and glass blowing but has now turned its hand to small manufacturing. At the top of a hill was St Martins, a church set in a tiny village of narrow laneways, stairways and a jumble of houses which seemed to be on top of each other. I was ready to light a candle in this ancient church but it was closed. I had the name of a lady who took in pilgrims but she referred me to another number at La Séguinerie, a small hamlet across the valley from St Martin. My host came down the road to greet me. His house was new with an extensive and profuse vegetable garden. He gave me a comfortable room with a Queen-size bed and ensuite, a luxury. I had arrived early enough for a siesta and to send a few texts to the family. This was my sixth day of walking and I had come over 100 kilometres. My room led out to a patio where I had dinner on my own. My host was an older grey-haired man who looked like a retired professional or businessman. I was not invited into the house. He was courteous and respectful but not particularly friendly and although I heard family noise I met no other members of the household. This was the first time I'd dined on my own. I wondered where Godfreid was that evening. I would have enjoyed his conversation. What you lose on the roundabout, you gain on the swings. Instead, I watched the hills opposite turn purple as the shadows climbed with the sunset and almost immediately the moon rose. I enjoyed the silence and the beauty of the evening.

Despite my comfortable bed, the night turned into a restless tussle with my anxiety about the next day, which I knew would be long and without any facilities. I left my luxury early for I knew I had almost 30 kilometres to cover. My host's tomato plants were loaded with fruit and, God forgive me, I souvenired two of them to supplement my bread and cheese lunch. The day was spent in forest and the climb was several hundred metres. There was no water, no villages, no houses.

I was fascinated by the silence and the extensive views. I was in high country. Without doubt the day covered one of the most beautiful stages of my Chemin. After crossing the bridge over the river Orb I walked on a carpet of leaves and pine needles through forests of broad leaved trees and conifers along ridges and over crests, about seven of them, into the heart of the forest of Monts d'Orb. Around me I sensed the forest was full of life and I came across startled deer which took off as soon as they saw me. I was in deep wild remote France away from towns, villages and people. I relished my solitude and vast silence. Behind the silence I could hear the gentle stirring of leaves losing their fight with gravity, the buzz of insects around my head, the songs of birds invisible among the tree branches. I was in communion with creation. I felt part of creation and creation part of me. It's tricky to describe this feeling. I sensed a Presence, something connecting like a field force, something elusive that was here before I got here and will still be here after I'm gone, inviting me into a different sense of who I am. I was not on my own. I'm not just living my own life by myself. Something Else is living in me and through me. I am part of a much bigger mystery, of which I can only sense a glimpse as my muffled steps tread lightly on the floor of the forest.

I meet one other person that day. We exchanged 'Bon Chemin' as he passed and I lost sight of him among the trees as he took a turn in the track.

Because of the constant ascents and descents, I picked up a stick to aid my walking. In all my years of bush walking and following the Camino, I had never used a stick although so many swore to their usefulness. The first stick broke as I leaned on it, so I searched among the leaves on the forest floor for a sturdier one. It stood the test of my leaning. I found it helpful both in climbing and descending and wondered why I hadn't used one before. I was grateful the day was without rain for I had to negotiate rough rocky slopes that could have been slippery and dangerous. On one of these slopes I was picking my way down, placing my feet carefully among the rocks, leaning for support and balance on my stick when it broke. Down I went, arse over tit. I tried to save myself. No avail. I tumbled down several metres. My first thought on coming to rest: *'No bones broken!'* I felt the sting of cuts and scratches on my legs. I remained where I lay, recovering from the shock, thanking God that I had survived without injury. I sat up and looked around. My pack was still on my back but it had burst open and its contents were strewn up the hill. Thank God for my pack. It had clung tenaciously to my body and saved me from bruising or worse. I found my first aid kit a few metres away and used all my band aids to stop the bleeding. The thought occurred to me. If I had broken a limb, I could have been lying there for some time. I would have been in deep shit. I was on my own for I had seen just one other person that day. I did another round of thanking God, then climbed up the slope, gathered my scattered belongings and returned them to my pack. I sat on a rock regaining my composure. The stuffing had been knocked out of my carcass. How I wished my bed for the night was just around the corner but I still had several kilometres. How pleased I was when Saint-Gervais-sur-Mare came into view. I would have arrived earlier but did an unnecessary detour around some ruins above the village and couldn't find my way back to the track. I'm sure the ruins were interesting and very significant, but I'd run out of puff and curiosity. I just wanted to lie down, bash the spine and flake out.

I was more exhausted than usual by the time I arrived at Saint-Gervais-sur-Mare. I found my accommodation down a narrow street, *Gîte d'étape* run by M Michel Bras. The combination of a hard day and the shock of a fall had me on bedrock but after a shower and change of clothes I found enough energy to explore the village and find a bar. I needed a beer (*Une bière, s'il vous plait, Monsieur*). The village itself is quaint. It seems to be heaped up on itself with stairs and covered walkways. M. Bras and his wife were warm and welcoming, an unsophisticated and homely couple. I shared the evening meal with them in the kitchen along with Pierre, who had passed me that day. Pierre was Italian and spoke French. He had set out from Italy and was making for Santiago. He had been on the road for weeks. I suspected he could have been a priest. We chatted about the Camino and about the beauty of the area, the Hérault district of the Languedoc-Roussillon region. I went to bed early and had a dreamless sleep. I was tired.

I left St Gervais late. After walking through the narrow streets, I was back in the forest and faced a demanding climb to the little village of Castanet-le-Haut. I followed the meandering stream at the edge of the village and paused to converse with a chap down on the banks cutting back a hedge that bordered the stream. He told he was the village handyman who had to keep the village looking neat. He had done a good job. The hedges, lawns and trees around the bridge and the adjacent square were well manicured. There were no shops but just as I was about to leave, an itinerant épicerie (grocer) pulled up under the umbrella of a large tree, lifted the sides of his truck and revealed a shop stocked with cheeses, sausages and other delicacies. Out of their houses came the ladies with their shopping bags and lined up to be served, exchanging the gossip as they waited in the queue. On the side of his vehicle was a notice listing the various villages he visited and the times. Thursday morning was Castanet-le-Haut's day. He stayed for 30 minutes.

I was grateful for my timing for I was witnessing the economic and social side of rural France in action. The épicerier was providing a public service to the families of these isolated villages. I imagined his day, travelling around the mountains from village to village and stocking his shop in his home village ready for the next day. Some form of travelling shop had probably been visiting the village for centuries and today it arrived in a diesel truck. I would have enjoyed staying here. My guide book listed two gîtes but at mid-morning it was too early to stop.

I waited for the ladies to be served and then bought a long sausage to munch along the way. For most of the way I followed the wheel tracks of the cart that Elias was pulling. I came across the couple a number of times as they were resting. She said that she would be stopping at Castres for her body had had enough, but Elias was planning to walk as far as Toulouse. I forgot to ask him what he would do with the cart if he only had his own pack to carry. The track climbed steeply for most of the afternoon up to a cross roads at a place named Ginestet. Mid-way between Saint Gervais-sur-Mare and Murat-sur-Vèbre lay two choices for a bed. To the south lay *Gîte d'étape Les Clèdes*, to the north lay a gîte at the tiny hamlet of Figairolles. Both were about 2 kilometres off the Camino route. I chose to go south.

When I mentioned to M Michel Bras back at St Gervais-sur-Mare that I would probably stay at *Les Clèdes*, he used the French equivalent of *'grotty'* to describe both the place and its proprietor. The year before I visited a third world country, Timor Leste. I discovered that my version of grotty was not really grotty. What I once may have thought was incredibly disgusting — uncleaned squat toilets, flush toilets not working and overflowing with shit, showering with a bucket of cold water in a mouldy bare concrete bathroom — became kind of run-of-the-mill.

M. Bras' gîte was comfortable, neat and clean. His wife's influence was evident in the lace table cloths and fresh flower arrangements. So I decided to approach *Les Clèdes* with an open mind, knowing that it would not match M. Bras' gîte in neatness and order. The sky was overcast, and although there was some hours to sunset, it became darker almost eerie as I left the sealed road and entered the forest. Crudely painted signs pointed the way. What the sign said was 50 metres ahead was more like 500. I felt I was in some magic woods as I walked more deeply into the forest with the curious eyes of a child, half expecting a spectre to emerge saying '*Go back! Go back!*'

The gîte was well hidden but eventually it emerged. The cement rendered building hadn't seen maintenance for years; the blue shutters and doors had not received a drop of paint for decades. The only sign of modernity was a satellite dish. I was greeted by two dogs. I entered the open door calling out '*Personne?*' (Anybody there?) and about 30 seconds later, the owner Monsieur Christian Edel appeared. He was like one of the brotherhood of the forest. He wore a cap and some clothes which could have been on his body for some time, a bushy moustache while an unlit half smoked hand-make cigarette hung from his lips. He reminded me of Jacques Prévert, a French poet and screenwriter whose poems are still read. On my previous Caminos, I met a few eccentric characters but M. Christian Edel was the first on this Camino. The evening turned out to be one of the most memorable. He warmly welcomed me into a disordered room set out with tables arranged like a restaurant and a bar in the corner. He took up a position behind the bar where he remained for most of the evening and poured both of us a drink, the first of many, from one of the many bottles from the shelves behind. The room was a den, the refuge of a single male, with none of the comforts provided by a mother or wife such as Mme Bras. The walls were full of leather jackets and motor bike helmets. I'm not sure if Christian received many guests but he was definitely ready for them with tables set and even menus. From his position behind the bar he entertained me. He hardly stopped talking. He told me he was an 'artiste,' a magician and a juggler and demonstrated his skills with cards. He showed me old photos of a younger Christian in action as well as a newspaper clipping reviewing a performance. He loved his dogs. His favourite had died but he showed me a tiny helmet which the dog wore when he rode with him on one of his motor bikes. I could see two of these machines through the window. Initially I wondered if I was safe, but concluded he was harmless — a lonely old man off the Camino route who craved company. He thought my pack looked heavy. His ancient rusty scales said it weighed 15 kilograms. If they were correct, no wonder I was stuffed climbing the hills. After a number of drinks, I asked if I could clean up. He took me upstairs to a large dormitory just below the roof with many beds packed close together. The 'bathroom' was at the end. It was on a slant. Hot water came from a makeshift heater and the shower was a garden rose. At least the toilet was clean. The blankets were old and grubby and I wondered about bed bugs. I chose a bed under a skylight which I opened because the room was airless, dark and gloomy. Everything was rough and make-shift.

Downstairs, Christian produced a casserole for dinner. After so much alcohol I needed some blotting paper, something to eat. Christian continued to pour drinks both for both of us. I made friends with his dogs. Christian told me stories, particularly about the little dog which had died. He used to take part in his performances. He expounded on his philosophy of life which was essentially to enjoy a relationship while one can. I told him my story. By the end of the evening we were mates. I had to concentrate on maintaining my balance in climbing the narrow stairs. The place was rough. It met all the criteria of grottiness but I had a bizarre but wonderful evening in the company of an eccentric yet gentle person. I slept well that night.

In the morning, Christian was having his first drink for the day while I was eating breakfast. He and the dogs gave me a charming farewell, waving as I made my way up the track through the forest to the road. I thought of Christian all day and the lonely life he lead. I heard later a sad story. His ailing mother had left the house some ten years previously for a walk one snowy winter evening and never returned. Imagine the impact on the son.

I had a shorter day ahead of me. I continued to walk through forest. There was more tough climbing to face. I reached the highest point at Cap de Faulat. The morning was overcast and gloomy and the same gloom descended on me as heavy as my pack. Why on earth was I here, walking in remote France? Back home I lived in a world of comfort on demand and instant gratification. There are many holiday destinations which offer just that! The minimum of facilities and the absence of other walkers contrasted so sharply with the Camino Francés through Spain where there was a bar every few kilometres. I had to admit, however, that I had worthy compensations. I valued the silence and the solitude of walking in deep forest, the magnificence of landscapes, the vistas of river valleys, the beauty of a line of stones across a gushing stream, the charm of coming across villages nestling in a forest valley as if they'd been there for centuries. As I crossed a road, a cyclist stopped and greeted me enthusiastically. He had walked the Camino himself. He was into cycling nowadays and was planning to cover the same Camino route in the saddle. I felt the bond of instant camaraderie. He wished me 'Bon Chemin' as he parted. Our meeting was therapeutic; my gloom had been unshackled and banished with the breeze, my optimistic positive self-restored. I don't let myself stay down for too long.

Eventually the forest cleared to make way for farmland. I overshot Murat-sur-Vèbre and had to retrace my steps but I arrived at 2.30 pm. I needed money but the 'distributeur' (ATM) was in the Tabac shop which opened at 4 pm. I had enough cash to buy a beer at the Snack Bar Chapy, then found the Mairie for the key to the Gîte Communal. The gîte was just around the corner and as I arrived, a group of teenagers from the camping ground opposite asked if they could look inside. I saw no harm in letting these French youngsters in. Curiosity satisfied, they thanked me and departed not before one tried her few words of English on me. Shortly after they returned and offered me a good sturdy walking stick. They had found it and thought I needed it. They saw that I had a stick from the forest, not to be trusted as I found out. I thanked them for their kindness. Off they dashed again. Another example of the way in which the people respect and look after their pilgrims. Another lesson in the true meaning of gratitude. I settled in. A neat kitchen lead on to an L-shaped dormitory. I decided to cook my dinner so I returned to the Tabac for some cash and visited the épicerie. I explored the camping ground and talked to my new young friends. They were enjoying the last few days of their holidays and would be back at school the following week. I found Elias and Agnes. They had camped and set up their tent, their cart to one side. I was the only guest at the gîte. I shared the toilet with the campers but I had the key to the shower. I enjoyed cooking for myself. I zapped a very acceptable microwave dinner Boeuf Bourguignon with eggs and cheese, accompanied by a bottle of good French red wine.

The next day the route was not as difficult. I was still in the high country. There were steep hills earlier in the day but the second half was almost all descent. It rained all day, a light misty rain, but sufficient for me to wear my Sydney Swans poncho for the first time. I met three ladies walking together. I could hear them talking from a distance. Later I met a German lady on her own. I walked through forest most of the day although around the mid-way point I edged a lake (Lac du Laouzas). La Salvetat-sur-Agoût looked an ancient town, buildings packed together, perched proudly on its rocky outcrop, its wet slate rooves shimmering in the afternoon light. I found the *Auberge de la Resse* about a kilometre out of town. It offered meals and accommodation to everyone with a special price and menu for pilgrims. The restaurant was busy that Saturday evening and the family was enlisted to help. The building needed maintenance but the place was comfortable and I had a room with ensuite. I even had a TV. Luxury! The day was my 10th and I had covered 180 kilometres.

Sunday found me in gentle rolling country with a few hills to climb and long downhill stretches. Mostly forest, but there was some farmland with cows, sheep and newly mown hay. I met no other walkers. I knew Elias and Agnes were ahead of me for the cart's wheels had left their mark in the damp earth. I arrived at Anglès about 3 pm Sunday afternoon to find a market in full swing. I met Elias and Agnes. They had booked into the *Gîte La Gariguette* so around I went and found Mme Nicole Collett who told me she had a bed available. I was not allowed to take my backpack upstairs as a precaution against bedbugs. Her gîte was quaint, furnished with a collection of knick-knacks gathered over a life time. I returned to the markets, found Elias and we went for a beer at the local bar which doubled as a Tabac. My first opportunity for conversation!

They had been walking the Camino for many years, covering a small section at a time. There were five guests for dinner back at the gîte including the German lady I met earlier in the day. Heidi preferred to speak English as her French was not good. A Frenchman named Gilbert had plenty to say. Our conversation focused on Camino experiences. My contribution was the night I spent with Christian at *Les Clèdes*.

The next day, I walked through forest where timber cutters were at work despite the rain. I passed three ladies slower than me. They knew me as the Australian who was walking alone. Even on the Camino d'Arles where there were fewer walkers, the grapevine worked.

My destination was Boissezon, the scene of many disasters during the wars of religion when the town was occupied in turn by protestant and catholic troops. I arrived at Boissezon, delightfully medieval in ambience, about 3 pm and found the gîte, the *Gîte d'étape et de séjour Le Saint-Jacques*. Although I had only met her the night before, Heidi greeted me as an old friend. Gilbert was there, too, along with 8 ladies including the three I'd met on the track. All the ladies knew each other; there was much laughter and loud conversation. The scene was chaotic. Everyone had draped their wet weather gear on whatever was available. They stuffed their boots with newspaper to absorb the dampness. The lady who collected the money arrived about 5. My presence annoyed her because I wasn't in her book. I had already claimed a bed and had unpacked my stuff so she let me stay. I had rung ahead for the first few days but as there was always room, I thought booking ahead was unnecessary.

The evening meal was organised by the local café. It was open despite its being Monday when all the shops in France seem to shut. It closed Tuesday afternoons and all day

Wednesday so we were lucky. The *Restaurant Les Deux Mousquetaires* provided a *plateau-repas pèlerin* (a pilgrim meal) to take away. You placed your order during the afternoon and they delivered it to the gîte. The meals arrived at the appointed time on airline trays. That night the camaraderie was high. The eight ladies were stopping at Castres so there were many farewells. Heidi, Gilbert and I were pressing on. The ladies were impressed that I was planning to reach Spain. I had a long conversation with Heidi. She preferred to talk to me as an English speaker. She was not comfortable with French even though I thought her French was as good as mine. She was an academic with a string of higher degrees. Back home she was highly respected and was addressed as *Doktor*, but on the Camino she was Heidi. She seemed to enjoy talking to an Australian unaccustomed to deferring to such learning. On the Camino all ranks are levelled. Pilgrims leave behind their status and standing in their communities and everyone is regarded as equal, sharing the same joys, pain and burdens.

In a small park on the outskirts of Castres I met three of the ladies from the previous night drinking champagne, celebrating the end of their Camino and waiting for the brother of Beatrice to pick them up. They offered me a drink and told me of a free bus service which could take me into the centre of town. The bus stop was nearby and, after checking that a bus would be along in ten minutes, I thanked the ladies for their company and their grog. The bus wandered around the suburbs but eventually dropped me on a bridge in Centre-Ville. I was feeling bedraggled and needed time and space to tuck in some of my loose ends. I had lost my Opinel pocket knife and my camera had packed up. I needed to find a computer to receive and send emails. I hadn't been in touch with the family for days. Rather than stay in a gîte I wanted privacy, so, hang the expense, I booked into the *Hôtel Rivière* which overlooked the river Agoût, lined with barges and tour boats. The private room was luxury. After a shower, I was able to wander around immodestly, spread out all my possessions and rearrange my pack. I ventured out to explore the town. Castres is quite a large town with an extensive shopping area. It is an important stop on the Chemin de Saint-Jacques because the abbey church constructed in the 9th century guards the relics of Saint Vincent, a martyr renowned in Spain. The name of the town comes from the Latin word castrum which means *'fortified place'*. That night I had a meal at Subway, cheap as against the expense of the hotel. The rowdy young male patrons of Subway weren't too interested in chatting to an elderly Australian, so I went around the corner, found a bar by the riverside for a couple of glasses of red wine with more congenial fellow patrons.

7

Blessed are you, pilgrim, if what concerned you
most is not to arrive, but to arrive with others.

Beatitudes of the Pilgrim

I'd been walking for thirteen days and covered 240 kilometres. I thought of staying an extra night and having a rest day, but decided to have a short day with a late start which would allow a sleep-in. I quit Castres about 11 am not before meeting Heidi. We had coffee together on the plaza in the town centre. She and Gilbert had stayed in a gîte. Gilbert pushed on but she needed a rest day. She was planning to take the train the next day to Pau and continue walking from there. We exchanged contact details.

Near Viviers-lès-Montagnes a farm offered pilgrims a demi-pension for 25 euros, but they were closed, so I opted for *Chambre et table d'hôtes Le Pasteillé*, the only other accommodation listed. I had to walk along a busy road, the D621, dangerous with its trucks whizzing by at high speed. *Le Pasteillé* was off the Camino route so I left the familiar markers to arrive just after 4 pm to a beautifully restored old house surrounded by gardens. The hostess Mme Joëlle Limes welcomed me graciously and for a time we sat and chatted in her beautifully appointed kitchen. The house was 200 years old, lovingly restored and elegantly furnished with drapes and antique furniture. She tried to speak English but her vocabulary was limited and we reverted to French. We joked about the similarity of our names — Joëlle and Noël. I was shown to my room. It was huge, with a heavy antique door, a king-sized bed, TV, and ensuite. The furniture was antique, far too grand for grubby pilgrims. I was used to utilitarian dormitories but, while I could, I enjoyed my surroundings. After a shower and some washing which I hung on a barbed wire fence, I sat in the garden writing my journal to the cackling of the chooks and ducks. Joëlle's husband, Patrice, arrived home and joined me in the garden and offered me a beer. He worked in Castres and enjoyed getting to his home in the country with his vegetable garden, small orchard, chooks and ducks. For dinner Joëlle had changed into an elegant dress and I felt as if I was a special guest, sitting down to a dinner party. We lingered over aperitifs and hors d'oeuvres, then she served a beautiful duck casserole. Patrice found his red wine and we lingered further over the dinner table with liquors. They were interested in my background and why had I come so far. I felt privileged to be in their home. The surroundings suggested that they were well off and I wondered why they allowed pilgrims in. I asked them why. Joëlle said she enjoyed meeting the people. They came from all over and had interesting backgrounds and stories. The night cost me 75 euros, the most expensive so far. I enjoyed the luxury and lapped up my hosts' attentiveness.

In the morning, I was farewelled and Patrice showed me a short cut through his back fence to get back on the Camino. The day was easy walking, mostly flat. I had left behind the mountains and had descended on to the plain. I paused at a tiny village for lunch and made use of a pilgrim shelter. One of the villagers joined me. His name was Danton and he was aged 7 (*sept ans*). He kept dashing off on his scooter and returning for a chat. He told me he went to school and when I asked why he wasn't at school today he told me he was on holidays. I could hear two ladies nattering in one of the nearby houses. Every now and then one of them called out to check on Danton,

I assumed that his mother thought he was safe. If ever she had advised him not to talk to strangers, Danton ignored that advice. Perhaps both he and his mother could see I was a pilgrim with my pack and shell, and that was okay. I wondered what they thought about stranger danger in this part of France. I walked for eight and half hours and covered 29 kilometres. This was the first time I passed through not one but two towns with facilities and I had been walking for fifteen days. Dourgne boasted a baker, butcher and small supermarket while Sorèze had two bakers, restaurants and supermarkets. I found a church and lit a candle for Maris, my first opportunity. A candle is a symbol of hope and love, of light and warmth, of memory and celebration. A candle is so powerful. It's like a parable. In burning itself out, it gives light to others.

Both Dourgne and Sorèze had chamber d'hôtes but no gîte. Having spent up big on accommodation the previous two nights, I pushed on to the communal gîte at Revel. Situated in the Haute Garonne, Revel is a small historic medieval city of about 8000 inhabitants. It boasts the largest covered market place in France. The entire town is constructed around the market place and is surrounded by arcades named *las Garlandas*, perfect for promenading. In contrast to other gîtes, this one was easy to find in a street just off the market place. After a shower and washing, I went exploring and did my own promenading looking at the shops, bars and stalls. The gîte is run by the Friends of the Camino de Santiago in Occitan (*des Amis du Chemin de Saint-Jacques en Occitanie*) and Joslin was the volunteer that evening. She was a warm welcoming inclusive lady. Staying that night were Gilbert, whom I had met two nights previously at Boissezon, and Robert. Joslin prepared a beautiful meal and the four of us sat at the table discussing our Camino experiences. Once again, we were a little family bonded together by our shared experiences. Joslin had the right personality for her role. Not only was she a good cook, she had the personality to facilitate conversation and to help everyone feel they were included. She enjoyed people and conversation. She loved her volunteer role and worked regularly. She had been at this gîte for two weeks, she said, the chief cook and bottle washer. This was her last evening (Thursday) but after two days rest she would be working again from Sunday at Baziège. She hoped she might see us there.

We enjoyed a convivial breakfast with Joslin. I was looking forward to the day because I would be following the canal la Rigole which eventually flows into le Canal du Midi. I found the canal and at 8 am began walking. Something was wrong. The sun was not in the right place. I worked out I was walking east instead of west and turned around and was back at my starting point at 9 am. I was annoyed with myself but, at the same time, thankful that I had wasted an hour rather than a whole day. As predicted, it was flat all the way. I had to share the path with stacks of cyclists. I met Sibylle. She said she was German although she spoke excellent French. Most Germans I had met so far in France preferred to speak English. We stopped at a restaurant by the Lac de Lencles and shared a cake.

I was making for Les Cassès which was off the Rigole for a gîte and chambre d'hôtes known as *La Passeur-Elle*. The guide book recommended this establishment so I was keen to see it. I was greeted by the proprietor Christiane. She was tall and slim and had a pleasant though commanding presence. I soon discovered she was a veteran, accustomed to organising pilgrims. There were four of us — Sibylle, Michel, Didier and me. She kept us and our packs outside in her courtyard. It was not unpleasant for she had a well-tended garden of vegetables, fruit trees and flower beds. There was time to wash and relax in the sun. Eventually Christiane allowed us to our beds but we were forbidden to take our packs in. We dined in the court-yard, the five of us. Michel was from Nice. He was chatty the same as Sibylle. Didier did not say much. He was German and didn't understand French well. Once again, we became a small Camino family bound together by our common journey.

There was nothing ahead in the way of cheap accommoda-tion. Christiane recommended a friend Danielle who ran *le Goutille* near Avignonet-Lauragais. She was new to the game and hadn't made her way into the guide books. The four of us left together in the morning and Christiane walked with us through the small village to a cross roads where la Rigole was visible below, easily identifiable by the line of trees which followed it. Didier forged ahead but I walked with Sibylle and Michel all the way.

Eventually the Rigole joined the Canal du Midi. The Midi is broader, about 20 metres wide and allows boats up to 30 metres long to move through its waters. Plane trees provide a beautiful shade. Crowds of cyclists filled the path. Every now and then, locks interrupted the monotony and often there was a bar or small restaurant, popular with the cyclists. The day was Saturday and we were not far from Toulouse so town folk were out for the day.

It's impossible not to be awed by the Canal du Midi. It's a major achievement of the 17th century, one of the finest con-struction works of the period and inscribed a UNESCO World Heritage site in 1996. Its construction took place between 1666 and 1681 during the reign of Louis XIV. 241 kilometres long, its original motivation was to foster the wheat and wine trade. It runs from Sète on the Mediterranean to Toulouse. Beyond Toulouse, other canals run as far as Bordeaux so that the whole system links the Mediterranean with the Atlantic. Once used as a means of transporting goods and people, the Canal is now mainly frequented by boaters and tourists.

The canals were a welcome change. I had no mountains to traverse while the beautiful plane trees provided shade and relief from the heat. Too easy! Nevertheless, I had thoughts of giving the project away once I arrived at Toulouse which we'd reach in about two days. My eighty-year-old body was tired from crossing the mountains, from walking through difficult and isolated country. What the heck was I doing walking with backpack along the canal while others of my age (and younger) were on the canal, sitting in cruise boats, sipping their cool drink, gazing curiously at the old people on the banks. Both Sibylle and Michel were in their late 60s or early 70s. We made a geriatric trio. Aging is a fact of life, but it doesn't mean you have to slow down to a complete halt.

As I listened to my footfalls on the path, a voice bombarded my soul:

Noel! Get real! Finish at Toulouse. No need to go further. You've already walked 1500 kilometres in 2010 and 2011 and by the time you reached Toulouse you would have covered another 360. Not bad for an old bloke! Toulouse is a major city with many attractions. You could use it as a base to visit Carcassonne and Albi.

But I heard another voice:

Courage Noël! You came to France to walk as far as Puente la Reina in Spain. Have a rest day in Toulouse. You'll feel much better and be ready to tackle the last 500 kilometres. Thank God that you took the punt to make this pilgrimage despite your age and the grim warnings of the guide books.

At one stage the Camino route left the Canal for Avignonet-Lauragais, but we chose to follow the variation which continued along the Canal. We left the Canal to follow the directions given us by Christiane to get to *La Goutille* up a steep incline, the first for the day. Down another incline and we arrived at a farm house surrounded by undulating fields of vegetables, their green foliage waving in the gentle breeze. Danielle was very gracious and welcoming but shy. It was obvious she was a novice in the game. Her house was charming. It looked as if it had been standing for centuries. The walls were crumbling but the shutters were freshly painted bright blue. The interior had been renovated and the furniture was new. The evening was warm and we sat down to dinner outside and had great conversation as the sun set and the surrounding hills and fields turned purple and darkened.

The three of us left together, climbing out of the valley and down to the Canal du Midi which we followed all the day. It was a fine clear morning, another great day for walking. Being Sunday, everybody was out cycling. The French expression for everybody is *tout le monde* which means literally all the world. All the world was on bikes that beautiful fine day. Most were steady and sped along in a straight line but others were wobbly and took up the whole path. We had to dodge them and be occasionally surprised as they come up on us from behind. Families were out, making the most of the last weekend of the school holidays, the parents encouraging their youngsters to keep pedalling. As we moved further west the banks of the canal were lined with more boats, moored, some with washing lines, satellite dishes, gardens, water and plumbing pipes installed. They were people's homes. Many had bicycles on their decks. What a quaint simple romantic life style, living on a boat and cycling to the nearest shop for provisions! More cruise boats passed by, their decks lined with deck chairs filled with elderly tourists. I had left the remote mountains and forests behind and was moving into civilisation, which was Toulouse.

We stopped in the shade by the banks and shared our lunch not only with each other but with the inquisitive ducks which swam from the other bank. We arrived in Baziège earlier afternoon and soon found the gîte, the *Accueil Pèlerin local diocésain*, a refuge solely for pilgrims run by the local church. Out came Joslyn. She embraced me with a big hug as if I were a long-lost friend even though I had only met her two nights previously at *Les Cassès*. How the spirits were lifted to receive such a welcome! I had time for washing, a siesta and a tour of the town. Everything was shut except the church, built of pink red bricks and intriguing for its five bells each in its own recess.

I rang Godfreid. We had parted at Joncelets two weeks previously but he was only a day or so ahead as I had seen his name a number of times in the gîtes' diaries. He had sent me a text and I rang to thank him. He was at Toulouse and was returning to Paris. He repeated his invitation to contact him when I arrived in the City of Light.

Joslyn created a beautiful casserole and found some wine in a locked cupboard. The four of us sat around the table well into the evening. The discussion was mainly about food and cheeses. Once again, we were a Camino family, bonded by our shared adventure. Joslyn reaffirmed her love of her volunteer role, caring for the pilgrims. She had no intentions of "retiring". It's people like Joslyn welcoming you at the end of the day that make up for all the fatigue and discomfort of long distance walking. She was keen to organise the next day for me and recommended a gîte in Toulouse.

I must admit that Joslyn's enthusiasm for her role of hospitalière had me thinking that was something I could do one of these days.

Michel left early for he had a train to catch in Toulouse. Because of time restraints he wanted to take the train to Auch and continue walking from there. After another warm farewell from Joslyn, Sibylle and I returned to the Canal du Midi. My preference was usually to walk alone but not today. We walked together. She talked all day. She was hard work. I had to concentrate. She had no English so conversation was in French. I had to reply. She had a habit of finishing what I was saying, which was not always correct. No time for meditation or reflection, or allowing my mind to slip into neutral. Just as well the way was so flat and it was impossible to get lost. The canal was always there. As we neared Toulouse the crowd of boats thickened and as many joggers as cyclists competed for space.

At the edge of Toulouse, there at Ramonville was a Metro station, its car park full of commuters' cars. It made more sense to take the metro into the centre of town rather than crawl the many kilometres through the suburbs. We took the escalator to the platform and boarded a carriage as full of passengers as any metro in Paris. We stood out with our packs, sticks and hiking gear. I chose to stand. It was easier with a pack on. Sibylle found a seat just below me. The elderly lady next to her befriended us. She loved *les pèlerins* (pilgrims), she said. She wished she could walk herself. Then through tears she told us about how lonely she was after her husband's death. Sibylle held her hand. It was comforting to think that we were able to support albeit briefly this lady who needed someone to talk to. I had some understanding of the journey she was on.

After three weeks, most of it in solitude, the shock of a big city was overpowering. Toulouse is the fourth largest city in France with 1,250,000 inhabitants. It's the centre of the European aerospace industry and boasts the third largest university campus in France. Little wonder I felt disorientated as I wandered through the crowded bustling vast rectangular Place du Capitale. The architecture of the city is unique. The buildings are made with pinkish terracotta bricks. Sibylle had already mentioned to me the nickname of *la ville rose* (pink city). She knew the city and we made our way to the address Joslyn had given us close to the church of the Jacobins. The gîte was known as the *Gîte des Jacobins*, not mentioned in any guide book. After much searching, we found it in a small apartment on the third floor of an adjacent building with access through an enclosed courtyard. Our host was Christian, friendly enough but preoccupied with his laptop. The bedroom was intimate. Just by the front door, it housed two double bunks and in a corner a spiral staircase led up to the attic which was a storeroom but doubled as a bedroom for Christian's son on his visits. The toilet was off a tiny balcony which looked over the courtyard to the church of the Jacobins. To get to the bathroom you went outside the apartment to the landing. You had to remember to take the apartment key with you. Sibylle and I both took the bottom bunks, no more than an arm's length apart. You could easily lean over from one bed to the other. I had slept in rooms with ladies before but, being so close to each other, we could have been in the same bed. This had all the makings of a spontaneous liaison.

After settling in we went out for dinner at a nearby restaurant, a haunt for students. A large room at the back was full of young people, making lots of noise greeting each other. The school holidays over, they were returning to their studies. Sibylle and I dined in a quieter room at the front. We discussed our immediate futures. Sibylle was planning to spend a day in Toulouse and take the bus home the day after. I, too, was planning a rest day. I could continue on or perhaps pause for a few days and take a trip to Carcassonne or Albi. Sibylle knew Albi well. As well as a museum to the painter Toulouse-Latrec, it boasted a grand medieval fortress cathedral. Or I could decide to give away my walking and do some touring before going home. As I lay in bed that night my two voices discussed the options. I heard the voice that said: '*I'll keep on going.*'

On the morning of a new day, we went our separate ways. My priority was to find an internet café. When I had checked my emails at Castres six days previously, I found one from my publishers keen to organise a print run for my latest book. The printing would be done in China and be ready for Christmas. A great idea but I hadn't seen a copy of the galley print for proof reading. It was supposed to arrive in Montpellier. I sent separate emails to my daughter Angela. She had seen the galley print and said there were a few small errors. I wanted ALL the errors eliminated. There is nothing worse for an author than to discover errors once the book is published and printed.

The streets of Toulouse were bursting with pedestrians and traffic. Tourists added to the throng. I met the same Australian lady from Coogee twice on my rounds of the sites which included the Cathedral of Saint Etienne, the Basilica of Saint Sernin and the Church of the Jacobins. Toulouse has a definite charm and one could be tempted to stay several days. Its history goes back to Roman times. I did a considerable amount of walking on what was supposed to be a rest day. I had lunch at Flunch, a chain of cafeteria style restaurants. I got to know Flunch at Chambéry as they provide a good range of meals at a reasonable price. The purists or gourmands of French style cooking would shun the mass production of Flunch, but I didn't come to France for its cooking.

Sibylle was back at the gîte when I returned. She was organising her stuff ready to quit the Camino. She had visited far more churches than I had and was keen to tell me in detail about them. As in any city there were many churches and places to visit. I was content to wander where my feet took me or to sit in a park and watch the people passing.

We had dinner together at a crêperie and then went for a stroll around the town. The streets were full of students out with their mates for the evening.

8

Blessed are you, pilgrim, if you discover that one step back to help another is more valuable than a hundred steps forward without seeing who or what is by your side.
—The Beatitudes of the Pilgrim

Christian gave us a chatty farewell and Sibylle and I left together. I walked with her through the early morning streets. I sensed she was sad to leave the Camino and wanted my company in this final stage. I escorted her to the bus station and saw her on her bus. She appreciated my support. The Camino had made us brother and sister. We exchanged email addresses. The railway station was nearby and I took the train to Pibrac, avoiding a tedious and lengthy walk through the suburbs. Toulouse represents both an end and a beginning on the Chemin. For many such as Sibylle, it's the finish. They have commenced at either Arles or Montpellier and have only a certain amount of time. Others begin at Toulouse and go on to Auch or Pau or beyond. So far I had met no one who was planning to walk all the way to Santiago. Although Toulouse has its charm, I was pleased to be leaving behind the bustle and noise of a big city, not to mention the solid bashing of my ears by Sibylle. I was looking forward to the countryside, to solitude and silence.

'It is in deep solitude that I find the gentleness with which I can truly love my brothers. The more solitary I am the more affection I have for them. Solitude and silence teach me to love my brothers for what they are, not for what they say.'
—Thomas Merton.

Two large churches dominate Pibrac. The multi-belled church of Sainte-Germaine and the basilica of Sainte-Germaine face each other. The people of Pibrac have a strong devotion to Sainte Germaine, a local, born in the 16th century. The church dates back to the 12th century but the Basilica is modern, began in 1901 in a neo-byzantine style and not finished until 1967. On the esplanade, in between, a market was in full swing. I tried to buy a tomato for lunch but the stall holder insisted on giving it to me as his contribution to a pilgrim's welfare.

During the days that followed I came across few other pilgrims. Perhaps this western side of Toulouse was just as sparse as the east. I saw vast fields of sunflowers. The countryside was magical, yellowed by the summer sun into a patchwork of many colours. One morning I passed through Monferran-Savès, one of the few places where a baker's (boulangerie) and a grocer's (épicerie) were open. I bought fresh bread for lunch. On most days, I had to carry stale bread which can be tough on the teeth. Just after Monferran-Savès I stopped at a sign inviting me as a pilgrim to pause. There was a bench made for the pilgrim. A shell had been set in the cement, the notice next to it read: *GR653: Chemin de Saint-Jacques de Compostelle.* This countryside oozed welcome. I accepted the invitation and sat on the bench admiring my surrounds and feeling part of it.

As I sat on that bench, backpack by my side, that negative voice of mine would not let go of the possibility of catching the train to Auch. Fatigue had found my left leg and the possibility of easing the strain always became more attractive as the days progressed and the body grew weary. I was relieved to arrive at the *Gîte du Grangé* just off the main route, on the recommended list of *Les Haltes vers Compostelle*. At the entrance to the property was a large bell sitting on a stool and just above a carving of a pilgrim and a sign. *Sonnez et Entrez.* I rang the bell and entered, disturbing some bantams on my way to the house which looked delightfully ancient. The rendering was peeling off the walls in some areas while a huge beam of unknown antiquity held up the roof structure. Andréas and Lili and young son Oscar were warm and welcoming, but they had their strict rules about backpacks not entering the upstairs dormitory. Two others stayed that night. Susanne was German. Her French was adequate. Carol was South African and spoke French with great confidence. In fact, she was a self-assured lady. We had an excellent meal outside on the terrace tucked in under the high beam. Andréas barbequed duck with the help of Oscar while Lili prepared beautiful salads, the produce of their small farm. The conversation was lively and in English. We discussed motivation. Why do people come all this way was Susanne's question. Carol's home was far enough but mine was further. Carol spotted my wedding ring and asked about my wife. I told she was dead but I consider her still my wife. I just have a different relationship with her. That led Carol to ask her cause of death. I told her about Maris' depression and suicide. That set off further questions, direct and not too sensitive. I felt uncomfortable. I am quite happy to talk about Maris when I feel I am in the company of compassionate and caring people. I had talked about her quite freely with Godfreid and Sibylle, but I sensed Carol's interest was based on curiosity rather than compassion and she was giving me the once over as if to determine whether I was worth spending time with. The good news: the gîte was excellent. That it was run by a young family with a baby Josephine gave it that extra homely ambience. The presence of young children makes things delightful but just a little unpredictable. They remind me of my own children and grandchildren. They can do a neat job of causing chaos and disrupting the most ordered of routines.

The gîte lived up to its reputation. Andréas and Lili continue to send me an annual email newsletter, as if I am now one of their extended worldwide family.

That night rain fell heavily. It was raining when I left. I wore my Sydney Swans poncho for the day. I was on my own, meeting no other walkers, submerged in my own little world under the poncho, not seeing much of the outer world through my wet glasses. That night I stayed at the *Gîte de Lamothe*, a kilometre off the main route through bare open fields. The other guests were Carol, the South African lady, and Gaëlle, a young French girl. There was no conversation nor camaraderie. Carol was chatty the night before, but that evening she was quiet and said little. She puzzled me. I wondered what her story was and why she was doing the Camino? The change unnerved me and made me uncomfortable, I'm afraid. Gaëlle was a doll but made no attempt to reach out. The meal was strange, abstemious. It seemed to be a soup made with beans and cheese, something like what the good medieval monks back at Prieuré Saint-Michel-de Grandmont would have eaten on their feast days, something that, back in Australia, could kill a brown dog. I would have enjoyed a red wine, even a cheap Red Ned, but we were offered none. The woman in charge was aloof and made no effort to get to know her 'guests'. The evening was as depressing as the weather, such a contrast to the previous night at the *gîte Le Grangé* with Andréas, Lili, Oscar and Josephine. Every now and then you have a bad night. That makes you appreciate the good ones.

On to better and brighter things, I hoped, as I left on Sunday morning. It was another wet day. Despite the rain the hunters were out and at one stage the shooting was uncomfortably close just on the other side of the hedge. Hunters and walkers don't make good companions. I sheltered for a while in the porch of a church which I shared with two other walkers. Jacques and Jean-Claude were in their sixties. Whereas Jacques was outgoing, warm and friendly, Jean-Claude was quiet. They were intrigued I was Australian. All that far? I met them again at the gîte that night. The *Relais d'étape La Croisée de Saint Cricq* was one of the best. On the recommended list *(Les Haltes vers Compostelle)*, it was off the route on the fringes of Auch. Christine was a warm friendly outgoing host, but she had her rules, one of which was to leave our boots and packs outside. Les Haltes vers Compostelle is a loose federation of gîte owners. They got together to work out policies as to how to provide the best service to pilgrims, one of which was to reduce the spread of bed bugs which had become a problem along the Camino.

Carol was the other guest, more outgoing tonight, although she seemed to ignore me and focus on Jacques. She spoke French with a sing-song voice as if she were flirting with him. I would have liked more time to get to know her. She was different. Her clothes and boots were top of the range and, in the morning spent far more time than other ladies with her make-up (which was impeccable). Alain, a nephew of Christine shared the meal. We had an excellent evening. Christine and Jacques sparked off each other and everyone joined in the banter with jokes *(plaisanteries)* about Frenchmen, Australians and South Africans. Once again, we were a pilgrim family made welcome by our Christine. We had some concern about where we might spend the next evening, but Christine was on the phone to a friend at Barron. She knew all the establishments along the Camino. She'd been in the game for a long time.

Christine allowed me to use her computer. Not so good news from home! My football team, the Sydney Swans, had lost their finals games and, equally distressing, the Australian people had elected a new federal government, and a new Prime Minister was now in charge. I told the others Australia had elected the wrong man. They knew nothing of Australian politics but Jacques' comment was that I should have been home to vote.

I wasn't sure which was worse. Perhaps it was the Sydney Swans' loss. A great thing about sport, if you can see that your team's winning, whether at the game, at home on the TV, on the internet or up there on the wall of a pub, you feel better. But when they lose...

We had such a farewell in the morning that it was hard to get away. The wet weather had departed and the day was cloudless and sunny. In no time, I was passing through Auch, a town with a history that goes back to pre-Roman days, a natural fortress dominating the valley of Gers. It took time to pass through. I visited the cathedral where I met Carol, Jacques and Jean-Claude. I moved away, lit a candle and sat before it, reflecting on my Maris and the life we had together. I miss her every day.

The guide book said to descend some steps to the rear of the cathedral. I descended about 100 steps on to another street. I walked along for about a kilometre but the streets did not fit the guide book's description. I decided that I had taken a wrong turn, not before finding an Aldi store where I bought food for lunch. I returned to the 100 steps, climbed them and returned to the cathedral where I found another set of steps, this time about a dozen. I descended them and the area did fit the guide book. Back on track, I was annoyed with myself for dashing off, but I quietened down as I entered a forest and I allowed the surrounds to absorb me. Autumn leaves were falling as I walked and made a soft thick carpet I was reluctant to disturb with my size 44 boots. Soon I found myself in farmlands interspersed with wooded patches in rolling hills. I joined Jean-Paul and Jacques and together we arrived in Barron. Of this ancient fortified village, the remains of the ramparts are still visible and we passed through the gateway along an avenue that was once a Roman road. We passed through the village of fine old houses. Everything was closed including the bar and there was no one about. On the way out of Barron we found the accommodation which Christine, our host from the previous night, had arranged for us. Mme Pean welcomed us into her ancient house which was in the process of being restored. It had a fine old garden, somewhat overgrown but nevertheless charming and picturesque with its autumn leaves fluttering to the ground. We dined outside to a beautiful meal, Carol, Jacques, Jean-Claude and me. Mme Pean and her husband treated us like special guests. They had left Paris four years before for a different life. Once again, we had a fine evening. The conversation seemed to focus on essential oils.

I shared a room with Jacques and Jean-Claude. They had some concern about future accommodation. They liked to plan ahead and book for several nights but they were having difficulties with Saturday night. Due to a big wedding, all accommodation had been taken. I had booked ahead at least one night when I began walking, but now on my 26th day, I didn't bother. There were so few walkers there was always room. Even when there was uncertainty about a bed and a meal, it always worked out. I was applying the lesson learned on my previous pilgrimages. Live for the present. The Camino will take care of the future. Be thankful for the occasions when someone arranges accommodation for you, such as this evening.

It was raining as we left the next morning. I walked along the road for a time and then the route left the bitumen. Usually

I followed the signs as closely as possible but this road was quiet with little traffic. By now the route would be muddy and the foliage that I had to brush would be damp and soon I'd be wet, too. The route would eventually re-join the road so I stuck to the bitumen and walked to L'Isle-de-Noé and Montesquiou where I fell in with three young people. We conversed in French for a start but quickly discovered we were all fluent English speakers. There were students from England and I enjoyed hearing their accents after having been immersed in French for so long. They were on holidays. The girl Kate had walked the Camino in Spain two years ago so she knew something of my pilgrimage. They left me to join some friends for lunch. Montesquiou was immersed in history as much as Barron, once a small fortress or castle dating from the 12th century on the hillside dominating the valley of the Osse. It is more famous for its being the preserve of the lords of d'Artagnan the most celebrated of whom is the musketeer who inspired Alexander Dumas' novel.

Montesquiou was picturesque and scenic but it was too early to stop. The afternoon was fine so I pushed on to Pouylebon where I stayed at the Camping de Pouylebon, which boasted a gîte and a caravan park. The site looked just a little decayed and had seen better days. I had the choice of sleeping in a gîte or an on-site caravan. Being cheaper, I chose the latter. Others were in their own caravans. I spoke to the people next to me. They were on holidays from Holland. Jacques and Jean-Claude stayed in the gîte and the three of us dined together to a meal provided by the owner whom seemed a grumpy chap without too many customer service skills. My appraisal was that he was sick of running a caravan park, etc. and had let the place run down. I was not surprised to hear that the site was for sale. I was cosy in my caravan but it became cold during the night and I would have appreciated another blanket.

It took time the following morning getting myself back on track and I found myself going around in circles until I got my bearings. Shortly after Pouylebon was the fortress church of Saint-Christaud which warranted a pause and an inspection. Constructed of red bricks in the Toulouse style, its high walls capped with corbels made it more like a fortress than a church. Unfortunately, it was not open. The day was fine with a gentle breeze, another day made for walking. Marciac is another picturesque village organised around a large rectangular plaza. It boasts a church with the highest spire in Gers. Marciac is renowned for its jazz festival in mid-August and attracts thousands of enthusiasts. It's impossible to find accommodation at this time, but as I had arrived in mid-September, I had no worries. I found the *Gîte-Refuge Le Grenier Saint Jean* in a street just off the plaza. *Le Grenier* is French for loft or garret. The place was well named for the gîte was as rough as they came. It reminded me of a converted garage. There was a sort of kitchen downstairs but no facilities for cooking. Upstairs were the beds in the one room, a ragged curtain dividing the area. The fittings were the work of amateurs with no regard for finish. There was no ceiling, just the roof tiles to stare at, and as I lay in bed, I could see light and even the top of the church spire through the chinks next to the wall. I was thankful it didn't rain that night. There was no heating so I imagine it could get cold. I've stayed in some grotty accommodation but this place took the dodgy award. However, the old bed was comfortable enough and I got a good night's sleep. Marciac was a significant marker in that I had walked 500 kilometres in twenty-eight days.

Next day I set out for Maubourguet. Apart from two stiff climbs the walking was flat. Mid-morning, I paused at the top of a hill at a small church (Eglise Saint Pierre de Samazan) and cemetery. From the cemetery one had a great view back to Marciac. Cemeteries are good places for a rest because there's usually a tap, an opportunity to refill the water bottle. As I sat on a tombstone, thinking about the family who had interred their loved ones here, a young walker arrived with his dog. Jean stopped for a chat. Out of his pack he produced a bowl, filled it with water and gave it to his dog, Nest. We had a chat about looking after pets on the Camino. I've seen a few people walking with their dog. They need looking after, too, making sure of water and food, caring for their feet the same as for humans.

I must have been getting close to the Pyrenees because shortly after Marciac I passed from the department of Gers into the department of Haute-Pyrénées. (High Pyrenees). It was to be a short visit because the following day I would be moving into the department of the Pyrénées-Atlantiques. I couldn't see any mountains, though. I stopped for lunch at Auriébat in front of the church which its elegant tower of 53 metres which could be seen from afar. Apart from the church, there were about six or seven buildings. Alas, no shops or bars. Along came another walker, Joan, an American, looking for water. I referred her to the cemetery. She returned and we ate together. Along came a number of horse-drawn carts with loads of people, both men and women. They could have been a troupe of entertainers.

Maubourguet was a reasonably sized town with most facilities. The town has been through the mill down the centuries. Originally founded as a Benedictine priory in the 11th century, it was fortified by the English in the 14th century and laid waste by the Protestants in the 16th century and again during the Revolution. During the Napoleonic Wars, it was a scene of skirmishes between the French and British armies under Wellington in 1814. Not that this chequered history was at the top of my mind as I went looking for the tourist office to get the key for the *Chalet pèlerin* which was in the municipal camping grounds. The grounds were attractive with a number of large spreading trees and was encircled by a stream. The sound of running water made a tranquil peaceful setting. The chalet was a small wooden cabin with two double bunks. The toilets and showers were a good walk on the other side of the grounds. No one was camping that night but shortly after another walker arrived. André was German and spoke excellent English. He preferred to speak English rather than French like so many Germans I'd met. He was an exuberant outgoing larger-than-life person with a strong loud voice. He started walking at Toulouse and was not sure how far or how long he would be walking. We got on well. We shared the little cabin, and together went looking for the internet café, important because I was still tracking progress with the printing of my book. The takeaways weren't functioning so we had a few drinks and dinner at one of the restaurants. Its bar was well patronised and I admired the young lady who did everything. She manned the bar, back-chatted the patrons, took the orders, went out the back to cook the meals and then served them. Back at the chalet, the sound of the running water just outside lulled me gently into sleep.

I left André still in bed when I departed early as I was hoping to reach Annoye, 26 kilometres away. He passed me during the morning walking at what seemed to me a furious pace, with long strides and using his two sticks as if he was leaping. I was happy to amble along at roughly 3 to 4 kilometres per hour with my one stick. Multiple hills made the day hard work but the fine weather compensated. During the afternoon, I missed a turn and probably covered an additional 4 or 5 kilometres, so I would have walked about 30 kilometres by the time I reached Annoye.

There were no shops, bar or restaurants at Annoye so I wasn't sure about an evening meal. I was tired when I arrived at the *gîte d'étape communal*, which turned to be one of the best, not only for the facilities but for the people I met. It had been recently refurbished and was well equipped. I was greeted by my fellow guests who were enjoying the sun around a table in the front garden. I knew André, the German, and Joan, the American from the cemetery at Auriébat. In addition, there was a couple, Mat and Laura, who had heard about me, the elderly Australian walking on his own. The gossipy Camino!

Where were Jacques and Jean-Claude? I hadn't seen them for two nights since Pouylebon. Nor had I seen Carol the South African. After my chores, I sat in the sun with Mat and Laura. Mat was English and Laura was Spanish. Mat seemed to me more like a boyfriend with his laid-back manner and ear rings, but they had been married for eight years. In that time, they had worked in Malaysia and India teaching English. They had completed their contract with the British Council and decided to walk the Camino before determining the next stage of their lives. They had walked the Camino before. In fact, Laura came from a small town not far from Santiago. They started at Le Puy-en-Velay but instead of walking towards Saint Pied-de-Port, they turned south to Montpellier to follow the Camino Aragonés. Two of the locals turned up to collect the money and to open a little shop from which we were able to buy provisions for dinner and for the following day. They had a well-stocked wine cellar. We had an excellent evening, cooking our meals together, sharing our wine and our stories. It was an all English night, so language was no barrier to communication.

The Camino family is a constantly changing and evolving group, as people join and drop off. We were building no permanent dwelling here, very temporary indeed, sometimes lasting only one night, but always developing a great sense of support and camaraderie. To me, it's the delight of the Camino. To embrace the spirit of the Camino, you need to reach out to those who are walking with you. It's a tiny step towards cohesion in a world where so many forces divide and force people into separate troubled warring tribes. As in the silence and solitude of walking, a spiritual dimension possesses these families, almost as if God, the Big Fellow upstairs, is hard at work. Acceptance of others, their looks, their behaviours, their beliefs, bring you an inner peace and tranquillity. They unite, heal, bring peace and nourish the spirit. Not only do they have an immediate effect, they reach out to all those whom our lives touch on the Camino and beyond. I am always filled with a profound gratitude.

9

The spirit is willing but the flesh is weak.

The following night (Saturday14th September) I stayed at Morlaàs and the night after at Lescar. The two towns are linked historically. Lescar was once the Roman city of Benearnum. It was razed by the Vikings in 841, after which Morlaàs became the capital of the ancient province of Béarn. It remained the capital until the 12th century. Today the church of Saint Foy is a witness to this period and is known for its imposing 11th century portal. Each of the two doors is surrounded by a tympanum with carvings on one side of the Flight into Egypt and on the other the Massacre of the Innocents.

I had the opportunity to visit Saint Foy (no candles, though!) for I arrived at Morlaàs about 2 pm on a bright sunny day and had time for washing, drying and a rest. Four of us from the night before at Annoye stayed at the *Refuge pèlerin, camping municipal* — Mat, Laura, André and me. American Joan had decided to push on for we had covered only 17 kilometres. As well as shopping at the supermarket next to the camping ground, we had an opportunity for rest and a chat in the afternoon sun. We discussed motivation. André was seeking a break from his busy work schedule and was keen to cover as much ground as possible. He had been tempted to push on to Pau which was not far but decided to stay as I think he liked our company. He seemed to know Pau well and had previously visited the city. Our conversation turned to spiritual matters and the journey of our individual souls. Mat was once agnostic but then he met Laura who had been brought up in the Spanish catholic tradition. He liked the Catholic Mass for its ritual. He once attended a retreat to delve deeply into the Faith. He knew that one was supposed to emerge as a believer but he was afraid to admit he went the other way. Still, he attended all the ceremonies with Laura as he enjoyed the ritual and felt the spirit moving others. He attended the pilgrim blessings along with everyone and having done the Camino before, he was drawn to walk again.

The lady in charge of the camping ground told us we could get a good meal at the Hôtel de France and that's where the four of us turned up for dinner. And what a night it turned out to be! Did they turn it on! The place was swinging. In the courtyard, a buffet meal was spread out along one side and at the end was an elevated stage on which two bands performed. The place was full of locals of all ages. What better place to spend Saturday night! Everyone welcomed us as pilgrims. We were the only strangers for everyone knew each other. Jacques and Jean-Claude turned up and we squeezed them on to our table. The first band were young, a support to the main band whose members looked veterans. They were excellent musicians. Their lead singer, a lady by name Patricia everyone knew and loved, judging from the enthusiastic applause. There was not much room for dancing but a few managed to find some space. Rain threatened to spoil the night but the band kept on playing and the people kept on eating, drinking, talking, singing and dancing.

The four of us shared a communal breakfast the following morning from the various goodies we had each purchased at the adjacent supermarket. I walked through woodlands that morning and, being Sunday, the people were out, too, including a group that were singing loudly and could be heard all over the forest. André passed me and told me he was all fired up and was going to push on. On he went with his long strides like the giant in seven-league boots. I kept on meeting Mat and Laura, Jacques and Jean-Claude. The track skirted the edge of Pau. That pleased me; I did not want to battle through a large city.

The five of us arrived at Lescar mid-afternoon where we found a fair in progress by the church. I was hungry and would have enjoyed something to eat but all the stalls were devoted to art — paintings, sculpture, glass work. Not a single food stall! Strange in a country like France which loves its food! In an adjacent field, we watched a group of young people dressed in mail and other medieval costumes jousting in front of some serious looking film cameras. Fatigue overtook us and our Camino family — Mat, Laura, Jacques, Jean-Paul, me — found the pilgrim refuge on the edge of town. Everything was closed but the hospitalière who arrived to collect our money told us of a pizza place on the other side of town. The pizza place was tiny. The floor was earthen and all the walls were lined with stacks of wood. It was like dining in a wood shed and a small one at that. However, the smell of the wood added its own flavour while the wine and food were worth the effort of walking across town. On the way back to the refuge we discussed our options for the next day. Monday was always a problem as the shops were usually closed. Furthermore, there seemed to be no pilgrim accommodation.

We stopped for coffee on our way out of Lescar then went our separate ways. I paused to book ahead on my French phone, one of the few times I had bothered. I missed a turn and walked extra kilometres and found Mat and Laura had done the same. Most of the day was devoted to forests. It began with fine weather but as the afternoon advanced the clouds gathered and by the time I emerged from the shelter into open fields, the rain fell heavily backed by a solid wind. I was the solitary pilgrim, my poncho flowing behind me and my hat pushed back by the wind, a cold wind that was too lazy to go around but went straight through me instead... I held my head up high as I wasn't sure where I was going, the track didn't make sense and passed through field after field of corn. I couldn't orient myself to any landmarks. I could have panicked but a reassuring voice within told me to walk on. With hope in my heart I pressed on. My hope was like a light within me guiding my steps through the storm. With gratitude, I found my way through the maze and arrived at *Chambre d'hôtes Relais Milord* at Estialescq. My hostess Françoise didn't mind my dripping over her clean floor and showed me a room with an ensuite. Luxury! Loads of pillows and fluffy bed covers. Jacques and Jean-Claude were in the other room. Françoise's husband, François, joined us for an excellent dinner. I left the towel warmer in the ensuite on all night to dry my washing. In all, an expensive but very comfortable night. I missed Mat and Laura. They were an open-hearted, charming and relaxed couple. I enjoyed their company and hoped to meet up again.

In the quiet of my bedroom, I reflected on the afternoon's storm. Despite its dangers and the possibility of becoming lost, I felt safe as if some Presence was guiding me through. Pilgrims often say to each other: The Camino will look after you. Someone was looking after me. I thought of the lyrics of that well-known song: *You'll never walk alone.*

It rained all night and was raining in the morning. I was pleased I was planning to walk only as far as Oloron Sainte-Marie, about eleven kilometres. Jacques and Jean-Claude had decided to push on, so we said good bye. I set off in the rain and soon entered a forest. I lost my bearings and couldn't find the way markers but I came across a road, the D24, where a sign pointed to Oloron so I took to the bitumen. I arrived about 1 pm but I had to wait for the refuge (*Centre d'herbergement Le Relais du Bastet*) to open at 2 pm. The restaurant opposite would not serve me any lunch because I was late!!! Meantime Mat and Laura arrived. They had stopped at La Commande, back about 9 kilometres before Estialescq.

The town has its origin in Roman days. Originally two separate towns, Sainte Marie and Oloron, they were merged under Napoleon. It was always a stopping place for pilgrims who chose the Col de Somport to traverse the Pyrenees on their way to Santiago...

Sharing the room with me that night was a Spanish man who had no English and a Japanese man who had no English nor French nor Spanish. He seemed disoriented and unorganised, but he tried hard to communicate and became frustrated with himself. I felt for him, lonely and isolated, and wondered what his motivation for walking the Camino was. In the other room was a Scottish couple (Clive and Barbara) and a group from Latvia. Mat and Laura had a room on their own. I looked out for them as I walked around the town to do some shopping, found them in the supermarket and had dinner with them. Laura was tired that night. They were having a rest day the following day.

I, too, was tired. I had already walked over 600 kilometres and had another 200 kilometres to reach my destination, Puente la Reina. Have I the will and energy to continue? I could easily catch the train back to Toulouse and become a tourist for the rest of my time in Europe. *'Pull out while you have time,'* came the nagging negative voice from the back of my mind. Besides, I would be leaving France and entering Spain in a day or two. I would have to dig out of my brain the little bit of

Spanish that I remembered. Daunting! *'It'll all come back to you,'* was Mat's reassuring comment over dinner. I felt encouraged. I loved his gentle caring manner and sense of humour. I had become very fond of Mat and Laura in the short time that I had known them. Their good company encouraged me and made me resolve: *'I have come to Europe to walk to Puente la Reina and that's what I will do.'*

I needed a rest day, too, so I stayed a second night in Oloron. I spent the morning at the library on a computer. The library has a beautiful location, I thought, as I looked through a broad glass wall on to the junction of two small streams (Gave d'Ossau and Gave d'Aspe) lined with overhanging trees, some dipping into the water. The scene would have been stunning on a fine day for the morning was overcast and already I had to dodge the showers crossing a small bridge to access the building. The library was large and silent but from the outside came the muffled sound of a small bulldozer fussing about in one of the streams clearing fallen branches.

That night the refuge was full (*complet*), the first time I had seen a full establishment in my 35 days of walking. Walkers were everywhere. Oloron was on a cross roads with routes going north-south, east-west. Some were going to Lourdes, others had come from there and were going to St Jean-Pied de Port. For thirty-five days, I had been walking west all the way from Montpelier, but the next day I would be turning south to cross the Pyrenees. I had resolved to continue. It would be a struggle and hard work, but I had a faith in myself that it could be done. Oloron was a turning point in more than one sense. I felt a sense of excitement as I drifted off to sleep. I was nearing the end.

The morning was gloomy and so was my mood. I reached the edge of town feeling somewhat discouraged, and as I faced the misty countryside, I realised I'd left my stick behind. That piece of wood had been my mate since the children gave it to at Murat-sur-Vèbre almost a month ago and I'd tapped my way along France for the last 440 kilometres. I had never used a stick previously but I had grown to value it. It helped me climb hills and steadied me as I descended. I wasn't going to leave my faithful friend behind so back I went to the refuge where I found a late leaving couple slowly putting on their boots and wet weather gear. They let me in. I found my stick in the corner among others left behind.

I liked my stick. Around the top a previous owner had carved a small niche and tied a piece of cord. Below the cord many hands had smoothed the surface to make a firm grip. Its length was just right for me, straight and sturdy. It was a comforting prop. It was different, unlike the metal expandable types that most people used. To me, my stick was natural, a tiny part of God's creation, fashioned for man's safety and support. To the ancient pilgrims their staff (*bourdon*) represented Christ on the job of supporting and protecting them.

I retraced my steps and faced a muddy countryside. The morning continued to be overcast. Its highlight was my coming across Mat and Laura who had stopped to look at an eagle soaring over the tree tops towards the mountains. I borrowed their binoculars. That bird had perfect flight. It soared effortlessly searching for prey. Sometimes it hovered motionless as if dancing in the air, and swooped almost to the ground as if to catch some small creature. It could have been playing, enjoying itself although it was probably engaged in the deadly serious game of hunting. A hungry brood of chicks was waiting in a mountain crevice.

One needs to stop the rush every now and then, and pause to immerse oneself in observing creation in action. God was manifest in that bird as in every creature. Discovering God where I happen to be has enabled me to catch a glimpse of a liberating mystery whose centre is nowhere, but extends everywhere — in the candle's flame, in the warm greeting at day's end, in the dripping forests, in the Camino's camaraderie, or on the mountains, in the gentle breeze of sunset or in the internal light, the murmur of hope that keeps one going in the belief that all will be well. There is a deep spirituality in the elements of everyday life. I can meet God in the silence, in my being's core, in the air that I breathe, or in the sun in my eyes.

The sun came out in the afternoon and the valley down which I descended responded to its light. The last few kilometres were tough. The route followed a small mountain stream (Gave d'Aspe) and the passage was narrow, like walking through a tunnel created by the thick vegetation above one's head. The thorns of over grown blackberries threatened to draw blood. At the same time, I had to watch where I put my feet. I was not anxious to have another fall. Sarrance is a small but important village. Placed so near to the Col du Somport on one of the major routes of the Chemin de Saint Jacques de Compostelle (Camino de Santiago de Compostela), it had seen conquering armies when it was pillaged and burnt. In modern time, it once boasted a religious community in an abbey but nowadays pilgrims are welcome at the *Abbaye Notre-Dame*. Eight pilgrims stayed on Thursday 19th September including Mat and Laura. There were two dormitories, one for the boys and the other for the girls; even Mat and Laura, the married couple, were separated. Alain was the hospitalier. He quizzed me because I had not booked but, as he could see, I was a genuine hard core pilgrim who had arrived by foot, carrying everything in a backpack, panting for a rest. There was a spare bed, he let me in. Mass was celebrated in the adjacent ancient church at 6.30 and later we sat down to a hearty meal prepared by Alain. Once again, as it had happened so often, we were a Camino family and we sat at the long table exchanging our experiences and discussing the remainder of the route. The Pyrenees were in sight. Discussion centred on whether to stay on the road as one climbed, which was the easier option but also dangerous because of the heavy trucks. The route through the vegetation was safer but more difficult.

I was apprehensive about the Pyrenees. We had one more day of walking along the valley and then we would be challenged with a very stiff climb — straight up, unrelenting, no undulations, just up and up and up! My eighty-year-old body would be taxed. It might be exhausted so severely that I could not continue. There was still time to end my walking and take the train back to Oloron. On the other hand, I could take the bus to the top, to Col du Somport, and then continue the walk-through Spain, less exhausted than if I had tackled the mountains by foot. Fatigue was eating into my old bones. I'd been walking for thirty-six days and was longing for the end. I had done well to get this far. I, knocking on the door of old age if not already inside, should not feel guilty if I quit now. But I did. The flesh wanted to give the whole caper away, but the spirit wanted to battle on. These anxieties and arguments spinning in my brain kept sleep at bay but they lost the combat and I fell into a deep slumber...

Our hospitalier Alain bid us a warm farewell. The morning was overcast, still and full of mystery with the mountains towering above us. The route followed the Gave d'Aspe along the narrow valley d'Aspe. A *'gave'* is the name given to the mountain streams of Bearn. They begin in the Pyrenees. Their flow is too rapid for boating but they hold plenty of fish. Not that I tried fishing from one of the bridges that I crossed that day.

That night I stopped at Borce, the last place before crossing the Pyrenees. The *Hospitalet St Jacques* was a tiny but cosy gîte with six places on the edge of the village. Mat, Laura and a German girl (Sybie) were already there. We decided to cook our own dinner rather than visit the restaurant in the equally small village of Etsaut just on the other side of the valley, found the shop cum bar and bought the ingredients including a generous supply of red wine. We had a fun evening busily preparing the food. Laura took charge and gave us our jobs. I peeled the onions. There was much chatter and laughter over our last meal in France and in our consuming several bottles of wine. We discussed the massive climb the next day. I said I was planning to take the bus from Etsaut to the top of Col du Somport as I had doubts about my body's ability to cope. Laura said she was tired, too, and might come with me while Matt walked.

The next morning, she decided to walk. They set off early, Sybie as well, for the bus did not leave until late morning. I did the final tidy up of the Hospitalet, leaving it cleaner than when we arrived, walked across the valley to Etsaut, found the restaurant where I enjoyed coffee and waited outside for the bus. Clive and Barbara turned up. They were taking the bus, too. Two other walkers joined us, an older man and woman, neither of them in good shape, and the five of us climbed on to the small vehicle which looked as if it had given many years of faithful service to the people of the mountains. It tackled the steady climb without hesitation and up and up we went. We passed two walkers, one of them Michel, with whom I had walked along the Canal de Midi prior to Toulouse. I saw no sign of Mat and Laura. I had an attack of the guilts for taking the easy comfortable way but, in the same breath, I could feel my body sighing with relief that it didn't have to face this particular challenge. I've faced quite enough challenges, thank you, I heard it saying. I probably would have tackled the never-ending climb for I'd crossed the Pyrenees before, but I wondered how long my body would take to recover. This time I trusted the vibes. Unlike the mind, the body doesn't lie.

The driver, who looked as ancient as his bus, changed down gears for the last steep 500 metres to the top. We five passengers descended. The bus departed. On the French side I noticed *Restaurant Le Chalet* and the *Gîte d'étape du col du Somport*. Further along the road just in Spain I could see a building that looked like a refuge. The older couple stumbled across to the *gîte d'étape* as if not yet ready to venture into foreign lands. Clive and Barbara walked on to Spain. I stayed on the side of the road and looked around. It was not the highest point in the Pyrenees but I felt as if I was on top of the world. The sky was cloudless and the sun shone brilliantly. Behind lay France and ahead the adventure of Spain stretched out before me.

10

Blessed are you, pilgrim, when you don't have words to give thanks for
everything that surprises you at every twist and turn along the way.
—The Beatitudes of the Pilgrim.

hat a contrast to the last time I found myself in
the Pyrenees! When I crossed in 2011 from St
Jean-Pied-de-Port I saw nothing but mist. Only
occasionally did the clouds swirl away to give me a glimpse
of what I was missing. Today I could see the world. The road
stretched down the valley, the walking track meandered along
its side, in all directions mountain peaks soared, great piles
of bare rock. In winter, I would have been in the middle of a
snow bound wonderland. There was no wind that afternoon
but the ruthless blizzards of winter would make this place a
dangerously exposed hazard for the unprepared. Right now,
the mountains were benign, displaying their rugged beauty. I
felt humbled, just a tiny speck of humanity. I was in awe. The
sheer size of everything around me reflected creation in all its
wild abandonment. Man's attempts to tame it in the form of
the road and a few buildings down the valley were puny and
insignificant.

I debated whether to stay in the Spanish refuge, the Refuge-
Bar-restaurant Aysa, but decided to walk to Canfranc Estación,
only 7.7 kilometres and downhill all the way. Clive and Barbara
were sitting on the balcony of the bar. They waved as I passed.
As I walked down the valley I came across an abandoned railway line — cuttings and bridges overtaken by weeds. In some
places the rails were still in place. I wondered if the rail service

ever ran. I was further intrigued when I arrived at Canfranc. It seemed to be in such a remote location but before me was a huge decaying structure in the Art Nouveau style.

The small village of Canfranc boasts the biggest rail station in Europe. The Canfranc International Railway Station was opened in 1928, the centrepiece of a railway between France and Spain. It was grand, glamorous and over the top. The Spanish government of the time was hoping to attract the wealthy of Europe to the station's hotel. Despite its grandeur, the luxurious station was over taken by warfare. Only eight years after it was opened, the station and the tunnel across the Spanish-French border were closed during the Spanish Civil War. After the War the 220 metres long station was reopened and enjoyed a brief period of success before the outbreak of World War II. At first, the train provided a lifeline for Jews to escape, but eventually the German occupation closed the border. During the 1950s and 1960s, the station finally returned to business. In 1970, following an accident on the French side, the line was cut and the International Station of Canfranc became the biggest "ghost" station of the world. On the Spanish side, the station is still available for some shuttle services but only a small local service operates. This immense structure with a platform 1200 metres long and 170 metres wide has been abandoned to burglars and graffiti artists and is crumbling before one's eyes. There has been talk between the Spanish and French governments of reopening the line but the respective railways of the two countries are lukewarm.

I found the *Hosteleria Pepito Grillo* where I shared a dormitory with Clive and Barbara, and a German girl. Monika was walking along the Pyrenees from east to west. She had been camping but that night she needed a comfortable bed under cover. She was a tiny person but she had a huge pack which included a tent and her camping gear. I was not surprised when she said her pack weighed 18 kilos. The four of us had a pleasant meal together in the bar which was full of walkers. This was definitely hiking country. Memorabilia was posted around the walls and various small items such as maps and compasses were on sale.

The next day was Sunday. My window faced west and I took a series of photos over an hour of the mountains emerging out of the night, the sunlight slowly creeping down the rock face and banishing the shadow. The valley was still in shadow as I set off late under a cloudless day deciding I should aim for Jaca, a distance of 23 kilometres. Eventually the sun rose high enough for me to feel its warmth. The walking was easy, mostly downhill all the way, but, as it turned out, the day was a catastrophe.

Walkers were taking advantage of the benign weather and the weekend. All were wearing day packs and mostly coming from the opposite direction. They provided an opportunity to refresh my Spanish as we passed each other. The path was level but rocky and you had to keep your eyes downcast to pick your way through. I looked up to note a noisy group approaching, tripped over a protruding rock and down I tumbled. I fell heavily, the weight of my backpack forcing me down. Last time I fell in private, but this time I had an audience. They rushed towards me, everyone shouting with concern and astonishment. No bones broken but my knees and hands were grazed and cut, the blood flowed liberally. Whilst doing my best to avoid getting blood on my clothes, (blood strains are a pain) I dived into my pack for my first aid kit, always at the top, and applied bandages and band aids, a crowd of well-wishers around me trying to help and offering advice. In my limited Spanish, I thanked them profusely for their kindness and concern, at the same time, hoping they would leave me and allow me to tend to my wounded pride in peace. Eventually they continued on, offering advice to the last.

I was shaken. I was embarrassed. Both my body and my ego had taken a bruising. To fall in private is one thing, but in public to be fussed over by well-meaning bystanders... I was knackered, feeling dizzy and faint, in shock, ready to conk out and give the game away. I needed to sit down, to take stock and to recover. I was indeed fortunate that I had the health and fitness to undertake a long-distance walk. Every day I was thankful for these gifts. But I was vulnerable. A conversation with a lady from my church just before I left raced through my mind. I mentioned I was undertaking another Camino, my third. This lady told me that when she first heard she was pleased for me. Later, she was angry: 'Does Noel think he is indestructible?' was her thought. Perhaps she had in mind her husband who was in early dementia. Was she asking herself why had Noel escaped the ravages of old age while her husband had not?

My fall was too close to home. People in their eighties are fearful of decay. They're not cracked up to what they'd like to be. They'd like to think that they are holding up well but every now and then they are forced to realise that's just bullshit. Was my walking hundreds of kilometres across countries an attempt to prove that age had not wearied me, that I could do just as well as the young ones? Just an ego trip?

Other walkers passed. They looked down at me in puzzlement, perhaps, not knowing of my fall and wondering what the old hombre was doing there just sitting on the side of the track in the dirt. Even though it was downhill all the way, Jaca was out of the question. The next village would be my destination.

I took my time to traverse the next five kilometres. I arrived at Villanúa. Signs directed me to the *Hotel Triton Plaza* where they were in the final stages of serving lunch. Yes, they had a bed I was advised rather indifferently, but the bar would be closed soon and no further meals would be served that day. (It was Sunday!) Rather than go hunting for a friendlier place, I stayed. I was sent upstairs and found a room with five double bunks jammed together. The other rooms had occupants but I needed privacy that night to nurse my demoralised tender ego. After dumping my bag and redressing my wounds, I walked back to the entrance of the village, a small shaded park. I was usually content with my own company, but this afternoon I was conscious of being in a foreign country where my command of the language was somewhat tenuous. I was lonely and badly in need of good company. I was hoping that Mat and Laura might come along. My prayers were answered. About 30 minutes later, I was overjoyed to see them strolling down the track into the village.

They didn't like the sound of the *Hotel Triton*. Laura checked her guide book and got on her phone. After a long conversation in Spanish with multiple exchanges, she confirmed that she had found a place with one double room still vacant. While Laura worked on the phone, Mat sat back enjoying the sun and watched his wife. His look was one of admiration. When she finished, he said: '*The joys of having a Spanish wife!*' I, too, was full of awe and respect. She had received instructions on directions, negotiated the price and was told where we could find a meal in this small village on a Sunday night. We agreed to meet at the park at 7 pm and together we would find this obliging restaurant. Mat and Laura set off for the other side of town while I returned to the hotel for a much-needed siesta. Lunch was over, everything was closed except the front door. No one was around. No one!

We met at 7 pm, walked about 500 metres to what looked

like a pizza parlour. It was open but we were told dinner wasn't served until 9 pm. Not to worry, we filled in the time with a few tapas and Mat and I enjoyed a few red wines. We spoke to the locals through Laura. They were good humoured and friendly. They, too, were waiting for their 9 pm meal, passing the time with a few drinks and a chat. Overall, a good night.

Together, we walked back to the village. We seemed to be wondering around, our brains somewhat vague and foggy. I thought Mat and Laura's place was on the other side of town but it turned out to be next to the hotel. Although I had plenty of wine and should have slept soundly, I had a restless night as my knee was stinging. I assured myself that the irritation was the body healing itself but that didn't help with sleep. I did not like this place. It was creepy and a street lamp outside filled the room with light. There were no occupants in the other bunks but their number squashed together made the room claustrophobic. Overall, a bad day, saved by Mat and Laura whose presence was like a light in the darkness.

In the morning, I was embarrassed to find that blood had seeped through my leg bandages through the night, had not only stained the sheet but had gone through to the mattress. I was leaving a mess for someone to clean up. The hotel had laid out a lousy breakfast. I spilt the coffee in the microwave. The coffee was foul. No one was around and eventually I let myself out the front door, happy to leave the place behind me.

As I walked with battered body, dented morale and sleepless night, I had reached a nadir. I debated whether I should finish at Jaca. There was still an opportunity to take the bus back into France to Oloron and then the train. I had already walked 685 kilometres. That was no mean feat for someone long in the tooth. Once I passed Jaca I would have to commit myself to the remaining 138 kilometres. My mood did not correspond to my beautiful surroundings. The sun had risen high enough to dispel the shadow of the surrounding mountains and had bathed the valley in light and warmth. My mind was in a gloomy fog, seriously playing with the idea of giving my Camino away. My steps were plodding and heavy, my pack was a burden. My mind was so involved with this inner dialogue that I paid no attention to the beauty around me. My eyes were downcast, half my attention given to the potential pitfalls on the path, the other half given to the battle confronting the spirit.

I came to a bridge. There was Michel. Our paths had not crossed since the canals before Toulouse except that I saw him, from the comfort of my bus, struggling up the road to Col du Comfort. He was resting against the wall. He looked tired but when he saw me approaching, the light sprung into his eyes and he jumped forward, shook my hand and embraced me as if we had been old, old mates. He wanted to thank me. He had enjoyed my company. It was a pleasure to meet me and I was an inspiration to him. His enthusiasm took me by surprise. I couldn't remember doing anything special in his company other than being myself. He seemed to know all about me. Sybille was our other companion at the time. I told her my story and I guess she told him everything. The Camino bush telegraph works very well.

I was comfortable speaking in French and I soon found the right words to thank him sincerely. I did not mention that I had taken the bus while he walked up the Pyrenees. We took each other's photo, exchanged cards, embraced each other again and then he picked up his pack and walked on while I stayed by the bridge for a further rest. Our conversation did wonders to my morale. I felt content with myself. Peace had been restored. Perhaps I was a worthier person than I gave myself credit for that morning. As I set off, both my pack and step were lighter. All my senses were alert. I saw the world as if it had been reborn and washed clean. I was aware of the beauty of the day, I could hear the song of every bird, the rustle of every leaf, the hum of every insect. I took my time to enjoy the mountains and a delightful fragrance drifting through the valley. Deep within our hearts there resides a gem that we can uncover by making continuous effort, never giving up nor allowing ourselves to be discouraged. Such perseverance gives us wisdom and the ingenuity to withstand any adversity.

I did not see Michel again, but we have been exchanging emails. I received the first shortly after I arrived home. He had made it to Jaca but his knees which had been troubling him all along became too painful. The approach to the Pyrenees had been too much. He told me they had taken the ginger right out of him, or the French equivalent. He had to stop and return home to Nice where he was recuperating. I felt a touch of guilt but then realised that missing the steep climb had been a saviour. I had recognised that I was not indestructible, that I was just as vulnerable as anyone who tackles the Camino regardless of age. I, too, like Michel, could have been forced to abandon the Camino and return home early.

To add to my day, I came across Mat and Laura having lunch. They were taking their time, too. Mat had removed his shirt and was bathing in the sun, stretched out on a beautiful piece of lush green grass. Laura preferred the shade of a tree. They presented a beautiful picture of enjoying the moment. I joined them for lunch and together we walked the last few kilometres into Jaca.

Jaca is where the col du Somport eventually levels out on to the plains. It's the Spanish starting point for the summer hiking and the winter snow sports in the Pyrenees. It's a pleasant town with plenty of shops and was once the capital of Aragon.

We arrived at the pilgrims' refuge about 2.30 pm and had to wait until it opened at 3. It looked freshly painted, with orange the dominant colour. I met Jan, a Dutchman who lived in Ireland and Jessica, a German. The six of us had dinner together. As always, I was the oldest, but I felt accepted (as always) by these younger walkers. Their good company confirmed my decision to continue walking to Puente la Reina.

The six of us set off the following morning for Arrés, about 25 kilometres away. The day marked the transition from the mountainous Pyrenees to the fertile plains of the Aragon river. Since Oloron in France I had been walking due south, but now the route turned to the west. I was on the home run. I had walked 700 kilometres, 135 to go. While a fatigue was seeping through my bones that made me feel like an old man, I was buoyed up by the enthusiasm, exuberance and vigour of my younger companions. How I valued their presence, particularly that of Mat and Laura! My affection and love for them grew with each encounter.

The walking was comparatively easy except for the last three kilometres. The route left a well-defined road to follow a narrow-overgrown footpath which wound itself round and round the hillside. We followed each other in single file, continually brushing aside the foliage to see our way through. Mat kept calling back to ensure I was okay and still on my feet. I had told him about my fall. There was no ending. Adding to the difficulty was the uncertainty of what was ahead. The guide book indicated the presence of a refuge that was not always open. It warned we should visit the shops in Jaca because there were none at Arrés. My backpack was heavier because I was carrying provisions for the night. I was stonkered by the time the track suddenly opened and descended into the village.

Arrés was a surprise. The village was no more than half

a dozen buildings along a ridge, but the refuge was exuberantly open. People were about, hanging out their washing or just sauntering around. The English hospitaleros, Laurie and Catherine, who had set up a table for reception on the small plaza, gave us the warmest of welcomes and showed us around. Everyone crammed into the small kitchen and dining area for a communal meal so I did not need any of the stuff I bought at Jaca. Catherine loved her role and the village. She took a few of us on a tour of village and unlocked the small chapel to show us its fresco decorated walls and icons. Seeing Laurie and Catherine at work reinforced my earlier thought that one of these days I could be a volunteer hospitalero, too.

I was further surprised to find that the village boasted a bar which sold a few groceries as well. As always, the lesson is never to worry; the Camino provides. Just be content to be. I need constant reminding of that message.

You do not need to know precisely what is happening, or exactly where it is all going. What you need is to recognise the possibilities and challenges offered by the present moment, and to embrace them with courage, faith and hope.
—*Thomas Merton*

The refuge was crowded, every bed in the dormitory taken. A young girl gave up her bottom bunk to me, the oldest by far, the granddaddy. It was a squash in that dormitory by the time every body and their backpacks had squeezed in. The night was noisy, not from snorers but from the creaky old bunks of metal and wire. I went to sleep dallying with the thought that if I were to furnish a refugio, I would install wooden bunks that were solid and didn't squeak.

11

When your determination changes, everything else begins to move in the direction you desire The moment you resolve to be victorious, every nerve and fibre in your being immediately orient themselves towards your success.
—*Daisaku Ikeda*

I decided on a shorter day and walk as far as Artieda, a distance of 20 kilometres. The others planned to walk a further seven kilometres to Ruesta. My spirit wanted to keep up but my body told me that 20 kilometres was more than enough.

A new challenge found me. Flies! Tiny midges, billions of them! They crawled up the nostrils and gathered under the brim of my hat, between my glasses and my eyes. I couldn't sit down to rest. The aussie salute was useless. They gathered around my face, neck and bare arms, dense clouds of relentless irritation. At their worst in the dense undergrowth, they were less intense in the open and the heat which offered some relief. On other days, I enjoyed the cool trees by a small stream, but today I dreaded passing into the shade where I knew the myriads were hovering, waiting.

When I arrived at Artieda early afternoon, Mat, Laura, Jan and Jessica had arrived before me, drinking coffee on the terrace of a bar-restaurant, taking a break before their final push for the day. My spirit wanted to join them, but my flesh said an emphatic no. Accumulated fatigue had worn me down and the day's additional burden, the battle of the flies, had diminished my resilience. We said good bye and, in case, we didn't see

each other again, exchanged addresses. With a heavy heart,
I farewelled Mat and Laura, watching them walk down the
valley until they disappeared. I was alone, my coffee went cold.

The bar-restaurant had an albergue attached. Others
arrived. Clive and Barbara, and a French lady whose name was
Marie. I shared a room with French doors and a balcony overlooking the terrace and entrance and a grand view down the
valley stretching to the mountains in the north. I was joined by
two dour Danes, rough diamonds, big men without much English, and John, an Irishman. He was grumpy; he had to take a
top bunk. He wasn't sure, he said, how he would get up there.
I was tempted to offer him my bottom bunk. I was probably
fitter and healthier but I would have given him ten years or
more. I allowed age to rule the day. He did make the top bunk
with a lot of grunting. He was quiet and even aloof, but he did
mention that he had returned each year for ten years to walk
this part of the Camino. I was intrigued. I could understand
returning to the Camino for its addictive powers, but why the
same part? Why not different routes? I would have asked more,
but his aloofness suggested he was a private man who had
erected a barrier to fend off intruders like me. The meal was
strange — strained, sullen and silent. We ate together, the six
of us, but no one talked. We could have been dining in a monastery on a silent retreat, waiting for a lector to read the life of
an exemplary saint. No effort to engage each other, so unlike
other Camino meals full of jocular chatter and camaraderie.
The dour hospitaleros made no attempt to interact. It was no
laughing matter, this looking after pilgrims. Even Clive and
Barbara were subdued and did not respond to my attempts
at conversations. Where was the camaraderie of the Camino?

The night was warm. I left the French doors half open for
the breeze. That suited the others for no one bothered to close

them. I heard the Danes very early stumbling around before
they departed. I went back to sleep but was woken by a call.
Something landed on my bed. Something banged on the wall.
I came up from the abyss and broke the surface like a fish
in slow motion returning to the surface. I lay with my eyes
open, listening and puzzling what the sounds might be, sleep
doing its best to pull me back into dreamless depths. Another
object landed on the floor. A stone! Someone was calling from
outside. *'Australian!'* I heard. I got up and went to the balcony.
The Danes were below. *'My hat!'* one said in a loud whisper. I
remembered a hat on the hook behind the door. It was easy to
find in the half light. I threw it down to him. The front doors
were locked, easy to get out but not back in. He thanked me
and they disappeared. I returned to bed for more sleep and
dreamed erotically of balcony scenes from films and literature,
mostly romance and trysts, where I was the gallant caller woo-
ing my way into a fair maiden's bed, both discovered naked
in the morning. As we began the day, John told me he heard
the Danes well before me, but as they were not calling him, he
didn't bother.

On the way again, the flies were just as bad. The route
wound its way between the dry brown fields and enormous
heaps of chalky blue clay, which made the day an arid, blighted,
semi-desert as if some mining company had fallen on hard
times and failed to restore the land. Deserted villages devoid
of life dotted the route. The way was level except that it kept
a nasty surprise to the end, a killer hill on the approach to
Undués de Lerda. It took all day to traverse the 20 kilometres
and I didn't arrive until 5.30 pm feeling like death warmed
up. Overall, an uninspiring, miserable day in a miserable
landscape!

A joyful surprise awaited. As usual, I was the winner of the wooden spoon. Everyone had arrived before me and was busy in the open plaza next to the refuge — washing, hanging out clothes, chatting, drinking beer, lying in the sun. Mat, Laura, Clive, Barbara, John, Marie, Jan, Jess, and two others, Ethan and Kily. Mat found me a beer. My fatigue fell away with his friendship, like a caring shepherd gathering a stray back into the fold, like a family welcoming a long-lost member back home. I was happy, I felt as if I'd just hit the jackpot. The bad news was that a wasp had stung Laura three times between the toes. Both she and Mat wore sandals. She appeared cheerful and okay, but I suspected a brave face.

I shared a room with Clive and Barbara. Barbara gave up her bottom bunk, an unanticipated act of kindness. Last night at Artieda, they seemed unresponsive, but tonight they were bright and outgoing as if they, too, were sensitive to the mood of their company. Even John the grumpy Irishman was ready to joke and handle Mat's banter. The eleven of us had dinner together in the bar opposite. The young hospitalero was versatile. No pussy footing around, he ran the bar, served the drinks, cooked and presented the meal, all jobs performed with enthusiasm and chatter. In contrast to the previous evening it was a noisy meal, everyone talking at once and speaking louder and louder as the wine flowed. Everyone spoke English except for Marie but those who spoke French kept her in the conversation. Camaraderie had been restored and I, too, was rejuvenated.

As I sunk into sleep I thanked God for returning me to my Camino family. The Camino, God or whatever name one might use was looking after me. The night was a gift, a recompense for a poor day. I was reminded of a prayer: *'Be a bright flame before me, a guiding star above, a smooth path below, a kindly shepherd behind, today, tonight and always.'*

Sangüesa was only 10 kilometres but it was worth the stop

as it had all facilities. On the way, I met Mat and Laura. Her foot was swollen and painful once she began walking. I stayed with them for their pace was slow. I tried to return the support they had given me. We made the refugio in Sangüesa late morning. The young hospitalera would have taken first prize for rudeness and indifference. She made no eye contact, played with her phone and just pointed to the registration book. I felt sorry for her that no one had ever taught her some basic courtesy. The afternoon gave an opportunity for rest and for Laura to find a doctor.

That evening I had dinner with Mat, Laura and Marie. Mat and Laura discussed their options. The doctor had advised Laura not to walk for three days. She thought she might take a taxi to the next stop while Mat walked. Their original intention was to walk as far as Santiago but now she was wondering if she might let Mat finish the walk while she took the train/bus home. Their ultimate destination was her parents' home in a village not far from Santiago. She was in two minds. She wanted to walk to be with Mat. She would see how she was in the morning.

I woke early and was keen to depart. I left Mat boiling eggs (he gave me two) in the albergue's tiny kitchen. He passed me later. He told me Laura was taking a taxi to Monreal and he would join her there. Walking was uphill all the way but I was pleased that I handled it well. I arrived at Izco about 2.30 pm, a distance of 18 kilometres. I considered going the extra 9 kilometres to Monreal, but the albergue looked inviting. Marie was already there. I was pleased I stopped, for the rain which had been threatening for the last two days fell at last. The only other guests were two very wet Spanish cyclists who arrived about 5.30 pm. The hospitalera opened a small shop which stocked enough items to purchase for dinner and breakfast. I make my selections and enjoyed cooking my evening meal in the well-equipped kitchen.

The rain had cleared by morning although the day was overcast. The walk from Izco to Monreal was downhill along a newly laid concrete path. As I approached the village I could smell a barbeque. On one side of the road was the fire, on the other a group of men had set up a table which was loaded with cooked meats, bread and bottles of wine. As I drew level, one of the men stepped out, addressed me as 'Peregrino' and ordered me to join them. He reminded me of a policeman pulling me over for a random breath test. Marie was already seated on a long bench. I accepted a sausage on bread but declined the red wine. If I drank alcohol mid-morning, that might be as far as I'd get. How strange to be invited to join these men enjoying a Sunday morning brunch! Another example of the generosity of the local people who accept and look after their pilgrims! Marie and I both left this jovial group just as the bells of the adjoining chapel rang for Mass. None of the men bothered; church was for the women and children.

The route became more difficult as it undulated around the edge of a hill. A pain in the arse, it went on for ever with one undulation after another. On the plain below an enormous freeway was being built. Eventually, I arrived at Tiebas, a small village dominated by a huge quarry eating away the hillside. Rock for the freeway? I found a brand new albergue only opened that year. Mat, Laura, John and Marie were already installed. We shared a room with four older Japanese cyclists on their way to Santiago. They had little English, no Spanish nor French but were very polite with much bowing and smiling. They looked so quaint, their older faces peering from under their helmets and their bodies clothed in lycra. Together we shared a meal at the bar just up the road. Another good evening after a hard day!

Monday 30th September was the 47th day, my last on the Camino. The walking was good, above a valley with magnificent views as if the best were saved for the last. Cultivated fields stretched across the valley to hills lined with wind turbines. Tiny villages, clusters of houses around a church with spire, dotted the valley and the slopes. I stopped for lunch at the Church of *Santa-Maria d'Eunate*. Dating from the 12th century, the building has been faithfully restored. Octagonal in shape, it is completely enclosed in a covered gallery. The church was locked. Cars loaded with tourists arrived. They walked around the building and took many photographs. I was the human interest, a pilgrim eating his bread and cheese.

I had planned to stop at Obanos. I stayed in the albergue two years previously when I walked the Camino Francés. I expected a significant increase in numbers as this is where the two routes, the Camino Francés and the Camino Aragonés join before continuing on to Santiago. I intended walking the three additional kilometres to Puente la Reina in the morning. However, I arrived early and decided to continue on. At the entrance to Puente la Reina was the *Hotel Jakue*, a large affair with a pilgrim albergue attached. Reception was in a kiosk in a very pleasant garden, which also served as a bar. The albergue was in the basement, an extensive windowless dormitory divided by curtains into cubicles of two double bunks. After selecting my bunk (bottom!) and doing my chores, I returned to the garden to mingle with the other pilgrims and to welcome Mat and Laura should they turn up. The others were mainly Americans and Canadians. They had started from Saint-Jean, Roncesvalles or Pamplona. They were at the beginning of their journey and were full of tales of blisters and of adjusting to this new vagrant life. They seemed impressed that I was at the end of my journey, my 47th day of walking, and, at the age of eighty, none the worse for wear. Among the crowd, I found three Australians, my first. I thought I was in Kangaroo Valley. Hugh and his wife Anna were recently graduated doctors. Luke was a chiropractor, all from Sydney. I was excited to meet fellow countrymen and, as they had just left Australia, keen to hear any news.

Dinner was very busy and a startling contrast to the smaller intimate gatherings of the last six weeks. A cafeteria-style meal served in a large dining hall full of diners, both pilgrims from the basement and tourists from the hotel. The car park was full of their cars and coaches. I had dinner with doctors Hugh and Anna. Our conversation covered the new political situation following the change in federal government. I had my first opportunity to share my misgivings with someone who was also a voter. I had voiced them to Mat on hearing the results of the elections. He joked about my becoming an activist when I returned.

The ambience of the Camino had changed. More pilgrims were tucked into that albergue than I had met in my forty-seven days. I felt a touch of claustrophobia in my bottom bunk in my cubicle. All beds were taken and there was only one way out, through a kitchen and a longish corridor to the exit. A fire would be a disaster. I was saddened to miss Mat and Laura to say good-bye. At least, I had their email address and phone numbers.

Fortunately, there was no fire, flood or other catastrophe that night. In the morning, I was a slow starter. My job that day was to find my way to Pamplona and find somewhere to stay. I knew where the bus stop was. Almost all the other pilgrims had left and after wishing a few 'Buen Camino' I was in the kitchen taking my time over breakfast and a coffee from the machine when in walked Mat, complete with backpack. 'G'day,' he said. 'We missed you.' They had stayed at Obanos and expected to find me there, too. They had to say good-bye. They left Obanos, saw a group of pilgrims outside the hotel as they came into Puente la Reina, and asked *'Did an elderly Australian on his own stay here last night?'* 'Yes,' they said. *'He's still inside.'*

I was thrilled they had gone out of their way to find me. In came Laura, and after hugs, I collected my pack and we walked out together. I said good-bye to my stick and left it in its place for some other pilgrim. Together the three of us walked to the bus stop, took photos of each other and got a passer-by to take a photo of the three of us. Laura's foot was better. She would test it that day. They left me with much waving. I had many Camino partings, but this was the most emotional. I felt I had made true friends of Mat and Laura, and that they had the same affection for me. Their presence was a charisma. I would probably never see them again, but I hoped I would. I felt the hollow anguish of loss in my heart.

I was at the bus stop about 8.45 am waiting for the 9.15 am. Marie arrived and together we travelled to Pamplona. I was pleased I had a companion, for, after such an emotional departure, a cloud of loneliness as thick as those flies would have settled on me. She was more organised than me. She had made all her bookings. I had my bus ticket for Pamplona but eventually I wanted to get to Paris. I recognised the surroundings of Pamplona as the bus travelled through the suburbs and I recalled the underground bus station. Was there a bus to Bayonne? I enquired at the ticket office. Yes, it leaves in an hour via San Sebastián, I was told. I was planning to spend a night in Pamplona but why remain? I knew Pamplona. I stayed there in 2011. I took the bus to San Sebastián and another to Bayonne. The bus passed through Biarritz. The three cities had joined together into one continuous megacity — all buildings and no countryside with occasional glimpses of the beach and ocean. Back to civilisation! Goodbye Camino! Marie was on the bus, too. We said good bye in Bayonne.

I had made the transition. I woke up that morning a pilgrim and by early afternoon I was a tourist. I was suffering minor identity confusion but, at least, I was comfortable back in France where I knew the language. I found the railway station and bought a ticket to Paris for the following day. The Hotel Côte Basque was opposite. I stayed there in 2011. I had arrived late at night and left early next morning. It seemed a dark and subdued place. It looked completely different in daylight. If someone said it had been refurbished in the meantime, I would have agreed. They had a vacant room. An internet café was nearby. I spent the afternoon sending emails to the family and exploring Bayonne. I booked accommodation in Paris at the Holiday Inn near the Gare de Lyon. The price just for one night paid for many beds on the road. I justified the cost with the thought it was time to treat myself to luxury.

The four-hour TGV ride gave me time for reflection. I had passed through many towns and villages, visited many churches. My memory of most would fade away but I would not forget the many fine people I had met, all pilgrims on the journey with their own story, some of which I had the privilege to hear. I thought of the millions of pilgrims who had trod the same path for up to one thousand years, all united in a common bond. We are many, but we are one. The Camino is confronting. It throws up challenges and uncertainties but they are what make the Camino interesting. Overcoming them gives the Camino meaning.

The Holiday Inn was luxurious, the clientele a contrast to the pilgrims I'd met on the way. The first night I dined in the same restaurant as in 2006 when I stayed at the *Hotel Corail* just up the road. I enjoyed watching some French TV. My first task in the big city was a haircut and shampoo to return a little respectability to my appearance. I visited Les Halles and bought shoes and socks as an alternative to my boots. I crossed the Seine to the fifth arrondissement where I visited Saint Etienne du Mont, my favourite church in Paris. I lit a candle for Maris. It seemed a long time since I last lit one for her. This time there was no wedding to force me to leave, so I had all the time in the world to sit before the candle, to reflect and to thank her for the life we shared. I found myself telling her about my Camino and the many people I had met. I mentioned Mat and Laura. She would have loved them, but, of course, she knew them because she was with me all the time.

Around the corner, I visited the bookshop in Boulevard Saint Germain which stocks the Camino guides and happened to see the guide book for Camino Portugués. I lashed out and bought one. It might come in handy one day.

I contacted Godfreid whom I met early in the walk. We had two pleasant evenings in a small bar/restaurant, one that Parisians used and way off the tourist track. Godfreid knew the regulars and I almost felt a local as I joined some of the banter with the other patrons. I enjoyed the discussions Godfreid and I had about his spiritual life while on the Camino. Over two bottles of good French red wine, we continued our discussion those evenings. He was into Zen, and he told me about the activities he and his fellow "students" undertook under their Zen master. In particular, two intrigued me. One was to live on the streets of Paris for a few days and to beg, to take no money or food, but to live on what people gave him. This was seen as a humbling and cleansing experience and an abandonment of the world's material objects in the journey towards purification. I had seen many beggars particularly at the entrance to churches and metro stations. I wondered how many of them were there, not because they were destitute, but for reasons of the spirit. Sometimes, one stood out as being too well dressed, but perhaps they had fallen on hard times. The other astonishing practice was to hold their retreats/meditation at Auschwitz, given its terrible history. Godfreid said the place was confronting at first but, later, he found that its ambience was cleansing and redemptive. Through emails, we are still in touch. He has moved back to Belgium and has formed a relationship with a Polish lady whom he met through his Zen classes. They have since married.

The next phase of my pilgrimage was a visit to Taizé.

Noel between Mat and Laura

12

All the darkness in the world cannot
extinguish the light of a single candle.
—Saint Francis of Assisi

Many churches around the world conduct services in the Taizé style. They use their music and chants. My church was one of them. Through these services, I came to know of the Taizé community. I visited Taizé after my 2011 Camino. I was keen to visit again, because I regarded it not only a highlight of the Camino, but a highlight of my life.

Taizé has become a meeting place for young adults from every continent. Each year over 100,000 young people make a never-ending pilgrimage for prayer, scripture study, sharing and communal work. The community is an ecumenical monastic order, composed of about 100 brothers who come from thirty different countries and from Catholic, Protestant and Eastern Orthodox traditions. The monastic order has a strong devotion to peace and justice through prayer and meditation. Their welcome extends in the main to young people but they tolerate older adults in their 'quiet' times. Hence, they were happy to welcome me, an old bloke.

Getting to Taizé involved taking the TGV at Gare de Lyon to Mâcon and then a bus to Taizé. On the bus, I heard an Aussie accent. I introduced myself to Evan, a cheerful young man from Newcastle, NSW. A girl had told him Taizé was 'great'. He impressed me as a good person, of no particular religion and definitely not a church goer, but he wanted the experience and to discover for himself what it was all about.

I saw Evan a few times but I never had a chance to discuss with him how his search progressed.

Visitors are encouraged to come for a week, Sunday to Sunday, in order to participate in the community's cycle of life. The structure of my two visits, two years apart, was identical. I arrived Sunday afternoon and went through a welcoming procedure that was well organised and accustomed to processing large numbers. I was surprised at my accommodation. I was expecting a tent or a bed in the barracks, but I was offered a private room next to the infirmary. I supposed they noted my age, thought this old chap will be doddery and will need extra care. Thankfully it wasn't like that at all. I didn't bother to tell them that I had just walked 800 kilometres and had slept many nights in dormitories with up to forty others.

The welcoming package included the following:

'Coming to Taizé is an opportunity to seek communion with God through common prayer, singing, personal reflection and sharing. Everyone is here to discover a meaning for their life and to find a new vitality.'

Pilgrims over thirty years of age were segregated. We dined apart from the younger pilgrims and had our own study programme. After our evening meal, we went to the church service. When I entered the Church of Reconciliation for the first time, I was struck by the silence. There were 500-600 people. By Taizé standards it was a quiet week, as they can accommodate over 5000 in summer, Easter and All Saints.

My first visit was phenomenal, the second just as amazing. What were extraordinary were the prayer sessions. They were simple, yet overwhelming. Three times a day, when the bells rang, the brothers of the community, dressed in white, came

and knelt down in the large expandable church, surrounded
by all the visitors. The prayer consisted of singing, a Psalm,
a scripture reading, silence, intercessions. The spoken word
came in many languages. There was no common language
but the singing and music made the prayer very accessible as
if reaching out to everyone. The simple chants were sung over
and over. In the evening the meditative singing went on until
late. On my second visit, I felt as if I had never been away. Time
had stood still. Like coming home!

Taizé is like a spiritual shot in the arm. Never in my life have
I looked forward to going to church so keenly, arriving early
and reluctant to leave. I was drawn to a Presence. The simple
worshipful atmosphere and daily rhythm of prayer/song led to
a deeper place of connection. There was no hurry, all the time
in the world to seek God with heart and voice.

Such a contrast with my normal religious practice! I go to
church most Sundays, part of the weekly grind. Sometimes the
service is brilliant and I feel connected and moved by the Spirit,
whether it be the music or the charisma of the preacher. Too
often, it's a matter of routine; the songs are slow and dreary, the
homily delivered dead-pan and boring, and my mind drifts off
to what I'll have for lunch or I must talk to Harry after church.

On my first visit, the adult group was about a hundred
in total from a variety of countries speaking a variety of languages although the majority were Germans as it was a holiday
season. Brother John who led our scripture study canvassed
the group and determined that most understood either English or German, so he gave his talk in those two languages.
He spoke for a minute or two in one language then changed
to the other. I was amazed at his flexibility. I noticed a small
group of Spanish speakers one of whom translated from the
English for her group when Brother John spoke in German.

We were divided into either English or German small discussion groups. These small groups were given communal tasks. Our group's job was cleaning up after breakfast. After each session, he gave us questions to discuss in our small groups. Our group included Germans, Norwegians, Americans, British, Dutch and Australian (me).

Choir practice was optional. Apart from my school days I had never been involved in a choir, so why not start now? For an hour each afternoon we practiced the songs to be sung that evening. The girls in charge divided us into four groups-sopranos, tenors, altos and bass. I joined the bass. First we sang the song, then each group practised their part, then we all sang together. Wow! We were amazed to hear how beautifully we sounded, as if the ear of God had heard us. And after just one practice! Then in the evening enough people remembered their parts to produce the same harmony. Amazing! No wonder those songs stuck in our heads.

We sang one of these chants each day as a grace before meals. Our group sang them while washing up. I'm sure if I told my family that we sang hymns washing up, they would have looked at me sceptically and said: *'Dad, don't you think you're carrying this religion thing a bit too far?'* I used to resent having to leave the morning session early because our group had to be the first to have breakfast to give us time to clean up before Brother John started his talk. We usually just made it.

My second visit made just as deep an impact and was just as fresh. I came away from the prayer sessions with the singing continuing in my mind as if it had become a prayer underlying our daily lives. Of the hundreds of people who shared these prayer sessions, I saw great respect and reverence. I saw examples of the love of God in human love. The brothers encouraged children to partake in lighting a candle, a symbol of the light of Christ. I saw one child thread her way through the throng of people sitting on the floor to her family next to me and she nestled into her father's lap, her job well done. Among the young people, I noticed many couples devoted to each other, sitting closely together. I prayed that God would bless them and that the light of Christ would shine on them. Seeing loving couples always makes me think of my Maris. We were a loving couple. She was with me in spirit. She, too, would have been moved by this sacred place

The people in my discussion group covered the full spectrum of belief. One lady was born in Holland but lived in Italy. She wore a collar support and brace, needed two sticks to get around and was in constant pain. She had travelled alone to Taizé. She was our atheist. She described God as a metaphor. The rest of us were perplexed. Why had she come, particularly as this was not her first time? She described Taizé as a place where heaven and earth met. (Another metaphor?) I can only guess at what she valued. Was it the tranquillity and the feeling of being in the presence of something greater than what the normal hurley-burley has to offer? At the other end were a Norwegian couple, staunch Lutherans. They had visited Taizé many times, so often that they had bought a house in the neighbouring village of Ameugny where they and others of their parish stayed. In between, others mentioned that they hadn't attended church for years but they were still seeking the divine. A lady from England was hoping Taizé would bring some peace into her troubled life. Others had mental health problems. People shared their lives in such an atmosphere of trust.

The same Brother John who led our scripture study in 2011 spoke to the adult group in 2013. Only a handful was not German. There was only one English discussion group and some German speakers joined to improve their English. Each

morning Brother John presented a scripture reading which
was followed up by a number of questions which we discussed
in our groups. Our group came from many countries — England, New Zealand, Ireland, Switzerland, America, Germany
and Australia (me!). For some, this was their first visit to Taizé,
but others had visited many times.

I wanted to take home a souvenir of my visit, something
of real significance. In the bookshop, I found the Coptic Icon
of Friendship, dating from the sixth century the original of
which is in the Louvre. Jesus is shown with arm around the
shoulder of a friend named Menus. His eyes are not severe or
judgemental but gentle. His face commands attention, not in a
triumphal way, but as a calm authority. I liked the icon because
I identified with that friend. Jesus is my friend. I used to tell
the others in the discussion group that Jesus was my mate and
he talked to me in an Aussie accent. He walked with me on the
Camino and kept me going.

I bought three copies, one for the parish Taizé group, one
for an old friend, Fr. Peter McGrath, and one to keep. I have
mine in a prominent place at home, a constant reminder that
Jesus is my mate and is always there for me. But he's not just
for me, Jesus is everyone's mate.

I am thankful for the opportunity to experience Taizé, not
once but twice. On both occasions, it was sad to leave, another
Camino parting. I am thankful for Brother John's input, for the
members of my groups. I receive a monthly newsletter and I
enjoy reading what is happening in the Taizé world in France
and in many other countries.

Perhaps, God willing, I'll return one day.

Intermission

The journey is far from over

13

It is only by going down into the abyss that we recover
the treasures of life. Where you stumble, there lies your treasure.
The very cave you were afraid to enter turns out to be the
source of what you were looking for.
—Joseph Campbell.

Sometimes I'm not sure what to make of my life over the last ten years. I stumbled around after the death of Maris. I was lost. My life assumptions, my identity had been shattered by her suicide. I had to put myself together again. I travelled. I was drawn towards pilgrimage. I was seeking an anchorage that would bring some stability into my life. I heard of the ancient pilgrimage route, the Camino de Santiago de Compostela. Modern day pilgrims were following the same routes. I joined them. At one stage I thought that my travelling was a reaction to Maris' death, a way of working my way through my grieving. It was more than that. The same longing (or restlessness?) which sent me on the Camino in 2010, 2011 and 2013, to Chartres and to Taizé continues to drive me as if I were on a quest.

Back home I was on another pilgrimage, trying to apply the lessons of the Camino to my life, making my life a pilgrimage and every step a prayer. I moved out of my family home of thirty years into a retirement village. I was ready to leave behind the memories of a life with Maris, to make the final sort of her belongings and to keep what I valued. The retirement village was nice, its gardens were beautiful. It is situated on the edge of a national park. My view looked straight into this national park and through the trees I caught glimpses of the ocean. The people were friendly. We had our own inner community, the residents of a group of nine units. We looked out for each other.

The management promoted the idea of comfort, security and taking the worry out of life. There was a finality in that message as if a life of adventure and inquiry was over... I wasn't ready to settle into God's holding paddock and be content with reminiscence and looking back. I like to think I still had a glint in my eyes.

The longing continued. My quest, my search was by no means finished. In 2013, three months after moving into the retirement village, I returned to France and followed another of the Camino routes from Montpellier and across the Pyrenees. Every day, I thanked God that at the age of eighty I had the health, fitness and enthusiasm for such a mad caper. The route was more difficult and some days, I felt I had nothing but a faith in God's care to keep me going.

Back in Australia I abandoned the security of living thirty years in Sydney. I moved out of the retirement village to the Snowy Mountains, adjacent to Mount Kosciuszko National Park. Such an action is at the heart of modern day pilgrimage, moving out of the safety of the familiar and diving into the unknown, with a trust/faith in God to support me. Life begins at the edge of your comfort zone.

Jindabyne is a small country town of about 2000 permanent residents. About 6000 come to work during the snow season. Approximately, one million people visit the Mount Kosciuszko National Park each year, for the snow sports in winter and in summer bush walking, mountain biking, and water related sports. Lake Jindabyne was formed by the damming of the Snowy River as part of the Snowy Hydroelectric scheme, regarded as one of the engineering wonders of the world. Once upon a time, Jindabyne was where the lake is now. The town was flooded and rebuilt up the hill.

This was my home. I moved into my house in August 2014. It fitted my idea of what a house in the bush should be. It's clad in wood, its roof is tin and a wide veranda extends the length of the building, giving a view of the lake and the surrounding mountains. It wasn't as if I'd drawn Jindabyne out of a hat. My daughter Jacinta and grandson Brody lived here. She had grown to love the mountains when she worked a number of winters. Two years before, she took the plunge and moved. I visited her often. Jacinta encouraged me to think about moving, too. '*You'd fit in well here, Dad. Brody would love to have Pa nearby, too.*'

The connections go deeper. Maris' sister, Catherine, is buried in a tiny isolated cemetery at Moonbah, about ten kilometres south of Jindabyne. She was the first of the three sisters to die by suicide. She married Ron, a member of one of the pioneering families of the Snowy Mountains.

My son Stephen loves the mountains. Although he lives in Rockhampton, Queensland, he visits Jindabyne each year as a ski patrol volunteer. I grew to love the mountains, too, while Stephen, as a student, was my companion while bush walking in summer. We disappeared for days in the back country. I was sad but happy for him when he married and got his first proper job. In fact, all the family enjoyed snow sports and loved the beauty of the region. I truly live in God's country.

In quitting Sydney, I was leaving Maris behind in the Frenchs Forest Bush Cemetery. I visited her grave regularly, and now I was separating myself from her, another step in the process of letting go. I knew that, whenever I felt the need, I could visit Cath's grave and grieve for her sister, Maris.

I was looking forward to the challenges of living in a small country town. Most people in their 80s look for the comfort and security of the familiar, but, here I was, moving into a new community where I had to make new friends and develop new interests. I wanted to make my contribution, to use my skills and experience. It was sad to leave my church, St Anthony's at Terrey Hills, which I had attended for thirty years and where I made so many friends. It was sad to leave my fifteen years' involvement with Lifeline where I felt I had supported so many people in crisis and perhaps saved some with suicidal thoughts from themselves. It was sad to leave behind my regular attendance at Sydney Swans home games. I was grateful for the warm welcome of the people. Every day, I look at the reflection of the mountains in the lake and am thankful this is my home.

Yet nine months after moving in I was about to return to Europe. The Camino hook was in, sharp and deep. If I were to resist, it would only dig in deeper. I knew the Camino was not easy. But so what? On my side, I had, I hoped, a goodly dose of persistence and above all faith in myself and in God.

My plan was to travel to Rabanal, Spain, and work for two weeks in a refugio for pilgrims, then travel to Lisbon and walk through Portugal to Santiago.

My pilgrimages add new meaning to my life. My deeply personal journey continues and I pray that I'll have the courage and momentum to pursue my search for understanding.

I guess I'll just keep on walking.

14

Blessed are you, pilgrim, if you search for the truth
and make of the Camino a life of your life.
—*Beatitudes of the Pilgrim*

A few days before departing, we had a visiting priest at the Catholic Church at Jindabyne. In his homily Fr Brien spoke on the value of community and of no man being an island. He was preaching to the converted. His congregation was composed mainly of local residents, most of whom met for coffee after Mass in one of the cafes. They were their own community. They discussed the happenings of the week, the health and well-being of each other and of friends and acquaintances. They looked out for each other and cared for one another. Some had been born in the Snowy Mountains. They bore the surnames of the pioneering families, other were more recent arrivals. I was the most recent arrival but I felt accepted. Many queried why I had moved. I asked myself that same question, but, as soon as I mentioned the family connections, they were content.

Every Sunday, Walter led the singing. He had asked others to stand in to give him a spell, but he had no takers. One Sunday I did the scripture reading. He asked me would I lead the singing sometimes because I had a strong voice and projected it well. *'I'll give it a go,'* I replied, my usual response whenever asked to do something different. Foolish Noel! I thought. My voice is extremely ordinary. I have never really sung before, and believe I have no talents in that area. I led the singing that Sunday. An ancient overhead projector projects the songs on

slides made in the last century. *'I'd give myself 40%,'* I said to
the organist, June, after Mass. *'Doesn't matter,'* she replied. *'We
are all sharing. We are all singing together.'* A profound answer!
The lesson? Don't worry about individual performance or what
people think; it's the effort to bring the church community
together that counts.

On this last Sunday as we sat around sipping our coffees
I was farewelled. Not everyone understood my motivations
but, nevertheless, they wished me well. They were aware of
my training regime — regular attendances at the High-Coun-
try Gym, daily walks with backpack around the lake and in
the mountains. I experienced pain in my left leg and in my
neck. I attended the local chiropractor regularly. I wondered
if my eighty-two-year-old body was cracking up, wasn't up to
the challenge. Deterioration wasn't going to stop me. I had a
check-up with my doctor. He thought I was among his fittest
and healthiest patients. That made me feel good. I sought a
referral to a cardiologist in Canberra. He had me running up
a steep, steep treadmill and said my body had the fitness of a
fifty-two-year-old. That made me feel better.

My pilgrimage began the moment I stepped out of my
door. After farewells from Jacinta and Brody, I took the bus
to Canberra and then the train to Sydney. I felt calm despite
the nuisance pain in my neck and back. At Central I took the
train to Town Hall where I was to take the 506 bus out to Ryde
to stay with my daughter Angela for the night. I had caught the
506 several times. As part of my preparation I attended three
intensive refresher courses in Spanish at the Sydney WEA and
stayed with Angela each time. After travelling all day I was
feeling frazzled as I climbed on the bus. I had arrived in the
late afternoon to encounter the masses of people struggling
home, a phenomenon I left Sydney to escape from. The route

did not look familiar. The bus arrived at a different destination. I had caught the 505, the driver told me. However, he took me back to a stop on the 506 route where I waited for the right bus. There were plenty of buses but they were all going to the Homebush stadium for a State of Origin football match. Lesson? When you are a little stressed, you can be vulnerable and make mistakes. Eventually, my 506 arrived and I made it safely to Angela's and family.

I had one day in Sydney. I visited Maris' grave. A fierce storm a few days previously had ripped up trees. Branches, twigs and leaves were scattered across the lawn. Despite the mess, the tranquil ambience remained. The storm had passed, peace was restored, and the birds had resumed their songs. I sat on the seat adjacent to her grave. Maris was dead ten years. In the first few years I spoke to her every day, less often now, but I spoke to her at length on that Thursday afternoon as I sat among the scattered storm debris and reflected on the forty-two years we shared our lives. I asked her to be with me as I walked the length of Portugal.

My son-in-law, Guy, drove me to the airport. On the flight to Madrid, I realised this was my 7th overseas trip since Maris died — a reflection of my restlessness, loss of anchorage and endeavours to find structure. Most of the passengers around me were Spanish. I mused over my Spanish lessons. I seemed to have forgotten it all. I couldn't even remember the word for "bed", a vital one because I'd be looking for one every night. Dark thoughts filled the long night, which I tried to counter with a reminder of one of the first Camino lessons: Take one day, one phase at a time.

My Spanish neighbours were helpful. Pedro and Marta sat next to me while José, Madelaine and Alphonse were in front. The plane was supposed to land at 8.00 am and I had booked a 9.30 am bus for Astorga. We left Bangkok an hour late, so I knew I would miss that connection. My neighbours helped me to compose an explanation for Ailsa, the bus company. José had good English. He admired my venturesomeness, coming to Spain on my own. He'd been to Australia, liked Sydney and the Great Ocean Road and thought I spoke a different lingo to other Australians because I was easy to understand.

I had to wait five hours for the next bus so I wandered around the airport, asking questions and buying coffee, a beer and a meal. People understood my Spanish. That was encouraging. There was considerable confusion as a host of buses arrived at the same time but, eventually, I was directed to the right one. The afternoon was hot, the journey sticky and uncomfortable. I was tired, my neck and left leg were hurting and my right wrist joined them. I'm packing up! The country-side was uninspiring — hot, dry, flat and treeless. I tried to talk to the guy sitting next to me but he didn't want to know me. I was pleased when we arrived at Astorga at 8.00 pm. I could have found a bed at the pilgrim refuge but decided on a hotel. I wanted a good night's sleep and I guessed I'd have a better chance in a private room than in a dormitory. I enjoyed a three-course pilgrim meal for 10 euros in a café on the plaza.

It was still daylight when I finished my meal. I needed to stretch my legs before retiring having sat for so long in cramped conditions. I walked through the plaza to the adjoining one and found the municipal albergue where I had stayed in 2011. I remembered there were a number of disabled people wheeling around in front of the albergue. I was intrigued at their presence, but I didn't have enough Spanish to ask the questions and none of the hospitaleros had the English to answer them. Next to the albergue was a park. I remember ordering a beer from a kiosk and watching a very disabled person doing the same. It's a simple well practised skill on my part to order a drink, take my money out of wallet, and return the change. But the same tasks presented an immense challenge to my disabled friend. The bar attendant opened his purse, took out the coins, poured his beer and returned the change to his purse. It was a poignant moment of that Camino. I had witnessed an act of love and compassion, and it seemed as if the girl was the hand of God stretching out to offer some comfort to one of His disabled sons. I came away from that park, thankful that I was able-bodied and had so many skills which I took for granted, and humbled that I wasn't able to help him. Tonight, in the twilight, the park was deserted, the kiosk was closed and in need of repainting. One of the plywood panels had peeled off. It looked as if it hadn't traded for some time. Only the ghosts of past drinkers were out strolling or wheeling that night.

15

The best way to find yourself is to
lose yourself in the service of others
—Mahatma Gandhi

When I walked the Camino through the north of Spain in 2011 I reached the small village of Rabanal del Camino on 3rd September. Staying in the *Refugio Gaucelmo* was a highlight. Gaucelmo was a fitting name because he was a 12th century local hermit who built a church, a hospice and hospital for pilgrims. His spirit lives on for I received a great welcome from the three hospitaleros, a couple from Denver and a chap from Liverpool. I was even given apple crumble made with fruit from the garden.

The refugio is run by the Confraternity of St James, an English-based organisation. It organises a roster of hospitaleros from its members. Volunteers stay for two weeks. Everyone at some stage has walked the Camino. Good idea! I thought at the time. I'd like to be a hospitalero one day. I'd like the opportunity to provide shelter and support for pilgrims and return that friendly welcome to others.

That day had arrived. Back in Australia I joined Australian Friends of the Camino, the local branch of the Confraternity and expressed an interest in being a hospitalero. In January 2015, I underwent a two-day training course in Sydney. The ability to converse in Spanish was considered a desirable attribute so I revised my limited knowledge of Spanish. In Sydney, I attended intensive courses in Spanish under the tutorship of Gabriel, a delightful, fun-loving Venezuelan whose role playing, guitar playing and ham acting made Spanish sound so easy.

Pilgrims come from many countries. The Camino is a multilingual environment. As part of our training we were given a five-language dictionary covering all the likely situations — Spanish, English, French, Portuguese, and German.

I woke late to a bright sunny day, a good start for my new adventure. I was feeling refreshed but hazy from jet lag. I could have walked the 21 kilometres to Rabanal but decided a taxi was a better option if I wanted to arrive in good shape. I did not know what demands the duties of a hospitalero would place on my tired body. The taxi driver, Carlos, had no English but he spoke French. I mentioned that on my last visit to Astorga I noticed a number of disabled people in wheelchairs. Carlos replied that there was a hospice next to the pilgrim refuge and that they were the special sons and daughters of the Astorga community. We passed many pilgrims on the way all wearing the distinctive backpack. I will be looking after some of them tonight, I thought.

I remembered the approaches to Rabanal. The road leaves the open countryside, passes two ancient chapels on the left and begins a gentle incline up through the village street lined with stone houses overflowing with red geraniums. Rabanal is beautiful. In the middle ages, it was a stopping place for pilgrims on the way to Santiago. It crumbled into ruins due to centuries of neglect but now, following the late 20th century revival of the pilgrimage, house by house it is being restored, including the refugio, a major project of the Confraternity. It was once the parish house and began operating in 1991 to fill the gap in accommodation between Astorga and Ponferrada, an exposed and rugged 54 km stretch of the Camino.

I was about to knock at the gate when out came Alison

pushing a wheelbarrow loaded with large black plastic bags. She was one of the hospitaleros I was replacing. I was keen to meet Alison for she is a fellow writer, the author of the Confraternity's guide books, one of the heavies. She was taking the previous day's rubbish to the bins on the edge of the village, she explained. She took me along, too, and in the short distance, delivered instructions at machine gun pace, that left me breathless on the hospitalero's duties and named the key players in the village whose cooperation was vital for the effective running of the refugio.

Back at the refugio, I met Julie. She's a heavy, too, as she organises the roster. I met my fellow hospitaleros, Hope and Finola. Everyone apart from me was English. The tutelage continued at the same rate for the rest of the day. Thank goodness that I had taken a taxi and was relatively fresh. How will I remember all this? I thought. I could feel the levels of panic rising from the stomach, through the chest and up into my head which buzzed with swarms of detail that I'd never remember. I heard that Hope and Finola had arrived on the Saturday and that their instruction had begun the moment they arrived. They were in the know and I was a day behind. I was at the back of the pack in a rat race. I felt disadvantaged, cheesed off. Those two girls, my fellow hospitaleros, if they were into playing power games, would have it over me. They would know what to do in a situation whereas I would be still at first base. How knowledge can be power! I tried to suppress these competitive thoughts. I tried thinking of the present. Take things as they come. If I make a blue, it won't be a catastrophe. They won't chop off my toes. The world won't end. I should have arrived on Saturday, too, although I thought I had done well to arrive when I did, given it had taken me five days.

I sensed tensions in Hope and Finola. Perhaps they were

experiencing the same confusion. They chatted while I tried to absorb everything in a silent, dogged fashion. As the day advanced the tiredness of jet lag crept up on me, which was just as well for my thoughts changed from panic to *'she'll be right'* and *'it'll all work out'*. I was sure that Alison and Julie meant to create the minimum of anxiety in their inductees. They are compassionate, caring people. They had a job to do — to teach us the ropes. In the end, they said the refugio was in our hands and to make decisions as we thought appropriate, even though we had a fifty-page book of rules, worked out over many years, to guide us.

The refugio is beautiful. Carefully restored, it has an extensive garden in which the many rose bushes climbing over the walls were in full bloom. The herb garden, Julie explained, is used by those who prepare their own meals. Gaucelmo offers accommodation for forty pilgrims. On the ground floor are the kitchen and a communal area called the salon which houses a fire place, chairs, lounges, benches and tables — a place for the pilgrims to gather. Upstairs a dormitory accommodates twenty in double bunks, a smaller room for four and two rooms for hospitaleros. Outside is another building called the barn with accommodation for another sixteen. At the time it was closed, recovering from fumigation and other chemical treatments against bed bugs. Beyond the barn was a large garden with the remnants of an orchard where the pilgrims were able to relax.

Julie took us on a tour of the village to meet the key players. The refugio maintains very good relations with the approximately thirty-five permanent residents of the village. Susanne ran the small shop around the corner. Her husband Ramón was the refugio's handyman. Sarah and her sister Anne ran the shop around the other corner. Antoine, Christina and Ivan (who was Susanne's son) worked in the restaurant/bar opposite while Augustine, Susanna and Manipaz ran the other restaurant/bar just up the road. Esperanza, Isabelle and Mercedes ran the other refugio (Pilars). Everywhere, there were lively, enthusiastic and friendly exchanges, all in Spanish. I missed most of it but I certainly got the gist of their warm, well intentioned welcome. We felt at home, part of the community, doing our bit in caring for the pilgrims upon whom the village depended for its livelihood and existence.

It was time to meet the pilgrims. When they enter the village, they have a number to places to choose. *Refugio Gaucelmo* is different in that it offers beds to bona fide pilgrims only, that is, those who have arrived on foot or bicycle, with priority given to those on foot. Pilgrims who use motorised assistance (such as luggage transport services) are not normally admitted unless there are health issues or other valid reasons. They are referred to Pilars.

A number were waiting when we opened the gates. They had dumped their packs and were sitting quietly in the shade of a large tree or on the steps of the church opposite. They gathered their belongings and formed a line to be processed. We gave them a welcome and a drink, a glass of water with a mint leaf. Alison and Julie left Hope, Finola and me to induct the pilgrims. Hope gave the run down on timings. Finola recorded details of each in a register — name, nationality, pass or passport number, where they started walking. I took them to their beds, showing them the kitchen and the salon on the way. I gave each a pillow case and asked them to put the pillow on their bunk beds in the case so that I would know which were taken. The bottom bunks went first. I showed them the showers and toilets. We only had 20 beds that first night as, in the changeover, there were five hospitaleros. It wasn't long before Hope put the 'completo' sign on the gate.

That became our routine. The pilgrims came from many countries and spoke many languages. In the two weeks, we welcomed four hundred and seventy pilgrims from thirty-six countries, including five Australians. Finola has good Spanish but no French, while both Hope and I had good French and limited Spanish although Hope was better than me. I was both surprised and pleased just how far I got with my limited Spanish. Although most pilgrims had at least a smattering of English I developed a little patter, jumping from language to language and frequently resorting to gestures. That five-language dictionary came in incredibly handy.

The pilgrims were wonderful to meet and thankful for what we offered — a positive, cheerful welcome, a chance to care for their aching bodies and blistered feet, hot showers, a place to wash their clothes, a lovely garden for warm days and a fire in the salon when the days were cold. Many said the welcome and its peaceful ambience made our refugio one of the best. Later in the week a Frenchman told me we probably did not realise what impact we were having. I related to his comment because I had experienced expressionless hospitaleros who tapped their pencil impatiently while I searched for my passport, who made no eye contact, who treated me like a blow-in, who played with their phones and pointed at the register, indifference oozing out of every pore. It was good to know we were doing something worthwhile and appreciated.

The afternoon's routine included English tea at five. The pilgrims were invited to sit around a large table in the court yard and were offered tea and biscuits. This was an institution on the Camino for many pilgrims had heard about this little ritual. To this afternoon tea came from next door some of the monks of the monastery. (*Monasterio Benedictino de San Salvador de Monte Irago*) I met the abbot Fr. Xavier. He seemed to me young for an abbot. Abbots were a venerable lot in my image. He had a delightful larrikin streak and a great sense of fun. Although Spanish he was fluent in German and English. I met Bro Marinus a young novice. He was German but fluent in English. A serious, thoughtful young man, he was interested in me, an Australian, because, like many German youth, he had visited as a back backer. He was up to date with Australian politics. He wanted to discuss immigration policies. He believed Australia's policies on asylum seekers and boat people were cruel, a paradox because it was at odds with his image of a generous Australian people.

I told him he touched on an issue about which I was passionate because I was an activist and attended demonstrations in Sydney and Canberra. I found myself giving Bro Marinus a tirade. With the encouragement of both major political parties, Australia has become blind to its responsibilities towards those who have come as refugees seeking asylum. Not only has it failed to honour international treaty obligations, but it has deliberately imposed physical and mental brutality on asylum seekers, incarcerated in off shore detention centres. In between passing cups of tea around, I mentioned the policy treats people who have committed no crime as criminals. Giving others a fair go is supposed to be one of Australia's core traits, but we are failing to treat others with respect and dignity. It's a moral blindness. To cap it off, our politicians claim the policy 'has stopped the boats,' enshrining 'the end justifies the means' as a core principle of government.

Around this serious discussion, there were many other conversations around the table. It was wonderful to see everyone coming together, discussing their experiences, sharing information, supporting and encouraging each other.

The monks held daily services in the village church opposite all sung in Gregorian chant. One of our jobs was to enlist pilgrims to read a prayer in their own language at the 7 pm Vespers. The Compline at 9.30 included a pilgrims' blessing.

We did not offer dinner but referred the pilgrims to our kitchen or to one of the two restaurants. We hospitaleros, too, went to dinner. As one of us had to hang around all the time, we developed a routine whereby two of us went together and then the third one later. That first night Hope and I went to dinner together and Finola went alone. The following night Hope and Finola went together and I went alone. Then I went to dinner with Finola and Hope went alone. We made a lot of fun with this arrangement. I raved on about my incredible good luck having two lovely girls to date. The girls rabbited on about my faithlessness and accused me of two-timing — a good start to developing good relationships and to working as a team.

We rotated between the two restaurants. We chose first the restaurant opposite run by Antoine, Christina and Ivan. The young Ivan served us at table. The restaurant offered a three-course pilgrims' menu at 10 euros. We were to discover that the other restaurant offered a similar menu at the same price. Red wine was thrown in. Over the meal, Hope and I shared our stories. She had walked the Camino a number of times and had trekked in Nepal thirteen times. I was impressed. That explained her rugged weathered features. Her style was direct and matter-of-fact but I sensed a warm, compassionate and perhaps vulnerable person underneath her rough and ready appearance. I told her about Maris and my subsequent search.

I mentioned my conversation with Bro Marinus. It disturbed me to think that he had aired a slur on my beautiful amazing country. Australia's international reputation was at stake. I did not expect to be discussing Australian politics with a young German trainee monk in a tiny village in Spain.

I saw parallels in my situation and that of asylum seekers. My displacement, loss of identity and search for sanctuary was on an emotional level, but, for the asylum seekers, poor bastards, it was a hard, cruel ruthless reality.

As I drifted off to sleep that night, I decided as a post-Camino resolution that I would continue my activism when I returned home — attending demonstrations and marches, writing letters, anything that would restore sight to Australia's moral blindness.

The next day Monday 1st June was our first full day of responsibility. We were up early to give our pilgrims a breakfast of bread and jam. The pilgrims departed by 8 and then we spent three hours cleaning and preparing the refuge for the next lot. My responsibilities included the down stairs toilets and showers and the barn. As the barn hadn't been used, I didn't have to clean it, but I nevertheless inspected it for bed bugs. We had been advised to wait until Wednesday before we opened it to pilgrims.

Standards of hygiene are very high. I learned many new skills relevant to industrial cleaning. All the mops, brooms and buckets had a colour code. Red was for the kitchen, green was for the bathrooms, blue was for the bedrooms. If we mixed them up, we used lots of disinfectant before returning them to use. I took the rubbish to the bins at the edge of the village. We kept the bread scraps and gave them to an old chap Oblines for his chooks. He lived in a tiny house on the way to the rubbish bins. I said 'G'day' (actually *Buenos Dias*) each time I passed. He had lots to say in reply. He spent his day either sitting on a bench outside his home or one of the two bars. He lived between them

About 11 am, after our burst of hard yakka, we rewarded ourselves with a coffee at the bar opposite. Back at base, I found a mower in the shed. This Spanish version looked complicated. Ramón came around and showed me how to start it. I mowed a little as the grass in the garden was getting long, but the movement hurt my neck which had been causing me some distress. I decided it was a big job

We opened the gate at 1.30 pm. Pilgrims were already waiting. Some arrived exhausted, looking green around the gills, but most were in good spirits. We registered them and showed them their beds. The barn wasn't ready yet so we were soon full at twenty-four. As soon as they had gone through their routines of showering, washing their clothes and hanging them on the lines in the garden, most chose the garden to relax, read, or just sleep. Our refugio was quiet and meditative, a real refuge, which is what our pilgrims seemed to appreciate. Such a contrast to Pilars, the other refugio! It was larger and included a bar.

A young Belgian, Axel, turned up. He had a tent so we allowed him to set it up in the garden. It turned out that he was the 143,000th pilgrim to stay at Gaucelmo. The Confraternity gives a certificate and a special badge to every 1000th pilgrim, so we made a fuss of him and had a little ceremony of presentation in the garden.

Finola and I had dinner together at the other restaurant up the road past Oblines' place. He was sitting with a few of the locals in the bar. A more private and matter-of-fact person, Finola was looking forward to the wedding of her daughter. She had walked the Camino several times and bush walked (rambling the English call it) through England.

We decided that we all didn't have to get up early to open the kitchen for breakfast, so we organised a roster. Only one of us needed to be up before 6.00 am to start breakfast; the other two could come down later. The kitchen was small and soon become crowded. It was a humble meal — bread, jam, tea or coffee — but the pilgrims seemed to appreciate it.

We quickly settled into the routine of cleaning and got through our jobs smartly. I did more mowing, but the vibrations hurt my neck. You had to hang on to the mower all the time, otherwise it stopped. I decided that the job was far too big for me, which was annoying because I wanted the challenge. Ramón arrived and finished the job.

In the afternoon, we were soon full at twenty-four. Among the pilgrims were five Koreans, none of whom spoke English (or Spanish or French). One of them tried to communicate, but the only point I could understand was that he had retired at fifty-five. They spent their time cooking. They occupied the kitchen and used all the pots and pans. Most of the pilgrims who cooked had a simple meal, but the Koreans prepared themselves several courses. We tried to discourage the pilgrims from cooking in the morning as the kitchen soon became crowded. The Koreans, however, were undeterred and prepared just as elaborate a breakfast as their evening meal. Nevertheless, they were polite, with lots of smiles, and cleaned up afterward.

Wednesday we opened the barn, hoping the bed bugs had vanished. It was hard work getting the barn ready, moving the beds for sweeping, turning the mattresses over and placing the bottom sheet. My neck hurt badly and I had to tell the girls and seek their help. Hope tried a massage but that made things worse. Finola offered me a head sock. To make things worse, I kept bumping my head on the low beams despite the warnings of red strips. We had thirty-six that night, including two campers and a dog. Among our pilgrims were five Australians — two women with their daughters and a girl from Melbourne.

In the morning, I offered the Australians Vegemite for

breakfast. I had more work that morning cleaning the barn and getting it ready for the evening. I seemed to encounter every low beam on the premises. Hope gave me another head sock to protect my head which by now had a scar or two. It was disappointing to find a live bed bug inside one of the pillow cases. I found another on the wall beside that bed. The three of us discussed the issue at length. Did the girl who slept there bring the bug with her or was it there all the time? Should we close the barn again and have another fumigation? Bed bugs are harmless but they are irritating because they leave tell-tale bites and their presence suggests lax cleaning and hygiene. The opposite was the case with Gaucelmo. The guidelines were very strict.

We decided to isolate that bed, place the mattress outside in the sun and hope that the strong light would take care of any remaining bed bugs should they be there. Fighting war against the bugs is like dealing with an invisible enemy. The barn was an old building with a rough interior surface where the bugs could hide away from the light. There was only one small window up high. To search for the creatures, you had to use a torch. Many pilgrims found the barn 'charming' and 'authentic' as it looked as if it had been standing for centuries. Personally, I preferred the bright white open space of the upstairs dormitory.

We visited the monastery, our next-door neighbours. Fr. Xavier invited us to inspect the monastery and to stay for lunch. I was looking forward to our visit to see for myself what mysteries lay behind the walls. We walked around tight passageways, up and down stairs, passing from one room to another. I was surprised at how much had been fitted into a small space. We finished in a courtyard where the lunch was laid out, lovingly prepared by the monastery's hospitalera.

Clair was a charming big German girl who came year after year in her holidays to volunteer at the monastery. She came to our afternoon teas, too. All the monks were present along with their pilgrims. The monastery accepted pilgrims but they had to stay at least two nights. The arrangement was ideal for those who wanted time out for reflection and meditation. They participated in the routines of the monastery. We used to hear their bells ringing through the day summoning people to this and that service. Before we left we invited the monks back to Gaucelmo for lunch the following Monday. We walked the short distance back to work. A large group was waiting and thirty-nine stayed that night.

Friday was our first overcast day. There weren't so many pilgrims on the road, perhaps, because of the rain. A toilet was not working upstairs so, while waiting for the plumber to arrive and fix it, we put the people in the barn first. As it was, fourteen stayed. We had afternoon tea inside in the salon. As well as rain, the weather turned cold so we lit the fire in the firebox for the first time. That was another learning experience as we worked out how to get the right temperature. In the guidelines book, there were dire warnings about the fire box getting too hot. The warmth allowed the pilgrims to dry their boots, clothes and any washing.

A massive storm erupted. The hailstones fell horizontally driven by fierce winds and managed to find every weakness in the building. We were running around discovering leaks, including one in the barn which flooded the lower section. In the meantime, the plumbers had done their job so we evacuated the pilgrims and transferred them upstairs to the dormitory. All but one! He was in a top bunk in the upper section. He had slept through all the excitement and when he eventually woke, embraced the idea of being on his own for the night and stayed where he was. I appreciated his decision. I remember the joy of privacy following night after night of dormitories.

Saturday morning was my turn to get up to prepare breakfast so my day started at 5.30 am. By now we had a well-practised routine and were able to finish our jobs early. We went for a walk together in the hills surrounding Rabanal. I was wondering how my fitness levels were going. I hadn't walked for ten days and soon I would be embarking on my Camino in Portugal. We had a full house of forty and the 'completo' sign was posted by late afternoon. Apart from our usual nationalities (Spanish, American, Italian) we welcomed our first Pole and Uruguayan. Four young Americans who had only graduated a month previously were walking the Camino to celebrate their success. They were remarkably courteous and respectful. Nothing like the ugly American!

Pilgrims display a variety of attitudes. Some you see at registration and that's all. They are self-sufficient and keep to themselves. Others you see all the time, fussing about, asking questions and wanting things done. Some you enjoy talking to, others are a pain. You have to remind yourself that, as a hospitalero, you reach out to all.

Sunday morning, we finished our chores in time to watch the Corpus Christi procession. The monks started at the church and, followed by the villagers, processed around the village and back. We had time for coffee at Anton's. While sitting outside in the sun, two Scottish pilgrims joined us with their broad accents. One concluded that you had to be 'daft' to do the Camino. We opened at 11.30 am to allow early arrivals to settle in and attend the midday Mass. Soon, every bed was taken plus two campers who pitched their tent in the garden.

A group of eight English speakers took up the lower section of the barn. They spent the afternoon in a corner of the garden drinking beer they'd bought at Susanna's. In contrast to the usual tranquillity, the garden was rowdy, full of chatter and laughter. The noisiest was Glen. He was Irish enjoying the '*craik*' and said he was a poet. He took a liking for me and whenever I was near, sang '*The First Noël.*' Finola and Hope were cranky because they were disturbing other pilgrims who wanted peace and tranquillity, but I must admit I was tolerant of our scallywags. They were boisterous and enjoying themselves and their company. I would have joined their shin dig in different circumstances. None of this group knew each other before the Camino. They had met on the way, Glen said, bonded and walked together. I saw them as a wonderful example of how the Camino breaks down the usual barriers. People reach out to each other, cast aside the usual suspicions and allow life to flow through them. Apart from their noise, they caused no other trouble. I saw no reason to tell them to shut up. They cleaned their area and disposed of the empties.

As we had been hospitaleros for a week and half way through our term of duty, Hope thought we should discuss how we had been working together and invite each other to raise any issues which might have been bugging us. I mentioned how I felt disadvantaged the first few days because I had missed out on some of the briefing. We decided that when it was our turn to hand over to the new hospitaleros next Sunday, we would give them that day to settle in and begin our briefing on Monday before we left them to it and departed Tuesday.

By now, the pain in my neck was gone, I had managed to avoid bashing my head but I was looking forward to leaving and getting on with my own Camino. At the same time, I wanted to pitch in as well as I could and get the most out of the unique experience of being a hospitalero. I wanted to be better today than I was yesterday and better tomorrow than today.

I had dinner with Hope that night. She was interested in Maris, asked a few questions and ventured to inquire how she took her own life. I was happy to tell people that Maris had died by suicide, that my whole life had been destabilised, that I was still searching for stability and that her death was a prime reason for my involvement in the Camino. I was not prepared to give any details. Her death was tragic, I appreciated people's concern (sympathy) but I did not wish to traumatise others with detail, nor myself having to live again the day that she died. Hope accepted my refusal and our conversation over dinner concentrated on our different versions of a healthy spirituality.

The major event of Monday was our return luncheon for the monks. We were anxious to offer a meal as good as they gave us. The girls spent lots of time discussing the menu. We did our usual chores quickly in order to prepare. Finola took charge. She had intended to prepare an aubergine casserole but Susanna had no aubergines, the oven wouldn't work and the macaroni was burnt. Instead she prepared a ratatouille with bread slices as an entrée. My task was to gather plenty of herbs from the garden. Six guests arrived, including their hospitalera Christina. My jobs were to say grace and to look after the drinks. The meal was delicious and our guests appreciative. We had no time to congratulate ourselves on our success as the pilgrims were clamouring at the gate (it wasn't really like that at all; they were waiting patiently) and we opened at 2 pm. A steady stream brought the numbers to thirty-one.

I had itchy feet the following morning as we saw our pilgrims off. I was keen to join them and was looking forward to my turn in a week or so. I was feeling on top of the world. I was comfortable in my role as hospitalero, my aches and pains, particularly in the neck, had subsided and any traces of jet lag had vanished. I had fully adjusted. We opened early at 12.30 pm but the intake was slow and we had only twenty pilgrims. While twiddling our thumbs waiting for customers, we discussed the way in which numbers fluctuated from day to day. Hope slipped around to Pilars, the other albergue. Business there was slow, too. Some days the village is overflowing, other days see a trickle. Today was one of the slow days. The forecast was for a cold snap, rain and storms. Perhaps that had some influence.

The forecast rain fell by dark and pissed down all night. It was heavy enough in the morning, the darkness of night lingered and dawn came late. Some fair weather pilgrims wanted to stay another day and we had to explain the policy of one night stands. Other pilgrims were philosophical; rain was part of the Camino. Some enjoyed walking in the rain. They fished out their wet weather gear — over pants, ponchos, pack covers, gloves, etc. and, looking like men from outer space, launched off into the misty gloom. I was a touch sympathetic as I farewelled the reluctant ones huddling into their gear, barely admitting to myself that I was glad I would have a dry day.

Our workload was light as we didn't have the barn to clean, but we were busy preparing for the arrival of damp pilgrims. I chopped wood in the shelter of the wood shed and brought a good supply into the salon. Each time I made the trek from shed to house, I passed our climbing roses. They were wonderful when we arrived ten days ago, proudly clinging to the walls and flaunting their huge red, yellow and orange blooms. Now, storms and heaving rain had inflicted their damage. Most plants had lost their grip on the walls and had fallen sad and bedraggled, their once lively blooms scattered petals on the path. We organised a stack of newspapers to stuff into wet boots. We opened the gates by 12.30 to avoid people waiting in the rain. A steady flow bought the number to thirty-nine, almost a full house. Strange! I thought that such an inclement day would see fewer starters on the road.

We had afternoon tea in the salon where pilgrims sought comfort from the fire. Among our guests from the monastery were Bro. Marinus' parents who had come out from Germany to spend a few days with him. The room was a buzz. No room for calm and tranquillity today. Every clothes rack in the house was covered with damp clothes drying in the warmth. Every boot in the shoe rack was stuffed with newspaper. Every light in the building was on, most power points were in use, fuses kept tripping which required a constant dash to the box out by the gate to turn the power back on.

My date was with Hope that evening. She told me about the thirteen times she had trekked in Nepal. I was interested in her experiences and motivation. I had given her a copy of *The Day was Made for Walking* the week before. By now she had finished reading and was keen to discuss my motivations and spirituality. She returned the book to me and I placed it in the library in the salon. Perhaps my story might inspire the odd discouraged pilgrim who is seeking to restore him or herself in the comfort of the salon.

Spain had turned cold by Friday and Rabanal was no exception. These last few days galloped headlong and merged into the weekend. We farewelled Christina, the hospitalera from the monastery. She came around to say goodbye. The day remained cold, so once again we lit the fire and held afternoon tea in the salon. Among the guests was Frank, an Australian, who had stayed at Gaucelmo six times and walked the Camino eight times including the Camino Portugués. He recommended refugios where I had to stay. Reiner told us that he had been walking for eight years. The Camino was his home and he, too, had stayed at Gaucelmo several times. Dominik, a young Pole, a bean pole, well over two metres in height, had covered 50 kilometres that day. He said he could walk long distances because he had long legs. The place was bedlam. The kitchen was frenetic; everyone wanted to cook. We tripped the fuse many times. Someone was sick in the shower and blocked the outlet. Result? The dormitory was flooded and we resorted to panic stations to prevent too much chaos. The fire got too hot and the gauge needle was off the scale. A Spanish lady arrived with suspected bed bugs. We went through the cleansing procedures of spraying all her belongings and placing her clothes in the dryer at a set temperature. We gave her clothing kept for the purpose. She was grateful for our care. A French father and son arrived late. Jean the son spent his time caring for his father Jean; he had bad feet and may have been in the early stages of dementia. In the midst of all, we celebrated the 39th wedding anniversary of a Brazilian couple.

In no time it was Sunday morning and our replacements arrived — Donna, Barbara and Susan all from Canada. We allowed them to settle in. Donna had just finished walking the Camino Portugués and gave me a few tips. We spent Monday doing the handover. Barbara shadowed me as she did my chores. The best way to learn the job was to do it. The three of them attended to the induction of the day's pilgrim and in no time the house was full.

For the first time, Hope, Finola and I had dinner together. I gave each a small gift — a head sock with aboriginal designs which I had bought in Jindabyne. Were we happy to be leaving? We had mixed feelings but two weeks was long enough. Were we tired after working as a hospitalero? There are two types of tiredness, mental and physical. Our cleaning chores took about two or three hours but the days were long; it was no bludge.

Then there was our duty of care for our pilgrims, of listening to their stories and attending to their needs and questions. Judging from the comments in the journal, our efforts were greatly appreciated. There was little time for ourselves. The pilgrims' needs came first.

Would we volunteer again? We asked each other. While working, we often thought we'd rather be walking than working. Being a hospitalero is not unlike walking the Camino. You forget the bad days, the 40 degree heat, the storms and rain, the discouragement, the physical pain, the fatigue, and remember the good times such as meeting wonderful people and receiving their kindness, the friends you make. Would I volunteer again? Possibly, but not necessarily at Gaucelmo. I would be comfortable working in a gîte in France where I was familiar enough with the language. Finola thought she would like to work at another refugio. This was Hope's second go and that was enough.

I attended Compline that night and received the pilgrim blessing from Bro. Marinus. I was preparing myself for the next phase. Before leaving the church, I lit a candle and thought of my Maris and of our forty-two years of marriage. In that darkened church, I missed her and felt the emptiness of her loss. My candle truly was a light dispelling the darkness.

Tuesday morning, I awoke with thanks. I was free, a strange sensation after our two weeks of responsibility. I attended the 9.30 am Mass for the first time for I had been busy every other day with my cleaning chores. I lit another candle for my Maris. I shed a tear I'm afraid. The day was Tuesday which happened to be the day when Fr. Xavier celebrated the Mass in English as all the locals were at the market in Astorga. He made a special point of blessing and thanking the departing hospitaleros. Outside, there were hugs and farewells, and then the three of us, Hope, Finola and I, walked 9 kilometres to the Cruz de

Ferro. It's an iron cross on top of a cairn begun in pre-Roman times, making it the most ancient monument on the Camino. Gaucelmo christianised it by placing the cross. The tradition is to place on the cairn a rock carried from home, which is what I did, all the way from my garden in Jindabyne. We said good bye. Finola continued walking to Ponferrada while Hope and I ordered a taxi to take us back to Astorga. I arranged to meet her for dinner and we said good bye. Another Camino parting! How often I had said good bye to someone whom I had known for such a short time but felt I knew so well. I was back on my own. I had a mild attack of loneliness as I walked back to the hotel. That night I had a vivid dream in which Maris had returned. She was busy helping me to prepare for a Social Justice Group meeting at my former church. I felt bitter disappointment when I woke realising it was just a dream

The three hospitaleros Finola, Noel and Hope

16

High school Latin teacher Raimund Gregorius (Jeremy Irons) finds his life transformed when he saves a young Portuguese woman from jumping to her death. After the woman disappears, she leaves behind her coat, and with it, an enigmatic book containing a train ticket. Gregorius spontaneously decides to take an adventurous journey to Lisbon, where he will uncover a mystery, discover love, and rediscover life itself.

This blurb appears on the back of the DVD for the film *Night Train to Lisbon*. On Saturday 20th June, I took the night train to Lisbon after spending three days in Madrid. I can't say I found mystery, discovered love or rediscovered life. Indeed, the train was one of the oldest in the Spanish network. No wonder the fare was so cheap!

The train stopped regularly through Spain at stations big and small. There was plenty of life in these towns and villages that warm Saturday night. At one of them, I caught a glimpse of police rounding up a group of young men. About 3 am the Portuguese police boarded and checked passports. Why? I thought passage between European Union countries was unrestricted. I was weary and disoriented when I arrived Sunday morning at Oriente station, Lisbon.

I recognised Mat's tall lean figure. I met Mat and Laura Edmunds two years ago, in the south of France walking the Camino. We walked together for three weeks. I found the going tough and was faltering, but their good company and support kept me going. Their encouragement was a gift that helped me over a threshold I might otherwise not have crossed.

We missed each other on my last day of walking, but they went out of their way to find me and say goodbye. I was humbled that they thought so highly of me.

We kept in touch. Mat continued on to Santiago but Laura took the bus to her parents' home in a village not far from Santiago in Galicia, where they stayed for the next twelve months. Laura was pregnant. That explained many things — Mat's attentiveness, her concern about taking medication after the wasp sting, the fact that she fatigued readily. When Maggie Rose was born, I sent her a soft toy kangaroo. The postage cost more than the toy. It was a great joy to see the photo of baby Maggie Rose clutching her kanga.

We exchanged emails. I mentioned my intentions to walk the Camino from Lisbon and to learn Portuguese at a language school. In the meantime, Mat got a job teaching English in Lisbon. He insisted that I should stay with them. I was looking forward to meeting again.

This lovely couple were the most generous of hosts. From the moment I passed through their doorway with Laura waiting and meeting Maggie Rose I became Uncle Noel, part of their little family. We had a wonderful reunion and spent hours talking, catching up on the details. After both Maggie and I had a siesta, we four went out. I was introduced to Lisbon on a summer's Sunday afternoon. Lisbon is a charming city, smaller than Paris or Madrid, shabbily genteel, a mixture of the old and new. The footpaths are cobblestone and cars stop for pedestrians at crossings. They found a park, a favourite of theirs, with an open-air theatre and an accordionist. We followed many paths winding their way through the trees and water ways and came across a restaurant where we had the first of many drinks together.

Next morning Mat, Laura and Maggie walked me to the

language school in Rua Actor Taborda just to ensure I didn't get lost. The entrance to the building was grandiose with a highly ornate ceiling with walls and marble columns leading up to the stainless-steel door of the lift. Up three flights were the CIAL Centro de Linguas in a plain utilitarian office suite of class rooms with not a single painting, poster or etching on any of the walls.

I was not unduly worried. I had attended enough language classes in France and Spain to know that I would be the oldest student by far and that would make no difference to my being accepted by the other students. Today, we were beginners, all learning a brand-new language. My teacher was Eugenia. She asked why we were learning Portuguese. She was excited by the fact that I was planning to walk from Lisbon to Santiago at the age of eighty-two, and learning a new language at the same time. She thought I was an inspiration. I enjoyed my first morning. I was pleased I had some knowledge of Spanish. The rules of grammar were similar, many words are the same but there are marked differences. I wanted to learn the survival stuff. My guide book hinted that you needed some Portuguese if you were walking through Portugal on your own. I hoped to learn the essentials such as asking for a bed, a flat white or a beer.

Back home for lunch and after Maggie' sleep, we walked into the city centre with its innumerable tourist shops and attractions and across the plaza to the river Tagus. This became a regular pattern. They worked their way around Maggie Rose's sleep times and Mat's work hours but went out of their way to show me Lisbon — all the usual tourist spots and the out-of-the-way places as well. In the evenings, Laura served a delicious meal and Mat produced wines made by his father-in-law. Every time they visited Laura's parents in Galicia, they returned laden with her father's wines and sausage.

I was so fortunate to be with Mat and Laura. What a difference it made to my visit to Lisbon! I would have stayed with a host family, organised by the school, as I did in Amboise, Pamplona and Montpellier. All my hosts had been open and welcoming — Danièle and Michèle at Amboise, Jacinto and Loli at Pamplona, Michèle at Montpellier. No doubt I would have felt just as welcome here in Lisbon. Nevertheless, to be accepted into a family was a gift, like living at home.

On Friday afternoon, Mat and Laura received another guest. Ed was the brother of Mat's brother-in-law (his sister's husband). Mat had talked about Ed. He was a musician and quite a character. As soon as I saw Ed, I sensed he was one of the brotherhood. He looked as if he had been through the mill. He was friendly and outgoing, had deep rings under his eyes and was keen to chat. In no time, we moved into deep water. He suffered from depression, had been an alcoholic and his father had died from suicide. His mother hadn't handled her husband's death well. He raved on about me, wished that his mother could meet me, someone who had lost a spouse similarly but was handling the situation very differently.

After Maggie woke, we went for a stroll up one of the hills (Lisbon is built on seven hills) to the Goethe Institut, one of Mat and Laura's favourites as it contained a beautiful garden with many ancient trees. That evening, Mat, Ed and I went out about 10 pm. We walked through the adjacent red-light district, the girls patiently waiting for business on the footpath, which Mat said was gradually being gentrified. We had a few drinks listening to a Brazilian band playing in the plaza just down the road.

Saturday the five of us (Mat, Laura, Maggie Rose, Ed and me) walked into the city, visited the church of Sao Vincente, one of the few buildings which survived the massive earthquake of 1755 and continued on to the river. We caught the ferry to Casilhas where we met Laura's friends (Helena — Spanish and João — Portuguese plus young Alec) and lingered over a long lunch under awnings that protected us from the 35-degree heat. The shade was most welcome as the fierce sunlight obliterated everything it fell on.

On the way back as we were walking along the river a bloke appeared out of nowhere, approached Ed and offered him hashish. After some quiet haggling Ed paid £50 for a plug. Ed later said that he always seem to attract dealers. I took a photo of the two in negotiation from behind. Mat commented it was just as well none of the dealer's mates saw me. They would have grabbed my camera and either threw it in the river or smashed it on the cobblestones, and while at it, cracked me on the head for good measure. What a lucky escape!

That evening after dinner we sat in the small courtyard to escape the heat and Ed offered his hashish to Mat and me. I felt sorry for Ed. Whereas Mat and I were enjoying Mat's father-in-law's red wine (no four-penny dark) with an occasional Belgian beer thrown in, Ed, a recovering alcoholic, was drinking soft. I accepted. I'd give it a crack. In my 83rd. year I smoked my first joint. What would my girls have thought of their ancient dad smoking whacky baccy? Jacinta would have laughed, Angela would have said, 'Go for it, Dad,' as she always did. The sweet-smelling smoke drifted up the walls of the building and alerted the neighbours all of whom had their windows wide open to take in the cooler air. The dope was pleasant, it took its time to have an impact but in bed that night I felt stoned.

The taste of smoke lingered in my mouth in the morning. Mat joked about leading young Noel astray and getting him zonked. Over a delicious breakfast of smoothies and pancakes cooked by Mat, he commented that whenever he smoked pot he always felt like taking up smoking again. I could appreciate his comment for I, too, had an urge to smoke a cigarette. I told Mat I had given up smoking fifty years previously at the age of thirty-three. At the same time, I gave up a language. When it was time for a smoko, I used to roll my own. We students used the makings and only smoked tailors if we were going out. If we were out of smokes, we would share our cancer sticks and coffin nails. I had started a new job where my colleagues smoked fifty Camels a day. I decided I had joined the rat race and, if I didn't give up the fags immediately, I'd be smoking fifty Camels, too. Lung cancer got them all.

Monday saw a new teacher and four new students. Virgilio was a charming gracious gentleman of the old school, a personification of a Lisbon that once was. He was respectful of our efforts and did his best to ensure that only Portuguese was spoken. Whereas Eugenia occasionally slipped into English to explain a point, Virgilio battled with our limited understanding. The four students changed the feel of the class. They were friendly and I joined them each morning at the break in the café on the street below. They were German and Norwegian and spoke to each other in English. They were interested in me, the elderly Australian who was planning to walk from Lisbon to Santiago the following week.

Laura stayed home as such a long hot day would be too much for Maggie. Mat and Ed picked me up after school and we took the train to Sintra. Sintra is a picturesque town set among the pine covered hills of the Serra de Sintra, to the west of Lisbon. The slightly cooler climate attracted the elite and nobility of Portugal who built exquisite palaces, extravagant buildings and decorative gardens. One is the Quinta de Regaleira. The uphill walk on such a hot day was worth the effort. It's a 19th century gothic extravaganza built by the once richest man in Portugal. Its main attraction is the stunning terraced gardens that contain an elaborate tunnel system. We enjoyed climbing down a shaft and lingering in the cool tunnels, and finding throughout the grounds some of its secretive religious symbols, concealed gardens and other mysterious objects. We arrived back at Lisbon at 7.30 pm where the temperature was 35 degrees. We needed a few beers to cool off. I felt sorry for Ed the recovering alcoholic. He contented himself with a couple of joints, which I declined. I had had my one joint which was enough. I thought of my son Stephen who told me he had tried marijuana once but his brain was addled enough without it.

The hot weather filled Lisbon with an amiable lethargy. I was lethargic on Tuesday, a consequence of the previous day's effort and heat. The class was lethargic, too, and Virgilio had his work cut out inspiring us. After class, I took the metro to St. Apolino just by the cathedral, the starting point for the Camino Portugués. I would commence walking Saturday but decided to cover the first few kilometres during the week. Despite the heat and fatigue I walked nine kilometres through industrial suburbs. The route around the cathedral displayed the old world rustic charm of Lisbon but deteriorated into nondescript industrial suburbia until I arrived at the surrounds of Oriente, which are both spectacular and modern. Opposite the futuristic railway station is the Vasco da Gama shopping centre both above and below ground, part of Parque das Nações. I was tempted to explore the Parque which displays Lisbon at its modern best, but I was tired and was content to walk to the river Tagus, admire a tree lined promenade along the river and the Vasco da Gama bridge to the north, then return to the Oriente station and take the metro home to my Lisbon family.

The week and my time with Mat and Laura were racing to an end. I was concerned that I was free loading. I refused to take for granted their generosity so, after class I went shopping for some gifts. Shopping is not a favourite pastime. The weather had turned and my wandering around the shops was beset by frequent and sudden showers which had the tourists and shoppers sheltering under dripping awnings. A group of students playing and singing some beautiful traditional songs had to quickly change their tune. That evening Mat was working late. I spent the time chatting with Ed. Although my anxiety was building up about Saturday, when I listened to Ed talking about his fears, my worry was minimal. I could always reassure myself that I had walked a Camino route three times previously and on each occasion I had the jitters but I always came through. For Ed things were different. I imagine that in earlier times he blunted his fears with alcohol. Now that he had resolved to drink no more, he had to face his demons with the occasional soothing joint. I admired him for his courage and felt sorry for his captivity. He was a prisoner of his terrors. He told me about his massive apprehensions travelling to Lisbon — worries about whether he would be on time, whether he was on the right plane, how to get from the airport, worries about the metro. He admired me for my ability to travel from the other side of the world. He wondered at my ability to travel on my own around France and Spain. That would be a nightmare for him.

Thursday I took Ed on a school excursion. There seemed to be no rules about non-students going on school excursions (I didn't ask in case). Along with the other students, we took a public bus that bounced its way along the cobblestones to the Monasterio de los Geronimos, one of the most popular tourist attractions in Lisbon. Along with hundreds of tourists, we made our way through the church with its single nave and six perfectly carved columns that seem endless. The church houses the tomb of Vasco da Gama for whose return from India the Monastery was built. The cloister of the monastery is breathtaking for its size and perfection.

After the excursion, we left my fellow students to take the train home. Ed's fears were manifest. He was worried that we wouldn't find the railway station, which we did. He was worried that we were not on the right platform, where we were. He was apprehensive that a train wouldn't arrive, which it did. He was concerned that we would take the wrong train, which we didn't. He was anxious that we would not dismount at the right metro station, which we did. That evening I said good bye to Ed. He would be leaving the next day and I probably wouldn't see him in the morning. I was sorry to see him go. He was good company, a friendly, talkative fellow who could have been a misery guts but for the jokes at his own expense about his shortcomings. That night I hoped and prayed that he would return safely and intact to his home in England.

Friday was my last day at school. Virgilio, always a gentleman of the old school, handed me and the other departing students our certificates. I had coffee for the last time with my fellow classmates. By now, the guy running the restaurant knew my preference and would produce my flat white (*mai de leite*, literally half milk) without my asking. I spent the afternoon sorting my belongings and lightening my backpack. It took two trips to the post office. The postage was outrageous, costing more than the contents of my two boxes. The lady justified the cost with: '*Australia's a long way.*' I didn't have enough cash, she wouldn't accept my National Bank traveller's card. The post office only accepted Portuguese cards. I had to leave the post office just on closing time and find an ATM which fortunately was opposite. I was flustered. I know that when I'm flustered I'm vulnerable. The traffic was heavy both ways, I managed to negotiate my way across and back without becoming a statistic. A passer-by warned me not to hold the cash and card in my hand. I understood her. I had learned more Portuguese than I thought. The post office had closed its door but the attendant allowed me in as he was letting the last of the customers out.

I spent my last evening with Mat, Laura and Maggie Rose. It was a delight to witness Mat chatting and playing with his daughter. Love's oozing out of every pore. Laura spoke to Maggie in both Spanish and English. The sounds she was making were a mixture of languages. Fortunate girl, I thought, growing up in a multilingual environment. When I arrived two weeks previously Maggie was taking a step or two. A fortnight later, she was running across the room.

I gave them my gifts — a set of Portuguese pottery to Laura, a bottle of scotch to Mat, and a dainty pink dress with matching hat to Maggie. They were astounded, cross and wanted to refuse. I sensed they were not just being coy; they were offended. I thought: 'God, I've blown it.' I replied I could not merely say thanks and go. I wanted to show my thanks sincerely for their generosity and acceptance of me as a member of their family. I pleaded with them to accept my gifts. Maggie eagerly grabbed Uncle Noel's gifts. She took a liking to her hat, christened it by plonking it on her head and ran around the room. Her enthusiasm and laughter lightened the mood. Mat said it would take a long time to forgive my clanger, but we were reconciled sharing a sample glass each of the whisky. I had chosen well, I was pleased to say. Over a final glass of his father-in-law's red wine, Mat mentioned that Ed went fearfully that morning.

I will forget the monuments, palaces and other splendid sights of Lisbon but I will never forget the welcome of this young family who took me in, almost a stranger, and allowed me to hang out with them. What a difference their home made! My time in Lisbon is a highlight of my Camino, indeed, of the later years of my life.

Mat, Laura with Maggie Rose

Act Four

Portugal and Spain

Camino Portugués
La Via Lusitana

Lisbon — Fatima — Porto — Santiago — Finisterre

Camino Portugués

17

Blessed are you, pilgrim, if you discover that
the Camino opens yours eyes to what is not seen.
The Beatitudes of the Pilgrim

I left by 8 am on Saturday, not before touching farewells, Maggie shyly waving good-bye. Mat and Laura insisted I keep in touch, particularly if I got into trouble. They would come and get me, and the nearer I got to Spain, the closer were members of Laura's family who would willingly be enlisted to help me. I must admit I felt vulnerable, an eighty-two-year-old, on the other side of the world from his home and ready to launch out alone with no other support than my own resilience. Their concern was comforting as I left the safety zone of their home and walked the hundred metres to the metro. Once more I was stepping out on my own. Like life, the Camino begins at the end of your comfort zone. Up to now I had been with other people in Lisbon and Rabanal, but now, on the 39th day of my trip to Europe, I was on my own.

Feeling in good nick, I took the metro to Estação do Oriente. This futuristic railway station was my entry and departure point for Lisbon. Across the way were the shopping centre (Centro Vasco da Gama) and the Parque das Nações. The Parque das Nações is the follow-up to the rehabilitation done in the north of Lisbon for Expo'98 and demonstrates the vision that was employed in preparing for the Expo. There are many buildings for the arts and entertainment, condo towers, office buildings, hotels and restaurants. I walked through to the River Tejo (Tagus) to the same spot as earlier in the week and proceeded to walk north along a pedestrian-way edged with gardens and sculptures. By far the most beautiful section of the day (for some days in fact), it generated a feeling of calm and order in the early morning. It would soon be busy with the arrival of hordes of tourists. There were magnificent buildings I could have visited, the Pavilhão Atlânico and the Oceanário de Lisboa, for example, but, having commenced my Camino I did not wish to linger and was content to walk under the shadow of the cable cars Teleférico to the Torre Vasco da Gama (tower), a gift from Brazil, to the Ponte Vasco da Gama, which stretches 17 kilometres beyond the horizon across the river Tagus to the distant shore, the longest bridge in Europe.

I had seen the old city, delightful for its rustic, old world charm and now I was departing through its modern hub. The wealth of Portugal was built on its colonial past and its sea ports were gateways for the lucrative slave trade. Portugal appears to be recovering more rapidly from the global financial crisis than its neighbour Spain. Economic growth is higher and unemployment is lower. There appears to be a greater resilience among the people and a preparedness to get on with things.

After passing under the impressive Ponte Vasco da Gama the route turns away from the River Tagus and follows a small tributary Foz del Rio Trancão. The signs marked the Caminho de Fátima, blue arrows to Fátima, yellow to Santiago underneath. The way passed through open land under a ring road and railway line at Sacavém and followed the Trancăo to a bridge (Ponte Sacavém) where the guidebook instructed to turn right over the bridge, immediately turn left and follow a small path along the far side of the river.

I encountered the first of many confusions where the ground did not match the guide book. Just over the bridge on the left were extensive road excavations which blocked the path. The blue and yellow arrows crossed the bridge and led to a ditch about three metres deep and about thirty metres wide. I could see an overgrown path beyond, which looked as if no one had trodden on it for some time. No one had bothered to mark a detour for the confused pilgrim.

The route was supposed to follow a wide farm track up a green valley *'where time seemed to have stopped, except for the aircraft landing at Lisbon airport.'* I couldn't see how to get to this idyllic spot. The map in the guide book indicated the route passed by the Póvoa railway station. I returned to Sacavém station and took the train to Póvoa where I hoped I would pick up the yellow and blue arrows.

At Póvoa de Santa Iria, the arrows were easy to find and I made my asphalted way through a flat ugly dull industrial wasteland. No farm tracks in green valleys here! The day was hot. I stopped in the shade of a tree in a factory car park, sat on the gutter edge and ate the lunch which Laura had lovingly prepared for me, her father's sausage being a significant component.

I continued on to Alverca do Ribatejo. The guide book informed me I'd completed Stage One of the Caminho Português, a distance of 31.1 kilometres. Earlier in the week, I had walked from the cathedral to Oriente — that was nine kilometres. Taking the train from Sacavém to Póvoa ensured another reduction of twelve kilometres. I had walked ten kilometres. And what dull drab walking it was! There was no accommodation at Alverca, but I could take pot luck at the off-route nearby industrial town of Verdelha de Baixo. Workers took up the accommodation but, being the weekend, there may be a few vacant beds if people were willing to open their establishments. The guidebook advice to work my way up the main street wasn't enticing. It was still early afternoon. I decided to continue on to Villafranca de Xira, but feeling hot and frazzled on my first day, the temptation to take the train was irresistible. Santiago (St James), forgive me! The guidebook indicated good pilgrim accommodation, but misgivings stirred when I read a poster at the station advertising a week long grand festival, Festa do Colete Encarnado- "red waistcoat" involving bull runs, horse riding, dressage, and lots of kids' attractions, commencing this weekend. I said goodbye to cheap beds. I would get an expensive hotel if I was lucky.

Sure enough, I walked out of the station at Villafranca to a town busy with preparations. The streets had been barricaded and covered in sawdust. Groups of horsemen and horsewomen pranced along the streets dressed in black coats over red waistcoats, cafes and bars were crowded with drinkers singing and listening to performers, the air was filled with music and expectation. The statue of a bull fighter dominated the small plaza. I felt daunted at the prospect of finding the hostel (*Pensão Ribatejana*) but a taxi driver pointed it out to me, next to the railway station. The owner spoke English. He apologised. He had just given away the last bed. All other accommodation in the town had been booked weeks ago. The nearest accommodation was at Azambuja, another twenty kilometres. I wasn't up to walking a further twenty kilometres. He suggested I take the train, a twenty-minute journey. My anxiety about a bed for the night had intensified. I accepted his advice. I was not interested in the history of this town, that it had links with the English crusaders who came this way en route to the Holy Land, that it's well known for the breeding of fighting bulls and for the 'Red Waistcoat' fiesta of which I had just had an inconvenient glimpse. I took the next train. All the passengers, mainly families, disembarked, all intent on joining the fiesta, leaving me with an almost empty train to Azambuja. On a roundabout at the entrance to the town I spotted the *Hotel Ouro*, a modern looking building behind a petrol station. That'll do me, I thought. I did not feel like hunting out the pilgrim hostel. I was tempted to take the taxi waiting outside the station but the driver decided it was knock-off time, locked his vehicle and disappeared into a house down the way. I walked back through an empty town, silent except for the traffic. Nothing was happening that Saturday arvo in Azambuja. Good! I thought. I'll have no competition for a bed. I reached the roundabout and walked through the service station. The hotel was semi-circular, gaudily painted maroon and yellow with a line of palm trees along the front, giving it the incongruous appearance of an oasis on the edge of an industrial desert. I entered the foyer under a maroon canopy. The foyer was equally gaudy with heavy furnishings and the suggestion of a Greek influence.

As I approached the desk I braced myself for the challenge of using my scant knowledge of Portuguese to ask for a room. Yes, they had a room, said the sullen teen age girl on reception. Did they have a special price for pilgrims? Yes, they did. A minor success! I was understood. She gave me a key. I walked up the stairs and along a corridor with maroon carpet and walls where the influence changed into Egyptian. The phrase '*misplaced bad taste*' from the Gilbert and Sullivan opera popped into my mind.

My first night on the road was not exactly in pilgrim accommodation. The room was very comfortable. An uninspiring view from my balcony looked out over the empty car park to the service station and roundabout beyond. The hotel was almost deserted. That night I was the only diner in the fancy silver service restaurant where the elderly waiter by the name of Octavio fussed over me. I didn't bother to explore the town stretching up the hill but remained in the hotel and reflected on my messy day. I had come 60 kilometres from Lisbon, mostly by train. I had the guilts about having walked only ten kilometres, so I decided to book into the hotel for another night and in the morning return by train to Villafranca de Xira and walk back to Azambuja.

The train was full of families babbling with excitement on their way to the fiesta. I found the arrows by an attractive park between the railway station and the river and followed the route under freeways and through roundabouts into broad farmland covered with tomato plants. I helped myself, I confess, to two of the rich red fruit. The red and white striped chimneys of a large power station loomed on the horizon. I left them behind and continued on a flat terrain through industrial wastelands where factory buildings were choked with weeds and decaying through neglect — the ghosts of former business ventures. Streets of industrial estates had been paved for future development but hope had succumbed to reality and they were now covered in weeds and rubbish. A brief respite was the charming village of Vila Nova da Rainha which could have been the set for a period film, but all too soon the route returned to the wastelands.

The dreariest part of the day was a dangerous slog of six kilometres along a very busy road, the N3, lined with operating factories. Large trucks thundered by and their draught threatened to blow me into the road side ditches full of rubbish. The number of discarded plastic bottles staggered me. Thousands filled the ditches. Questions plagued me. How did they get there? Why such criminal community neglect? Were the Portuguese indifferent to their environment? Did such degraded surroundings not bother them? Did they ever have 'Clean up Portugal' days?

It was as if I was walking through a vision of hell, a heavy industrial version. All that was needed was for two of the trucks to collide, burst into flames and set the countryside blazing, to have a modern version of Dante's Inferno. I was thankful that most of the factories were closed. If I was coping with Sunday traffic, I shuddered to imagine what Monday's was like? My body was holding up although my right hip was sore. However, my resilience was in jeopardy with the constant dim and threat of annihilation from swaying trucks. What was worse, I didn't have to walk these twenty kilometres. It was only to make me feel better about myself. On the contrary, the day had diminished me. I felt ground into the dirt. This Caminho Portugués was uninspiring. I hoped there would be more to see than bitumen, dangerous roads and industrial waste. This ugly wasteland failed to open my eyes to any mystic insights. Where was the solitude of forests of earlier Caminos? I felt trapped. Where were the beautiful fragrant flowers of freedom?

At last the *Ouro Hotel* sign appeared on the right and I was more than content to return to my room for a siesta. Body and morale restored, I sought the bar for a few beers and a meal. No one was about. I was the only diner and I noticed the adjoining restaurant was empty. I had to assume that the *Ouro Hotel* did all its business during the week.

I went to bed pondering the following day. According to my guide book, the next stop was Santarém, the route traversed the flood plain and followed '*delightful farm tracks through this agricultural area with its crop fields, fruit, tomatoes and vineyards.*' It would be a lovely change from hideous traffic-filled roads. However, there were neither facilities nor shade. One needed to carry food and water.

I was vulnerable, not yet track hardened. I listened to the

competing voices arguing in my head, one wanting to take the train directly to Santarém, the other reckoning I should walk. I succumbed. The leisurely start enabled me to explore the town. I walked up the hill from the hotel, found the pilgrim accommodation adjacent to the church and the tourist museum with portraits of the famous bull fighters of the town. Azambuja has its own running of the bulls but it's held the last week of May. I walked about two kilometres of the route to where the Camino joined the river and could see the 'delightful farm tracks' to the north. I was tempted to continue as the body movement had lifted my morale but retraced my steps back to the railway station.

At Santarém station a tough climb to the town centre 100 metres above the flood plain waited for me. Santarém is a charming historic city, straddling a fortified hilltop well out of reach of the floodwaters of the Rio Tejo(Tagus). I admired extensive views of the valley and river below, especially from a viewpoint called gates of the Sun (Portos do Sol) with extensive gardens on what was once the Moorish citadel. The town was once a centre for Julius Caesar and the Romans while, in later years, it was taken by the Arabs in 715 and became a stronghold for Islam until it was recaptured by the first king of Portugal Dom Afonso Henriques in 1149. I found the Santarém Hostel behind the tourist office. Mario ran this new pilgrim friendly hostel. He showed me around, particularly the spacious outdoor courtyard where I was able to do some washing. After a brief siesta, I explored the town and some of its impressive historic buildings and monuments, all witness to the important past of this town. For the first time, I met other pilgrims. Some were going to Santiago, and others were detouring to Fatima.

In the morning, I had to check I was on the correct path.

Two routes continue the Camino to Santiago; one goes directly to Coimbra, the other detours to Fatima. I chose to follow the blue arrows to the latter. They were easy to follow. The yellow arrows were more difficult to find, but they did not worry me as I was on the route that suited me.

I had two guide books, one in English, and the other in French. The English version described the direct route, the French described the detour. I put the English away for the moment. Interestingly, the French version was more detailed and seemed to contain more accurate descriptions of what lay ahead.

The first two hours were boring and hazardous. I walked through built-up suburbs with the constant roar of traffic passing a metre or so away. The brief silences between vehicles were broken by dogs, just behind a fence or hedge. Shrill yappers, deep brayers, all were loud, sharp and piercing. Every hound and yap dog in Portugal was challenging me. No friendly welcome here! Which was worse? The trucks or the dogs? The more I walked the more my nerves frazzled. Where were the silence and the solitude which I had found so precious in previous Camino routes? What hope did the sounds of silence have of being heard? Where was the quieter plane that would lead me to the centre of my soul? Where was the spiritual adventure? Where was the ecstasy of creation? My body was adjusting to long distance walking, but the grinding suburban crawl was tiring, and the shock of constant sudden noise of dogs and trucks had me spinning.

What was I doing here? I could have stayed at home back on the other side of the planet and found plenty of hazardous roads to walk on and millions of Aussie dogs to bark at me.

At last, I reached the countryside and passed through vineyards, olive orchards, fields of sunflowers, courgettes and other vegetables and eventually found myself in forest. I was hopeful that even though Lisbon was 100 kilometres to the south I had finally quit its suburbs. With those canines and trucks left behind I felt relieved, refreshed and relaxed as I climbed the gentle slope. I was ready to listen to the rhythm of my steps, to the truths within me, to the voice of timeless wisdom in our lives and for spiritual adventure.

I met one other pilgrim. I heard her sticks tapping and eventually she drew level. We greeted each other warmly. She was German but spoke good English. I said I was on the way to Fatima. She said she did not have enough time for Fatima, she was going directly to Santiago. I told her she was on the way to Fatima. She was incredulous. She thought she had been following the correct signs — the blue and yellow arrows. The waymarks were confusing. Some included the blue and yellow arrows, other had the blue arrow only but they all had the word *Fatima* or *Caminho da Fátima*. She was disappointed. She had lost time. She decided to retrace her steps back to Santarém to find the right path. I wished her *'Bom Caminho'*, but half an hour later she was back. She had changed her mind and decided to keep going. I wished her *'Bom Caminho'* a second time. I didn't see her again. I was concerned for her as without a guide book the route was tricky. She was the only pilgrim I met that day.

As I descended a hill I saw a roadside stall on the opposite slope. I had seen such stalls before in France and Spain where a local resident spends his or her day stamping the passports of the passing pilgrims. Sometimes they provide water and local produce which they either give or sell to the pilgrims. This one was no different. Under a large tree and a bush shelter, an old chap was sitting on a chair beside a small table. Next to the table was a board with lots and photos and religious pictures and rosary beads. Behind was a stack of cardboard boxes. Above was a collection of flags, among which I recognised the Portuguese and Spanish national flags. He was friendly enough but he had nothing to say, this old chap, and when I asked him with signs to use my camera to take my photo he did not understand. While I was there, a young lady arrived by car with the old fellow's lunch. She smiled and went her way.

My destination was Arneiro das Milhariças, an easy enough walk at 21 kilometres. However, immediately before Arneiro das Milhariças was Casais da Milhariça which I confused with Arneiro das Milhariças. The instructions were to follow the road with the sign to the cemetery (*cemitério*), which would pass the *Casa O Primo Bazilio*, where I was planning to spend the night. I had already rung the Casa and in my broken Portuguese told them I was coming. I found a cemetery sign in Casais da Milhariça which led nowhere. I was hassled, cursing the authors of guide books for providing useless information until I realised I was yet to reach Arneiro das Milhariças which my French guidebook said was *tout droit* (straight ahead). There I found the road with the *cemitério* sign and everything fell into place. I begged forgiveness of guide book authors for my sin of hasty judgement. I found the *Casa O Primo Bazilio* where I introduced myself as the pilgrim (*peregrine*) who had telephoned. The very old host and his equally aged wife welcomed me with enthusiasm and showed me to a comfortable room which overlooked a courtyard with an enticing pool. How I wished I had brought my swimmers! The day was hot and sweaty. The pool was sparkling. I was tempted to jump in in my birthday suit but did not wish to offend my hosts who may have belonged to a generation that did not appreciate skinny dipping. Had my Portuguese been better I would have asked the old bloke if he and his wife objected to my swimming *pelado* (in the nude). There was no one else to offend as I was the only guest

My interest in exposing myself in public departed once I'd had exposed myself in private to the shower and was clad in fresh clothes. Refreshed, I explored the *casa*. Downstairs was a large room which served as lounge and dining room. The furnishings were shabbily genteel, dark and heavy and probably fashionable when my hosts were newly-wed. The most intriguing part of the surroundings was a series of photographs of King George VI and family. The princesses Elizabeth and Margaret were children, so the photos came from the thirties. What were they doing here, portraits of a British king's family in a Portuguese bed and breakfast? Did they have lots of elderly English guests for whom a former king and family would create a touch of nostalgia? My Portuguese was not good enough to question my hosts on their connections with British royalty.

I went exploring the town. Quaint! I thought. I was thinking English, reading French (in my guide book) and trying to speak Portuguese. I was a walking example of the fight against dementia. There wasn't much to explore. Arneiro das Milhariças was a clean town. There wasn't a discarded plastic bottle to be seen. I soon found the café, supermarket and church, all just up the hill from the *Casa O Primo Bazilio*. I enjoyed a beer at the café. The barman/owner was a friendly and exuberant fellow, and this encouraged me to inquire about an evening meal. I probably spoke in a mixture of Spanish and Portuguese but I was understood and was told to come back at seven. In the meantime, I visited the supermarket to buy something for lunch the following day. Supermarket was too grand a name for such a tiny shop. The lady was a friendly soul. She guessed I was a pilgrim. She had no English but could speak French. We had quite a conversation. She told me she had worked in France but preferred this little Portuguese town. She was keen to hear a little about where I lived in Australia. '*C'est loin!*' (It's a long way.) Back at the café, my meal was ready and I was the only diner. At last, I thought. This is rural Portugal where everyone knows everyone else. This was the only watering hole in town and half a dozen were sitting at the bar with their after-work drinks. How I wished I had more than two weeks' tuition in Portuguese behind me so that I could talk to these drinkers and find out something of their lives.

In the morning, my ancient hosts fussed over me as I ate my breakfast of toast and jam. I was away by 7.45, walked up the hill past the café and church, and then down again to the edge of Arneiro das Milhariças. The signs were very unclear and I paused to consider the alternatives that would find me a way out of town. A window opened on a second floor and, like a voice from heaven, a woman shouted at me and pointed in one direction. I shouted back '*Muito obrigado*' and followed her advice, wondering if she maintained a vigil every morning to help puzzled pilgrims deliberating over signs that pointed in two directions.

I was planning to walk 17 kilometres to Minde. The way was in the main quiet and rural. A highlight was Monsanto where I stopped for a spell by a fountain at the entrance to the village. What was remarkable was the blue tiling on the walls enclosing the fountain. They were painted with scenes of rural life. Since my arrival in Portugal I had noted the penchant the Portuguese had for this tiling (*azulejos*), squares of earthenware painted with a vivid blue. They paved the walls, floors and ceilings of buildings, railway stations in most places I had visited. I would continue to come across them all the way to Santiago. This ornament was originally imported by the Moors and spread throughout the Iberian Peninsula. It was King Manuel the First who started the craze for tiling. He visited Seville in 1503 and was so dazzled by the beauty of the Spanish Moorish ceramics that he adapted them for his country. The art has become an integral part of Portuguese culture.

The shaded surrounds made the place a tranquil place to rest and recuperate to the gentle sound of running water. I could have stayed on and found a bed for the night but the dreaded fierce ugly roar of passing trucks filled with rocks destroyed the calm. My tiring body was faced with a steep climb. Every challenging step was a struggle. I concentrated on trusting in God and in placing one foot in front of the other. I stopped at a cemetery just out of the small village of Covăo do Feto and sat on a tombstone to eat my lunch of sardines and bread. I needed that sustenance and rest among the dead for I was feeling half-dead myself. I thought of my Maris lying in a cemetery on the other side of the world. One of these days, I would join her. My son Stephen once described her grave as being a double bunker. Mum was in the bottom bunk and Dad would go in the top.

Immediately after the village I was confronted with a killer hill of the most lethal variety. Not only was the route steep, it was rocky and treacherous. Even my French guidebook, in a typical understatement, described this section as '*un peu difficile*' (a little difficult). One foot after the other, I chanted like a mantra as I zig-zagged up the slope. At least I was able to cling to the stone wall for support and rest. Two young walkers passed me. They looked at me as if I was an odd bod, no spring chicken who needed his head read for tackling such a climb. They leapt from rock to rock like mountains goats and vanished ahead of me in no time. One of the voices in my head protested furiously, but the other was calmer. '*Noel, you should not treat the hills as enemies. You should meet them as friends, because you'll see a lot of them and you should be on speaking terms.*'

It took me two hours to slog my way to the top but I was rewarded with a panoramic view like a postcard from God and an opportunity to rest at a picnic table before I descended down an equally rocky and precarious path. Avoiding a fall was uppermost in my mind as I watched where I placed my feet. A stumble would have me tumbling, the contents of my pack spewed down the hillside. I passed through a silent forest and was happy to walk along a quiet paved road into Minde. My guidebook told me that rooms were available at the bar *Estaminé*. At the outskirts of the town I asked an old chap for directions. He said nothing, didn't bat an eyelid, just led me, threading his way along alleys and laneway, to a plaza where the sign bar *Estaminé* was prominent on an orange panelled building. How I enjoyed a beer in that bar, run by a family of three generations all of whom were fussing about. My room above the bar was musty, the furniture was well worn, the door handle was broken, the door didn't close as if someone without key had given it a decent shove but the bed was comfortable. I ventured out to explore the town. I found the supermarket myself and one of the customers led me to the fruit shop.

I was the only guest so I dined with the family that night in the bar. They were pleasant and friendly enough but not a word of English among them. I was feeling sorry for myself, lonely and aching. I could almost hear Maris scolding me. *'Stop worrying about your aches and pains. Enjoy yourself and reach out.'* Reprimanded, I made a few clumsy attempts at conversation in my broken Portuguese but they fell flat.

After five days, I had met few other pilgrims. On my previous Caminos, I met many and enjoyed night after night in their company where we developed an instant camaraderie and became a family. The spirit dissolved all fatigue and we were wonderfully restored after the grind of the day. Nothing like that so far!

On the other hand, Mat and Laura continued to offer me the gift of their encouragement, this time by texts.

18

A faith which does not doubt is a dead faith.

— *Miguel de Unamuno — Spanish Poet*

A solid uphill walk conveyed me from Minde to Fatima, thankfully through the silent blue gum forests, a minor joy that gave a sting to my walking. Blue gums are prolific in Portugal, covering about 7% of the land. I met four pilgrims. I stopped for a breather in a patch of saplings where freshly cut logs provided the seating with two Italians, exuberant young men, big Rambo types, both with dreadlocks and scungy shorts. They were rough around the edges and I was pleased I didn't come across them in a darkened alley in Rome, but they seemed caring and who knows, they could have been seminarians doing their own pilgrimage. Another lesson of the Camino: never judge on appearances. I met two Spanish ladies who looked to be mother and daughter. They were on the other end of the sartorial spectrum, well coffered and wearing the latest hiking gear. The day was promising. I was meeting other pilgrims. I was hoping to meet more at Fatima.

The closer to Fatima the more home-made signs I passed as if zealous locals were anxious pilgrims were heading in the right direction. They stirred in me excitement and anticipation. I was curious about Fatima. I was fascinated by Lourdes in France and I was interested in visiting this other famous Marion site.

Fatima is important both for Portugal and the Catholic Church. A place of pilgrimage and of veneration in its own right, it's one of the world's most important catholic shrines.

Fatima's Sanctuary welcomes up to four million visitors each year, drawn by apparitions of the Virgin Mary that appeared to three shepherd children, Lucia and her two younger cousins, Francisco and Jacinta, on the 13th day of each month between May and October of 1917. The Virgin exhorted the faithful to change their lives and to say the rosary daily. The children later said that the apparitions were preceded by 'an angel of peace' in 1916. The Virgin is said to have revealed three secrets to the children, which consisted of prophesies about the future and have been the focus of intense interest.

Devotion to Our Lady of Fatima received unprecedented papal support. Pope Pius XII encouraged devotion to her in 1946 and again in 1950. Pope Paul VI prayed at the shrine in 1967. Pope John Paul credited Our Lady of Fatima with saving his life during the assassination attempt in 1981. He came to Fatima as a pilgrim in 1987. Pilgrims visit Fatima all year, but the feast days of 13th May and 13th October draw up to 75,000.

After walking through the forest, I found myself on the edge of a vast open space. Most pilgrims arrive by car or bus, judging from the parking areas surrounding the town. I arrived on foot and walked through Car Park 9 to reach the sanctuary. There weren't many vehicles in the car park on Friday 10th July. I guessed it was a quiet time.

I came upon a large open plaza. Two enormous basilicas facing each other across this plaza dominate the sanctuary. At the other end, the Basilica of Our lady of the Rosary is a gleaming Neoclassical church flanked by monumental colonnades. Building commenced in 1928. I was disappointed to see it was not open for business, being covered in scaffolding and enclosed within a fence. It was undergoing a major renovation, in preparation, I would imagine, for the centenaries in 2016 and 2017 of the apparitions. Opposite and beside me was the

Basilica of the Most Holy Trinity, such a contrast in its simplicity and minimum of decoration. It's so modern it doesn't appear in many of the official guides and web sites. In between I could see the open-air Chapel of the Apparitions, built on the site of the apparitions. It's the hub of the sanctuary.

I had planned to spend the afternoon looking around, get an early night and continue walking the following morning. However, something was enticing me to stay. I felt like a fish drawn to the lure, a lamb led to the slaughter (Not really! Perhaps it was God remaining anonymous). I decided I would like to attend some of the services and stay Saturday. Besides I needed a rest day. There are many forms of accommodation for the four million annual visitors, ranging from up-market hotels to humble hostels. I walked around a few streets looking for the *Bread of Life hostel*, map in hand, and couldn't find it. I was sick of walking and in need of laying down my body, so I approached the *Santa Noite Hospedaria* close to the Sanctuary, asked for a pilgrims' discount and booked for two nights.

After a brief siesta, I felt refreshed enough to explore the town. There were many hotels for the pilgrims as well as a stack of shops and stalls full of religious objects and souvenirs, ranging from the tacky to the beautiful. That night I slept ten hours straight. I was certainly in need of a rest day.

At first, I was the detached observer, like an anthropologist studying the practices of an ancient culture. It was also a challenge to what I regard as my progressive faith as I expected to find myself in a time warp when Catholicism consisted of many devotions such as the daily rosary and novenas. This was the Catholicism of my youth. By lunch time I was hooked. I accepted Fatima. I decided to participate, to dive into the depths of the experience, boots and all, to go with the flow of my feelings, to rediscover the rosary and my 'old-time religion'.

I spent the day in the sanctuary. I caught half of a Mass in German, then a rosary and Mass in Portuguese. Mid-afternoon the Mass was English, concelebrated by five priests, all American. I spoke to John, an outgoing friendly soul who said he was the vice-rector of a seminary in New Jersey, visiting with a group of seminarians. He told me about another English Mass at five. Here I spoke to some English speakers who came with the World Apostolate of Fatima. They were on a pilgrimage of one week and came every year. Other groups surrounded us, singing in a variety of languages (mainly Portuguese), carrying banners and wearing special uniforms.

I realised that up to this time I had been thinking only about myself and how I was coping. It was time to think about and pray for others, particularly the family. Because I knew I would be saying many rosaries, I bought some beads from one of the innumerable souvenir stalls. Sadly, they were made by Señor Shoddy and fell apart after a couple of days.

I prayed for everyone — family, friends, Mat, Laura, Maggie and all the pilgrims who I had met and would meet,

In the evening, everyone flocked to the Sanctuary for the International Rosary, recited in ten languages, each language limited to five Hail Marys. The statue of Our Lady of Fatima was taken out of its glass cupboard above the altar and carried around the sanctuary, the people following with their banners and carrying lighted candles. They waved their handkerchiefs as the statue was returned to its place above the altar. Some wept.

That night, I reflected on my rest day. What better way to pass it than to immerse myself in tradition. I've always been a member of the Catholic Church. In my youth, I accepted the Church's teaching that it was the one true church, that its way of believing was the only right one. In those days, God was an entity completely separate and external to any human. He was a bearded old man in the sky who stood in judgment of our actions and would reward or punish us accordingly.

There was no need, I thought, to hurry on the next day and continue my pilgrimage to Santiago. I had arrived. I needed more time to reflect. Why not stay for the weekend, for another two days to savour the experience and depart Monday? The next morning, I booked in for two extra nights at the *Santa Noite Hospedaria*.

Sunday morning I needed exercise, so I walked out of town to the Way of the Cross where a series of small chapels represent the Stations. Although I met some groups, the place was quiet and contemplative. Bordered by groves of olive trees, it was an ideal location to sit on one of the low walls and meditate. I found a rotunda where the apparition of the angel is said to have occurred. I heard part of a Mass at the Hungarian Chapel. Back at the Sanctuary, feeling the need for mercy and forgiveness, I went to Reconciliation. They were well-organised for large numbers. A nun ushered and organised the people into their respective language groups. Red and green lights indicated whether the priests were busy. There were several rows waiting for the Portuguese version but there was no one in the English queue, the light was green so in I went straight away to an Irish priest. He wasn't at all busy and was ready for a chat.

Although thousands of pilgrims milled around me, they had all arrived by bus or car. I met my first walking pilgrim. I guessed others had removed their backpacks and melted into the crowd. My pilgrim did not speak English so there wasn't much communication except to say 'Bom Caminho.'

Although Friday was comparatively quiet, thousands arrived for the weekend. People approached the Chapel of the

Apparition on their knees down the long slope of the open plaza. Every seat was taken and row after row of people stood behind. At the International Rosary and Procession in the evening, the crowds were even larger. Everyone was respectful and many seated people gave up their place to the elderly or disabled.

Sunday saw an International Mass celebrated outdoors on a temporary stage in front of the barricaded Basilica. The cranes, drills, and earth moving equipment were in respectful silence as hundreds of priests both local and visitors concelebrated before a crowd stretching up the plaza to the new Basilica. The readings and prayers were spoken in a variety of languages including Latin. The homily was delivered in Portuguese and English. Distribution of the host at Communion was well organised. The many priests descended into the crowd, each under the shelter of a large white umbrella, and spread themselves through the plaza, making it easy for the faithful to take the host at the nearest point avoiding the chaos of everyone pressing to the front.

After Mass the statue of Our Lady of Fatima was taken down and carried on a bier around the plaza, all the priests following together with thousands carrying their own banners. Somewhere an organ was playing at full blast. I guessed it must have been in the basilica and amplified outside. The people waved handkerchiefs or tissues as the statue passed and more vigorously as it was being taken back to the Chapel of the Apparition. Some wept. To my surprise, I found myself gripped with emotion and crying, too. Why? I think I felt some of the joy of the people around me. I was in awe at their unflinching devotion to the Virgin. I remembered the small statue of Our Lady of Fatima which my mother kept in a special place at home, how she decided from time to time that we should say the family rosary in its presence. I was experiencing the same emotions and devotions that I had as a child towards the Virgin Mary.

I hadn't lit a candle for Maris since Rabanal. Here, I lit plenty. They were in large quantities, available before the Masses and the Rosary. People held them, or carried them as they processed behind the statue of Mary. There was an opportunity to place them in racks but in the heat of so many candles the wax melted, created a mini furnace and the flames rose and consumed everything. Candles were a large operation. What was missing was the intimacy of a small chapel where one could light a candle in the silence, meditate, pray and reflect.

In all, I stayed at Fatima for four nights and three days.

What kept me?

What kept me was the nostalgia, the exposure to tradition. I hadn't said the rosary for years. I've forgotten the names of the mysteries. What kept me was the contagious devotion of the people. What kept me was the opportunity to pray with so many other people in so many languages. I felt the presence of God, not because of the statue of the Virgin, the apparitions, and all that stuff (though it was the catalyst) but because the bond of devotion and love engaged so many pilgrims from all parts of the world. We were many but we were one.

It was sad to leave. As the euphoria settled down, I reflected. Fatima reminded me of the struggle that I and many other Catholics have with both a traditional and progressive faith. Many have moved away to a new reality and have allowed old thought-forms and dogmas to die, but they are still drawn to Fatima because of its unflinching devotions.

If ever there was a time to delve deeply into my spiritual development and world view, it had to be here at Fatima. I was in the middle of a Camino, a pilgrimage, a spiritual adventure where one could expect epiphanies or, at least, challenging moments.

As I grew older, I began to question. I tried to look beyond the doctrine presented in neat packages to look for explanations. I did not quit my church. To leave the church was akin to throwing the baby out with the bathwater, but I needed to keep seeking further truth, accepting the risk that just over the horizon could be a truth that would completely turn all my beliefs on their head. I embraced doubt, entertaining the possibility that those beliefs might be crap.

I was no Jesus freak, but, on the other hand, I embraced fully my church's teaching on social justice. Jesus' teaching was radical. To accept it and understand it, you had to give it far more than lip service. 'We are all one.' What is done to help anyone helps everyone. What is done against anyone hurts us all. I want to see all people as one, or the universe as one, all part of the same thing. Harming other people is detrimental. Harming the environment is detrimental. Everyone and everything is connected. Everyone and everything should be included in my concern, not just my group, not just me.

On the way, I have met many people who belong to no church and do not believe in a God. They don't need a God or external authority to prevent them from falling into chaos and depravity. They have their values and have made their own rules. They, too, love their neighbour and hear the cry of the poor.

The Catholic Church has given me a set of lenses. I chose to remain in my church, in a traditional organised religion, not because I believed I'd seen the 'Real Truth' and therefore feel compelled to follow that path. I accept that the Catholic Church presents one way among many towards seeking God. They're approaching truth from different angles. There are recurring themes and truths within all of the world's religions. The lenses that the Catholic Church has given me aren't necessarily better than others, but they are mine. They have provided me with a base from which I can view the world, a path that I can follow and a reason to stay on it.

'The diverse paths of religion are fingers of the loving hand of one
Supreme Being, a hand extended to all offering completeness
of spirit to all, eager to receive all.'
—Kahlil Gibran

God is no longer a bearded old bloke in the sky who judges our every move. God is an elusive, slippery character. My definition constantly moves. Sometimes I think of a separate entity with human qualities such as love and compassion; sometime a personal entity, that is, part of my own being; sometimes something of which I am a part; and sometimes tied up with the incomprehensible mystery of creation and the entire universe. In any event, the 'God' whom my mind is wrestling with is not judgemental, does not get angry or need to punish me for my wrongdoing, does not expect worship, impose rules or demand any particular type of behaviour from humans.

Often on the Camino I felt that I was not alone. I certainly felt a Presence in the prayer sessions at Taizé and here at Fatima. Without bothering to define what it was that I was feeling — something beautiful, awesome, immense, all embracing and unimaginable.

I use the word 'Faith'. A good part of the beauty of my faith is that it is based on doubt. My faith is restless. It continues to grow and to evolve. It rejects the notion of settling into a comfortable position. I continue my search aware that I may never find definitive answers. I like to think I'm not afraid of the unknown. I'm not afraid of uncertainty. I don't want to be given firm answers in a neat package about what to believe. I want to keep searching, to keep walking the Camino.

The beauty of life lies in an ever-developing understanding of Reality (what is), ever knowing it is a search for something that I will never fully know. I hope to leave myself open to the myriad of ways that the Divine Reality moves, inspires and challenges.

19

We must accept finite disappointment,
but never lose infinite hope.
—Martin Luther King Jr.

Fatima was all embracing. In departing, I left the past
and returned to the moment. I was fired up, ready
to tackle the challenges of the Camino with joy and
gratitude, to accept that every problem had a solution. A quote
hovered in my brain: *'When faced with a mountain of problems,*
look at it, study it, think about it, pray about it and you will find a way
to climb over it.' The Camino Portugués had been disappointing,
but I hoped for something better. I resolved to see it through.

My task was to return to the main route to Santiago. Para-
doxically, I wasn't looking forward to walking. Taking the bus
as an alternative aroused a niggle of guilt. What the heck! I had
already taken the train. This pilgrimage was different from my
previous Caminos where I walked every step of the way. I did
not feel driven to follow exactly the mode of travel of the ancient
pilgrims. I had to take my age into account. I'd done pretty well
for an eighty-two-year-old. I could hear my Maris chiding me:
'Noel, let good sense prevail! Be easy on myself. Push yourself when you
need to. Tell others that you took the bus to make up time.'

The bus to Coimbra reduced four days using Shanks' pony
to two hours. Because Coimbra has an interesting history,
once being the medieval capital of Portugal, and famous for
its university, it warranted time to explore. I was in no mad
rush. Coimbra's charming old town is a World Heritage site
and I jostled with a host of tourists ambling along the cobbled

streets, viewing the many shops and restaurants. In the heat of the afternoon, I climbed the hill to the university, the oldest in Portugal. The buildings are magnificent and imposing but the students provided the atmosphere. They lounged in bars and cafes, chatting and drinking coffee, seemingly carefree and living for the moment. They reminded me of my own student days. I longed to join in their fun. They painted graffiti on the walls, words of protest about 'police terrorism' and homelessness (*Where was the justice in people without houses and houses without people?*) They were a reminder that Portugal had not long ago emerged from a dictatorship. In the balmy evening, I wandered about the streets and listened to Fado music flowing from the bars — sad songs dwelling on a nostalgic past, on people who had disappeared, or impossible loves, sung by men, solo or in small groups.

I left Coimbra refreshed. The walking was on level ground with one long slow rise. I was delighted my body was coping, without the need for frequent breathers. Was my self-belief prevailing? Was I getting into the swing of things at last? I met three walkers on their way to Fatima. I conversed for a time with Alec, a young American. He was excited about walking to Fatima. I told him he would not be disappointed. He left my company, his enthusiasm white hot.

I met Suzette, a French-Canadian lady, who was having problems with her knees. A Danish couple were walking as far as Oporto. The four of us had lunch together sitting outside a small bar, a rare opportunity to converse with fellow pilgrims. I enjoyed our brief meeting, a glimpse of what the Camino should be about — forming community, sharing the joy of our triumphs and supporting each other in our difficulties. So far, my pilgrimage had been a lonely one without a compensating solitude. I was hoping as I neared Santiago the numbers would increase and I would enjoy more opportunities to build the camaraderie that was a vital part of my previous Caminos.

Bacchus seated on a barrel and imbibing from a horn in the middle of a roundabout announced the approach to Mealhada, a sign that the district boasted of its wines. The four of us stayed in Mealhada at the *Albergue Peregrinos Hilário* where Nino and Diego were our hosts. They had a restaurant, too, and the four of us dined together. To the Danish couple, their Camino was a few days walking as part of a longer holiday. They had left their car at Oporto and would use it to tour the rest of Portugal. Suzette was worried that her knees would crack up and force her to abandon her Camino. She had them bandaged and made liberal use of pain relieving ointments. Nino and Diego supplied plenty of house red with our meal and we were soon in congenial chatter, a reminder of the many previous evenings of conviviality. I thought of the wonderful people I had met, particularly Mat and Laura, my wonderful hosts in Lisbon, of my one-armed mate Michael from Denmark, whom I just missed at Rabanal, and of Ed and Clair, detective and teacher of disabled by day and folk singers by night. We would meet up night after night as if we were old friends, the relationship growing stronger by the day, and saddened when we had to say goodbye.

I did not see my dining companions again. Suzette had opted for a rest day in the hope her knees would benefit. The Danish couple had to forge ahead to adhere to their tight schedule. I had the time but this day tested my resolve. The route was level with gentle undulations and many kilometres of asphalt as the way passed through several industrial areas. At Anadia I was confused by a set of old markings which led me up a crumbling cliff. The markings were definite enough but the path looked seldom used. After a slide and a tumble, I muttered '*No Way!*' I abandoned these old way markings and detoured through the town where I managed to get on course again. A few vineyards, vegetable gardens and patches of blue gum relieved the monotony of the asphalt. I arrived at Agueda and, following the guide book's instruction, crossed the bridge except that it was the wrong bridge. I spent an hour of confusion and frustration. The area bore no resemblance to the guide book's description. It dawned on my foggy mind that perhaps there was another bridge. I retraced my steps and found it.

How comforting when the guide book description and the ground co-inside! The town was nestled around the river and I found the right street to follow to my bed for the night. The guidebook didn't prepare me for the long walk out of town to the *Residencial Celeste*. It reminded me of the frustration of early Caminos. The hours of walking over mountains and plains and the frustrations of losing one's way were nothing compared to when the end was in sight. I would see the village and hope filled my heart that the day's efforts would soon be over. I would calculate how long it would take me to arrive, that time passed and I was still not in that village. I would recalculate and the village still seemed out of reach.

At long last I reached the sign *Residencial Celeste* by the road side and below it the building which tottered on the edge of a steep hill falling away to the river below. I was thankful for a shower and rest.

In review, the day had its blessings. The weather was hot but tempered by a breeze. I learned that the east of Portugal and Spain sweltered in forty-degree heat. Here, I was thankful for the influence of the Atlantic Ocean which kept the temperature down to the late 20s, perfect for walking. My body was tired but had coped with the fifty kilometres of the last two days. I was encouraged by the warm greetings of locals — garbos waving from their truck, ladies leaning out of windows pointing the way. These are friendly country folk, I thought, not unlike the people at home.

It was a long way back to the nearest bar or restaurant and McDonalds was about a kilometre ahead, but the hostel organised a take away home delivery meal. You placed your order with the hospitalera and she telephoned through. I took my delicious omelette and joined the other pilgrims. There were six of them, who were walking together, all young, shy, tired, and keen to get to bed early. I had my second wind, ready for a good chat and discovering just a little about their lives.

In bed that night, before I slipped into sleep, I thought of the frustration of the afternoon, of never seeming to arrive at my goal for the day. It dawned on me that I had violated one of the pilgrim's first principles. Value the journey rather than the destination. I had stopped concentrating on the journey and was caught up in my destination. I should have been focussing on what was happening to me at the moment. I was missing out on the moment, too concerned with the goal of the day. I should have paused, perhaps, and focussed on the scene I was passing — the bird song, the orange flowers in the gardens, the coloured bunting draped in celebration over people's houses. I settled into sleep to the chant of: *'It's the journey, not the goal.'*

Next morning, McDonald's was the indication to turn off to the right. On the outskirts of Agueda I passed by a row of former grand houses but now closed and in decay. My guidebook mentioned many Portuguese who had made their fortunes in colonial Brazil built these houses but in recent times the families had fallen on hard times, On the wall of one of these houses, MacMansions Portuguese style, some disgruntled citizen had written in English in large red letters. *'Fuck the police.'*

For much of the day, I was walking on asphalt through built up areas. Relief from their monotony came in the form of a beautiful stone bridge along the original Via Romana XVI across the Rio Marnel, a lovely contrast to the busy roads. I paused to absorb the calm ambience and antiquity. Shortly after, I found myself in blue gum plantations. Solitude is inspiring. In the midst of the forest, you have a chance to filter through the dim of traffic, the noise of people and their smart phones, the clutter of modern life, the expectations and influence of others, the cycle of busyness in our lives. We hear our hearts speak more clearly and are better equipped to show patience and love to others.

Remembering my reflections of the previous night, I paused for a time in a cleared area filled with stacks of sawn logs to watch two men loading the wood on to a truck. Value the experience of the journey rather than the destination which that evening was Albergaria-a-Velha. I admired their skill in manoeuvring the heavy logs with the help of a small crane, all under a cloudless sky. Once I left the asphalt, the day was ideal for walking

I enjoyed my time in Albergaria. On the edge of town was a new hostel for pilgrims. *Albergue D. Teresa* looked inviting, but as I had arrived before opening time, I continued on to explore the town. My guidebook said the *Casa da Alameda* no longer offered accommodation, but it did. Their registration procedure was slack (there was none), the place was run down and in need of TLC. The carpets were worn and the floors creaked. However, I had a room of my own and the bed was comfortable.

The old and the new blend well in Albergaria. It was founded in the 12th century by royal command of Dona Teresa to provide hospitality and refuge for pilgrims. They continue to follow that command centuries later for mine host at the small restaurant (*Restaurante Ponto Final*) welcomed me with enthusiasm. He gave me a three-course meal and kept returning to refill the wine jug and only charged me 7 euros. '*A pleasure to meet you*', he said in his limited English as I left.

After dinner, just before the *Casa de Alameda*, I paused in the beautifully maintained central gardens. The irises were in full bloom, the low hedges were manicured, the cobbled paving was spotless. This was a tidy town indeed with not a speck of rubbish in sight, such a contrast to other towns I'd passed. Buildings in the art-deco style edged the gardens. The row of tall trees gave the appearance of an avenue. In fact, the word *alameda* is Portuguese for grove or avenue. On a column was a whiskered bust of Napoleăo Luiz Ferreira Leăo, a 19th century emigrant to Africa where he made his fortune which he left to his home town.

In the morning, I passed through the gardens, the entrance marked with the shell symbol. Initially I walked through blue gum forests but much of the day was on asphalt and through continuous built-up areas as if the towns and villages had merged. I had to cross the busy road (N1) and railway line many times. Along the track weeds grew continuously. It looked abandoned, as if the service had been discontinued years ago but I was told that the trains still ran. I never saw or heard any.

The day was cool and overcast with the threat of rain. The rest of Southern Europe was sweltering in 40 degree heat while this part of Portugal remained cool. The terrain was more irregular as the route passed through several river valleys and up some steep climbs, including a sharp one into Oliveira de Azeméis where I stopped for the night. The *Residential La Salette* was dilapidated and closed. The *Pensăo Restaurante Anacleto* wasn't much better. That left the *Hotel Dighton*, an imposing ten stories edifice with a 4-star rating. What's a top end modern hotel doing in a shabby town like this? I thought as I gazed up at the hotel name and star rating spread in bold letter across the side of a windowless wall. In the imposing foyer I asked for a pilgrim discount and they gave me a room for 45 euros. My room was high-class, modern, furnished with dark wood furniture, a mini bar, air conditioning and ensuite, all the trappings of a top rate hotel. I could have been anywhere in the world, totally isolated from the surrounds, instead of in a small town in Portugal between Lisbon and Porto, between the mountains and the sea.

I gazed out of my room window on the fifth floor on the red tiled rooves of Oliveira de Azeméis. The buildings were a good deal older, some were in decay, such a contrast to this luxurious edifice. Puzzled by the incongruence, I explored the hotel. It had two restaurants, one on the top floor, an imposing bar, a health centre which offered massages. Not the usual pilgrim accommodation.

Around the hotel were a mixture of the old and the new. Opposite was a tiny park with a nude statue of Ferreira de Castro, a famous Portuguese writer who was born in this town. The image was another sharp contrast with the whiskered bust back in Albergaria and other pompous images I'd seen on the way. Along the laneway past the *Residential La Salette* was the *Durga* Lounge Bar and further along the church. To get to it, you had to climb a long flight of steps, a challenge for the infirm. On the plaza in front of the church you had a good view of the roof top of the building housing the *Durga* lounge where they were setting up for a disco, competition for the Mass celebration later that evening.

Hotel Dighton's dining lived up to its high-class reputation. The restaurant on the top floor was closed, but the grill in the ground floor restaurant adjacent to the bar was fired up and ready. There were more staff than diners and the tables were laid with white starched linen and silver service. I chose from the extensive menu and I had to pay for the wine, another contrast with the many establishments I'd dined in where wine was thrown in. No house wines here! Only a wine list! I was still puzzled. What's a fancy restaurant doing in a town like this? There weren't many diners for a Saturday night, or guests in the hotel.

The *Hotel Dighton* was like an oasis, the folly of someone with too much money.

After dinner, I approached the man behind the desk in the foyer. *'Fala inglés?'* I asked him. *'Yes, a little,'* he replied. So I posed the question which had been plaguing me ever since I'd arrived. *'What's this hotel doing in a town like this?'* He smiled and told me that it was built by a local son, an emigrant to America who had made his fortune and returned to his home town where he made his contribution by building this hotel. Since then a company had taken over and promoted it extensively. It had become a tourist attraction in its own right. I accepted his explanation and went outside for a short walk before retiring. The disco was in full blast that shook the air and rocked the surrounding buildings. Even the road seemed to vibrate. I ventured along the laneway past the *Durga* lounge bar. It was the entry to the disco. A number of lads were blocking the lane, noisily drinking. I felt mildly threatened but they took no interest in me, an old bloke, as I elbowed through them. Security guards were on the doors vetting the would-be patrons. The bar was supposed to be a place for relaxation and intimacy, but not tonight. The noise was damaging and oppressive. I remembered previous encounters with discos on my earlier walks. The worst was when the relentless music was just outside the albergue's window. Sleep was impossible. Here in Oliveira de Azeméis about 200 metres separated the source from the *Hotel Dighton*. I was hopeful I would hear only muffled sound in the secure cocoon of my bedroom. As I settled for sleep, my mind ranged over the many places where I had found a bed. *Hotel Dighton* was unique, by far the most luxurious.

I had a restless night. Every time I woke through the night I could hear the thump of the disco. Discos are relentless. No one has to take a breather like live players. I woke late and left late, not before enjoying a silver service breakfast — the final indulgence. After an all-night pummelling, the town was quiet and exhausted. I had only a short distance, 9 kilometres to São João de Madeira, but the day was a struggle under the overcast and humid sky, while at ground level I walked through built-up areas. Where has the countryside and wilderness gone? I met no walkers, not for two days. 'Where have all the pilgrims gone?' I sang to the tune of Pete Seeger's 'Where have all the flowers gone?'

São João de Madeira is an historic town of Roman origin but the ambiance is modern. The town has enjoyed prosperous times. The way led to a pedestrian only central square with large rotunda flanked by two hotels (two star and four-star luxury), several café-bars, and the *Residential Solar São João*. I had my taste of luxury at the *Hotel Dighton* so I opted for the *Residential*, with its air of shabby gentility and the furnishings of the old school. My room had a high bed with iron lace head and foot while the chandelier boasted four branches, ideal to hang my washing. I wondered how many cafés would be open Sunday night but, later I explored the streets around the square and found a neat restaurant where the set menu was spare ribs which they cooked on a barbecue on the footpath.

Monday was a repeat of previous days — walking through built-up areas and occasional patches of forest. The *hostel*

António Pires run by the *Confrario de Santiago* was easy to find. The guy next door had a key and let me in. On the other side was a small shop which closed at 3 pm Mondays. Lucky I read the notice in the hostel and just made closing time. Furnishing was basic. The rooms had bunks, no blankets or linen, no doors, but the kitchen was well equipped. I read a notice that Mass was celebrated at the monastery (Mosterio São Salvador de Grijó) at 5 pm.

José Tavares, the hospitalero, came around to collect my money. Almost everyone in the parish (*Paroquia S. Salvador*) was on the roster, he told me in reasonable English, and today was his turn. I asked him about the Mass at the monastery. He said it was not far but he offered to come back and drive me. Back he came with his wife.

The monastery offered physical and spiritual nourishment to the medieval pilgrims and today's pilgrims can find peace and respite from the traffic in the extensive parklands. After Mass, José Tavares introduced me to a number of his fellow parishioners and offered to drive me back to the hostel but I declined and walked the short distance. Back at the hostel I found that two Polish cyclists had arrived and occupied the other room. They were friendly and amazed I'd come all the way from Australia. In the meantime, I cooked myself a dinner of sardines, potatoes, tomatoes and eggs.

Despite the proximity to Porto I found myself walking on stretches of the original medieval pilgrim route, a relief from the jarring noise of the roads where you had to forget reflection or contemplation and stay alert to the danger of fast moving traffic. At one stage I found myself on a narrow road without footpaths. I had just that moment made a Camino resolution to refrain from swearing at any frustration when I saw a car fast approaching me. The female driver had veered to my side to avoid the oncoming traffic but she did not alter speed and just managed to avoid me. I felt the rush of wind. *'Jesus fucking Christ!'* came out of my mouth before I could think. So much for my resolution!

20

Blessed are you, pilgrim, if on the way you meet yourself
and gift yourself with time, without rushing, so as not
to disregard the image in your heart.
—The Beatitudes of the Pilgrim.

I gave thanks for my persistence and safe arrival when I reached the bridge crossing the river into Porto, the logical end of the Lisbon section. I had walked on more asphalt than on any of my previous Caminos and tempted fate far more often in my encounters with fast moving dangerous traffic. How many pilgrims have been killed or maimed on these roads? What can be done to ensure a safer passage?

I paused to admire the panoramic view of the southern side spilling down to the river. On the far side was Porto, Portugal's second city, with the cathedral prominent on the right. Below the cathedral, the old quarter tumbled down to the river wharfs. Porto is a beautiful city, situated on the banks of the Rio Douro (river of gold). It's a modern city, full of life and vigour, yet has a long history. It was here in the 12th century that the independent nation took the name of Portugal. Henry the Navigator was born here and by the 15th century the city played a major role in the maritime exploration of the New World. Well established trade routes ensured the rise of a wealthy middle class and many substantial civic buildings. The historical centre is a World Heritage site.

I sat on a low wall for a breather before taking on the city. Others were admiring the view, all tourists, except for one. He was a young man, complete with backpack, a cross around his neck and clothes he'd been wearing for a while. We greeted each other as pilgrims. He had good English. He was Spanish, José-Luis, and had walked from Lisbon. He was the first pilgrim I had met for a few days. Together we walked across the bridge into the city, along impressive boulevards and plazas, flanked by imposing buildings to the tourist office. José-Luis was looking for a seminario which offered free accommodation to pilgrims; I was looking for a reasonable hostel. The rather bored girl gave us some directions. We wished each other *"Bom Caminho"* and went our ways. I walked a distance to find the first hostel. It was vibrant, pulsing with rock music and youth, but it was full. The girl on the desk was helpful. She said accommodation would be difficult to find as Porto was overrun with tourists, but she would contact a nearby hotel for me. She rang. There was room. I was hoping for cheaper accommodation, but I was in mild panic as I walked again. It took a while weaving around the city but eventually the *Hotel Moov* came into view. Rooms were 57 euros and there was no pilgrim discount. I was tired and anxious, so rather than leave and look for other accommodation, I took the room which happened to be fitted out for the disabled. What were they trying to tell me?

I found a restaurant opposite. Nothing swanky, just a place where normal folk would eat. The square was vibrant. Apart from the tram, group after group of runners and walkers came through. There was no distinction between footpath and road. Pedestrians and traffic were everywhere until late.

I spent the next day (Wednesday) as a tourist. It was supposed to be a rest day but I spent as much energy walking around the city, jostling with the crowds of tourists, dodging the metro and traffic, and visiting the sights. I caught the end of a Mass in the cathedral and spoke to some English

ladies who were on a whirlwind tour and didn't have too much
time to dally. I rode on the metro for the experience. On the
same square as my hotel was a church *(S. Ildefonso)*. The lady
manning a piety stall at the entrance welcomed me. She had
no English, but she spoke French. She was interested that I
had walked from Lisbon through Fatima. I told her about my
shoddy rosary beads. She produced a set and guaranteed they
would not fall apart because she made them herself. I had no
option but to buy. She told me of rosary and Mass later that
day. I gave the rosary a miss but I attended Mass where I had
the opportunity to light a candle for Maris, to thank her for
guiding me safely thus far. I asked her to stick by me.

I enjoyed this quiet time, vaguely aware of the din of the city
outside, and the opportunity to renew intentions for the inner
journey. My detour to Fatima was an encounter with tradition
which was like a shot in the arm to my spiritual life. The way
had its challenges but I persisted. I was not always conscious
of my reactions and thoughts. Some were good and led to a
sense of peace, others not so good and lead to frustration and
negativity. *'Nothing good comes from negative thoughts,'* I almost
heard my Maris saying. I tried to make every step a prayer and
in reciting the rosary, I endeavoured to shift the focus from
me to others. I hoped I could continue to accompany my steps
with wordless prayer.

I was disappointed with the physical journey so far. Most
people walking the Camino Portugués start at Porto, so perhaps I would meet other pilgrims, walk with them and we'd
come together as a Camino family. I was hoping I had left
dangerous roads behind.

My guidebook suggested options for clearing the city. I took
the metro and spent the first 12 kilometres in comfort watching the dreary suburbs pass by. I descended at Maia, found

the wayside markings and walked 14 kilometres to Vilarinho. At first, I found myself walking on asphalt and, for variation, granite cobblestones. I was in the suburbs and the traffic was frustrating, just as intense and scary, particularly where there was no footpath. What's the road kill like in these areas? I wanted to ask someone. I managed to remember my resolve not to swear when rapidly approaching vehicles came dangerously close, but only just.

A pilgrimage is an adventure. We expect the unexpected because that's where life is. When we walk, we open ourselves to risk, adapt to new situations, to changing weather, to wrong turns, to getting lost, to grotty accommodation, to dodgy food. It's the unexpected that makes a pilgrimage an adventure and it's the ability to adapt and persist that has us happy to arrive, knowing that we have met the challenge and survived. However, this menacing traffic was becoming drearily predictable. Adapt! I was commanding myself. Get used to this life-threatening traffic and be thankful you have survived! In between moments of saving myself, I thought of the ancient pilgrims who had travelled this road a thousand years before. They had plenty of dangers to face — wild animals, unfriendly robbers, vicious storms, lack of shelter. Their chances of arriving at Santiago were less than mine. They certainly had to face the unexpected, to adapt to their changing world. They put their trust in God just as I should. We both had to face menaces, the ancient faced the brigands and the medieval conmen, I had to walk on narrow roads heavy with traffic and drivers indifferent to my presence. We both had and have to trust in God. I paused to clear my mind of the anger I directed at the dangerous drivers. I tried to prepare my mind for peace.

On a quieter stretch I saw a figure coming towards me. A young man on his way to Fatima? Then I heard him. He was singing loudly. Complete with stick and backpack, he was wearing shorts but no shirt. The straps of his pack crossed his bare chest and stomach. He wore no hat, just a large crop of long hair. As he came towards me, he stopped, grinned and embraced me. I was conscious of his red sunburnt skin and sweat. Without breaking his song, he continued on past me, the words of an unfamiliar language floating over the shoulders. A brief encounter of the unexpected kind! We exchanged no words but a wonderful greeting. His smile and embrace cleared my mind of negativity. I was at peace and tackled with heightened patience the journey to Vilarinho, where I rested in a central park. I sat on a seat, cooled by the shade. The trees were a green silhouette against the blue sky and it was a great thing for it to be afternoon, to be resting and to feel the breeze in my face.

I was about to go looking for the hostel when a lady approached me. She was Antonia, English and a pilgrim and had just been to the little shop. She was just as pleased to meet a fellow pilgrim as I was. She was staying at the *Casa de Laura*. The place was very nice, she said, the lady was lovely and she offered to take me the short distance. I had noticed advertisements for *Casa de Laura* stuck on trees along the way. Laura had no English but I felt caring warmth in her welcome. The hostel was a small building in her backyard. There were two rooms, one a dormitory with four bunks, the other with a double bed a bathroom in between. Antonia had taken the double bed and I had the dormitory to myself. We sat outside in the peaceful garden of green lawns, vegetables and chooks down the back. Laura offered us port and cake, the first time I had drunk port in Portugal, the home of port.

Antonia and I had dinner together in the small café across the road. She, too, had started at Lisbon, but several days later than me, and being a fast walker, had caught up. She, too, was disappointed at meeting very few pilgrims. She, too, had become adept at dodging the traffic. She was on her way to Santiago and was planning to forge ahead. Back in the garden, Laura had not cleared away the glasses. They were covered with ants. Portuguese ants are just as smart as the Aussies.

As I drifted into sleep I thought about that shirtless young man with the baggy shorts and shoulder length hair. Every now and then you meet someone on the Camino who has a strong impact. I'm not sure what struck me. He seemed to have no cares; he was living in the moment, enjoying his walking, bursting with song and taking everything in his stride, including me. He just stopped to give a wordless greeting and continued. His shirtless body suggested he didn't have much baggage, both literally and metaphorically. I envied him for his carefree nature. It was hard to define his charisma. He gave me his full attention for the moment and then powered on. He didn't seem too worried about his next meal or bed. He may have had no money. Something about him was inspiring, like a minor epiphany, like meeting Jesus on the road to Damascus. Live for the moment. Don't be too concerned about what might be ahead.

What I worry about never happens anyway.

Antonia had departed by the time I stirred. I started late as I was planning to walk only 12 kilometres to São Pedro de Rates. I walked in misty rain and for the first time used my wet weather gear, bright orange Sydney Swans 2012 premiership poncho thrown over both pack and body. The roads were quieter and passed through blue gum and pine forests but the surface was mostly asphalt and granite cobblestones. I passed over a number of bridges including *Ponte D Zameiro* and *Ponte São Miguel de Arcos*. The original crossings dated back to Roman times but more substantial construction began in the 12th century. I paused to admire the solid structure and to absorb the quiet and peace, an experience which had been comparatively rare on this Camino Portugués. These bridges were like oases in the modern desert of noisy traffic. I lingered to watch the ducks swimming in unison in the still water. I paused at the church (Igreja de S. Pedro) as I came into São de Rates. A solid robust building, it was originally built as a monastery in the 11th century. The door was open so I ventured in for a quiet prayer. I would have lit a candle for Maris if they had been available. In France, I found many opportunities, but not in Spain or Portugal. The churches were not open. A line of small children hand in hand were entering the school room as I passed on the way to the albergue.

The albergue had accommodation for fifty in various small dormitories. It was well equipped with a living/dining room and kitchen with a large courtyard on the other side of which was a museum displaying objects typical of rural life in the area. Twenty-six pilgrims were registered for the night, the largest gathering I had encountered so far. I suspect that most started at Porto. In the bed next to me, was a Polish man who had no English, Spanish or Portuguese. Others in the dormitory included a German, Anthony, who was walking with his son Til. An American, Angela, who lived in Germany, was walking with her daughter Courtney. In the dining room I met Freya, a blond German lady. She was struggling with her pasta and insisted on sharing it with me.

Sleep was elusive as the albergue was on a busy road. Through the night, trucks thundered by the window. You could hear the approach, the noise increased, then the full thrust of the engine and road noise. They passed regularly early in the night but often enough later to ensure that sleep was interrupted.

On the way to Barcelos the following morning I enjoyed an hour and a half of forest and countryside. I prayed they would last but by mid-morning I was back on dangerous roads. There was a message of hope, however, in the road signs warning motorists to be careful of pilgrims, suggesting that the Barcelos Town Council (Camara Municipal de Barcelos) took seriously their responsibility for the safety of pilgrims passing through the municipality. Several times I passed the sign:

Camara Municipal de Barcelos Cuidado Circulação de Peregrinos

I stopped at a café in Pedra Furada where I shared coffee with Angela and daughter Courtney. According to my guidebook, the proprietor António Martins Ferreira, along with other concerned residents of Barcelos, is part of an association formed to coordinate efforts to improve the pilgrim infrastructure in the area. Initial projects included the safety of pilgrims walking the stretch of main road. I gave thanks to António and his mates and to the good town councillors of Barcelos.

At Barcelinhos I crossed the Rio Cávado by the medieval bridge into Barcelos. Before the bridge was built the medieval pilgrims took the ferry. Barcelos' history is immediately obvious. The town retains its medieval ambience. It occupies an elevated site above the Rio Cávado and was the first Portuguese County established in 1298 but its origin goes back to Roman times. The moment one crosses the bridge one is surrounded by antiquity, a bonanza for the history tragic. First, an open air archaeological museum, then a number of 14th and 15th century palaces and churches. You pass a 15th century granite tower (Torre de Porta Nova), which is the only remaining medieval entrance into the town and come to the extensive market square Campo da Feira known as Campo da Republica. The whole area becomes one of Portugal's best-known and liveliest markets, Feira de Barcelos, every Thursday. I missed the market because the day was Saturday. I admired the stone fountain and an octagonal Baroque church dedicated to Good Jesus of the Cross (*Templo do S. Bom Jesus da Cruz*), quite a contrast to the sombre granite of the other churches in the region. This is the site of the 500-year-old Feast of the Crosses that takes place each year on 3rd May and is named after the miraculous appearance of a cross in the soil of an adjoining market square.

I passed several images of the Barcelos cockerel. Its story is similar to the one I heard back in 2011 at Santo Domingo de la Calzada on the Camino Francés. I photographed a notice in Portuguese and English telling the miraculous story of the roasted cock that rose from the table of the judge who had wrongly condemned a Santiago bound pilgrim to hang from a nearby gallows. The pilgrim had protested his innocence and that if he were hanged then a dead cock would rise from the judge's table as a sign of his innocence. The innocent lad was hanged and sure enough a roasted cock stood up at the judge's table at dinner that night. They hurried to the gallows to find the pilgrim still alive, a miraculous intervention of St. James.

Eventually I arrived at the *Albergue Cidade de Barcelos*. Facilities were basic. I shared a room with Feya, the blonde German lady. Across the corridor were Angela and daughter Courtney, Anthony and son Til were with a couple from New Zealand. The day was hot and sweaty, so I enjoyed a few beers in the *Café Araujo* next door. Later, I found a massive supermarket in the modern part of the town but I could not cook my own dinner at the camp stove because there were no matches in the kitchen, so I had dinner in the *Café Araujo* with the New

Zealand couple. Tony and Joyce were on their way to Santiago but weren't planning to walk all the way. Back home, they were into high-tech farming and keen to talk about it. One of the family running the café, on old lady, congratulated me on walking the Caminho at 82. How did she know? She must have had access to the register.

Sunday 26th July was Maris' birthday. In contrast to the previous week, the day was cool and overcast. The walking was excellent. The beautiful natural landscape was like an elixir which lifted my spirits and much of the route was on pathways through tranquil forest and vineyards. I felt at home, attentive, alive to the moment, a rare opportunity to clear my mind of clutter. I felt I was just being myself, free of anxieties and expectations. I was alone but not lonely. Maris was walking with me, and I was content to allow my mind to drift through memories of the highlights and catastrophes of our lives together. Ours was a forty-two-year story of deep romance and genuine collaboration. She would have turned seventy-six.

The next town was Ponte De Lima, 33 kilometres but there were accommodation options in between. One was *Casa da Fernanda*.

I'd heard about *Casa da Fernanda*. Back at Rabanal, one of the pilgrims, Frank, an Australian, had stayed at *Casa da Fernanda* several times. Run by Fernanda and husband, Jacinto, it was a must. Frank had donated an Australian flag which now hung on one of the walls. Donna, one of the Canadians who replaced us, had walked the Camino Portugués just before her stint as a hospitalera. She, too, had stayed at *Casa da Fernanda*, one of the best, she told me. I just had to stay there. I was looking forward to the experience. Its reputation was widely spread, so I rang ahead to reserve a bed, the only time on the Camino Portugués that I bothered with a reservation.

En route, I ran into Angela and Courtney several times. We stopped at a café and met Michael, Laura and Eva, all Americans from California. I told everyone about Casa da Fernanda. The pleasant walking continued along country lanes past stone churches and chapels, over an ancient bridge (Ponte das Tábuas) and a brand-new drinking fountain, compliments of the parish of Balugães (Junta Freguesia Balugães). I stopped by the fountain to ring my daughters, Jacinta and Angela. Being Maris' birthday, I longed for her physical presence but was aware of her presence in spirit. It was still Saturday evening in Australia, but they had remembered mum's birthday. Hearing the voices of my daughters was a bonus. They have the same caring compassionate nature as Maris. I tell my friends: '*She bought them up right!*'

A hand painted sign *Lugar do Corgo Casa da Fernanda* by the side of the road indicated that I had arrived. Stepping under an archway of vines I found myself in an extensive vegetable garden and modern bungalow beyond. Angela, Courtney, Michael, Laura and Eva had already arrived along with three others. They were sitting around in a courtyard in front of the pilgrim accommodation, a timber chalet, eating cake and drinking wine. Fernanda, an extroverted lady with a beaming smile and excellent English offered me cake and wine, too. Despite the threatening rain, we sat around, laughed and chatted, Fernanda in the midst. This is as good as it gets. What a tired pilgrim values most is an exuberant welcome, a feeling of being accepted as a real person. More than once, I had been regarded as a necessary nuisance and greeted with indifference. Not here!

Fernanda got around to allocating beds. We were all to go into one dormitory. No bunks. I mentioned that I heard there was a room with an Australian flag. She peeled me off and pushed me into the room next door. Sure enough an Australian flag was hanging on the wall. The room had two beds, one a double and its own bathroom. It was certainly a privilege to be an Australian at *Casa da Fernanda*. The others were envious. For a time the ladies debated whether they should banish Michael, the only other male, from their dormitory, and segregate the sexes, but eventually they allowed him to stay.

Jacinto, Fernanda's husband, was hovering around doing various jobs. He grabbed everyone's washing, put them through the machine and hung them out on the line. He was also cooking dinner.

That evening we sat down to a wonderful meal, a banquet with a range of dishes including casseroles, salads and cheeses spread over the table. Jacinto and Fernanda presided and led the conversation. Interaction with the pilgrims was something they treasured. Fernanda had better English but together they told their story. They had been welcoming pilgrims for years. They had no set fee, the pilgrims contributing on a donativo basis. Their pilgrims had to arrive on foot, carrying their own pack. They accepted reservations but always tried to keep one or two beds for pilgrims who might turn up late. They loved their job, were open seven days with a break in winter. The vegetables came from their own garden and they always tried to use local produce. Someone asked if they prepared the same menu each night. No! said Fernanda. That would be too boring. They liked to change. They had already planned some pasta dishes for the following night.

After dinner we sat outside in the courtyard drinking port. Jacinto found his guitar and both he and his wife entertained with song after song. They loved to perform. Then it was our turn and we were all supposed to contribute. I fell back on Waltzing Matilda. One of the Yanks sang John Brown's body.

Back in my room, I checked the flag and found that earlier guests, including Frank, had written their names and the date in the white of the stars. I did the same. *Noel Braun. Jindabyne 26/07/15.* What a wonderful evening! It reminded me of the times in earlier Caminos when nights such as this were the rule rather than the exception — warm welcoming hosts, pilgrims ready to interact, communal meal and everyone joining in song. Language differences were never a barrier. Indeed, the various backgrounds and cultures added layers of richness. We were truly a Camino family. The fatigue of the day was forgotten, the aches were washed away in wine, camaraderie lifted the spirit. The body was ready for tomorrow.

In the morning, they farewelled their family. As I walked out under the vine archway, Jacinto wished me well. '*Bom Caminho, Australiano!*' My mind travelled back to Moissac in France. The *gîte d'étape Ultreia* was run by an Irish couple, Rom and Aiden. We had an evening of great camaraderie. In the morning, Rom reminded me of a father seeing off his children as he said goodbye to his guests. When I commented, he replied that while his guests were with him they were his family, except that after they departed in the morning, he never saw or heard of them again. Did Jacinto have similar thoughts?

The walking was fine, warm with a breeze. It involved a stiff climb to Facha, then a slow descent to Ponte De Lima, 14 kilometres in all. On the way as I entered woodlands, I passed a large bill board:

'Pelas nossas florestas, Pelo nosso futuro
Lutar contra a indiferença'
(For our forests, for our future Fight against indifference)

Behind the wording were two large photographs, one of

a flourishing forest, the other a wasteland. I was pleased to read that message. I was beginning to imagine that the Portuguese weren't too concerned about their environment judging by the amount of rubbish lying about, particularly plastic bottles. Forests are beautiful, a part of creation and it is our responsibility to ensure their protection for the benefit of our grandchildren. The greatest enemy is indifference, in Portugal and everywhere.

The Lima valley is full of natural beauty and towards the end of my walking I was in a beautiful riverside. My guide-book describes Ponte De Lima as *'a delightful market town that retains a sleepy medieval atmosphere'*. It was far from sleepy on Monday 27th July. As I approached along a pleasant pathway shaded by large spreading trees by the Rio Lima I ran into a huge market with hundreds and hundreds of stalls stretching through to the sandy beach. I had to jostle my way through the throng and follow the colour and clamour of countless spruikers right to the town plaza. This market claims to be the oldest extant in Portugal. As I crossed over the medieval bridge and looked back, I could see how far the canvas tops of many colours stretched along the river sands and through the trees bordering the river. Ponte De Lima's market made up for missing Barcelos' on Saturday.

I arrived in Ponte de Lima at 1 pm. I was planning to stay at the town albergue. It didn't open until 4 so I looked elsewhere. I crossed back over the bridge, strolled through the town plaza and along the narrow-cobbled streets until I found the *Pensão São João*. My room overlooked a small plaza. After a shower and siesta, I returned to the market and made my way leisurely through the thong of tourists many of whom were English. The market impressed me — the largest number of stalls I'd seen in the one place. One could buy just anything. Later, I had dinner at a restaurant below my window. Michael and Laura ambled by. My Camino family was scattered that night. After dinner I strolled back to the market. Perhaps there was some entertainment. It was gone — everything and everyone. Only the garbos remained, removing rubbish from under trees stirring gently in the evening breeze.

In the morning, I let myself out of the Pensão at 6.15 am. I left early because I knew I had a massive hill, the steepest climb in one ascent to date. I was now in beautiful countryside, walking along lanes through vineyards and forests. At one time, I was criss-crossing under an elevated freeway far above, but around me the many trees and forest undergrowth were nourishing the spirit. It's difficult to find spiritual nourishment on a busy road, facing oncoming traffic and hearing the roar of vehicles from behind, trusting in God that no driver, impatient behind a slow truck, would cross the road to pass and fail to see me in time. Here in the countryside my focus was not on self-preservation but on the view around me, feeling part of creation rather than an alien.

I came across a few pilgrims that day, four boys walking together and three couples. It was good to greet them with 'Bom Caminho!' I took my time. Everyone passed me. 'Il faut marcher doucement et lentement.' One must walk gently and slowly was one the first lesson I learned about the Camino when I took my first steps back in France in 2010. Slowing down enables you to observe the world around you and to listen to your body. I was following the Camino for the love of the journey and was not for the mad rush to get to Santiago.

The steep incline was through a pine forest, at first along a road then on a bush track that wound itself up the mountain to the Alto da Portela Grande and then a gradual descent into Rubiães. There were many signs telling walkers about a bar ahead and the distance. The last sign announced it was only 200 metres ahead, and there it was, a caravan in a backyard. I ordered a coffee and before it was ready, Michael and Laura strolled in. They had set out from Ponte de Lima at 8.15 am, two hours later than me. I felt good, to put my backpack aside, to be drinking coffee in good company, to feel the sun on my back.

As I walked towards Rubiães, my thoughts soared to the sun. We take it for granted. Its sunlight shines on the earth. It is the source of all light, power and heat. All life on the earth comes from the sunlight, giving rise to the vegetation which lies at the food base for all living creatures, which in turn reach out to the sun, such as flowers. Even the light and heat from fossil fuels are drawing on stores of ancient sunlight. It's all pervasive. No wonder primal people regarded the sun as a god, offering light and warmth and life within the nurturing encompass of the earth.

Back to earth! One of the first buildings in Rubiães was a three-storey white *Residencial O Repouso do Peregrino* (pilgrim's rest). The large sign announced in four languages rooms were available (*quartos, habitacion, chambre, room*), and underneath the shell symbol and *Caminho de Santiago* for good measure. Why bother to go further? Michael and Laura had the same thought. They were already seated in the little courtyard, Angela and Courtney came later. I met my first Australians, Cory and Simone from Bellingen in northern New South Wales. Cory was well tattooed and usually rode his motor bike but was walking this time. They had just attended motor bike rallies in Poland and had decided to try the Caminho before returning to Australia. It was refreshing to hear the Aussie accent and to talk about places with which the three of us were familiar. A touch of home! '*Aussie! Aussie! Aussie!*'

The rooms were out the back, motel style, all with shower

and ensuite, at 15 euro. Another suite of rooms was being constructed but it looked as if no work had been done on them for a while. They did not serve dinner. Instead, they provided a car and driver and took us to a restaurant about two kilometres down the road. The other diners were pilgrims. Among them were the German Anthony and son Til whom I hadn't seen for a few days. Many knew me as the older Australian walking solo. Between Michael, Laura and Angela, they knew everyone, pilgrims they'd met on the way, mostly Americans, and in no time, I knew them, too. On the Camino, your friends are my friends. At our table were Sue and Audrey, two exuberant Americans. They had heard of me and quizzed me. Why had I come so far? I countered with the same question. They, like many Americans, had seen the film *'The Way'* and were inspired. Everyone enjoyed another fun night of camaraderie.

The next morning at breakfast I said goodbye to my fellow Australians, Cory and Simone, who were *'forging ahead'*. I walked downhill past the restaurant where we had dined the previous evening and also the albergue where everyone else had stayed. The *Albergue Escola* was in a former schoolhouse. That day the walking was mostly on natural earthen pathways and quiet roads through farmlands and forests, over well preserved Roman bridges and, for the most part downhill, a delightful change from murderous traffic. I tried to bypass Valença to get to Spain, but somehow I managed to end up walking right through this busy town. The narrow-cobbled streets were lined with bars, souvenir shops and hotels. The streets were full of tourists. An interesting place to stay a day but I wanted to push on to Tui in Spain on the other side of the bridge crossing the Rio Minho. Just before the bridge was the impressive fortress Fortaleza standing guard over the Rio Minho. Occupying an elevated position on the border of Portugal and Spain it has been a major military defensive establishment from the earliest times. Here I came across Angela and Courtney. We explored the fortress together and admired the view across the river into Spain. We found a way to descend to the road and rail bridge. The Rio Minho was broad. Looking back we could see just how dominant and imposing the fortress was — an ideal place in turbulent times for the Portuguese to check what was happening on the other side.

21

The water wears away the stone.
—*The Book of Job. 14:19*

A large sign in need of paint welcomed us into España. The river was now the Rio Mino and we had to advance our watches an hour. I was happy to switch from Portuguese to Spanish. Whenever I asked for a flat white coffee I could now order a *café con leche* instead of *mai de leite*. I could expect the signposts to be a mixture of Galician Galego and Castellano.

Tui is an historical border town. It has a more modern profile than Valença but at its heart is the well preserved medieval town, the centrepiece being the Romanesque cathedral. Angela, Courtney and I made our way to the tourist office next to the cathedral. Along the way, we had seen many advertisements for the *Hotel Alfonso I* at 35 euro a room. It was out of town but they picked you up if you rang. So I rang. Initially, I was not understood and then there was confusion about where we were. We settled down on the steps of the cathedral to wait. The car arrived and we were taken well out of town to the *Alfonso I*, a three-storey hotel with a broad plaza in front, set in a light industrial area.

The owners seemed keen to break into the pilgrim trade, but we were the only pilgrims, the other guests being business men in their suits. The interior furnishings were lavish, gaudily over blown, but comfortable. The three of us shared a pizza in the bar and as the day was Courtney's seventeenth birthday Angela arranged a cake. I felt privileged to share the occasion — a gentle low key celebration. I felt a distant uncle instead of an acquaintance of a few days. That's the Camino. You feel close to people you've just met.

In the morning, we were taken by the hotel bus, not back to the cathedral, the starting point for the day's walk, but to a point on the route not far from the hotel. The gesture saved us about three kilometres. The day was overcast but we made steady progress through countryside, walking along the ancient road, the Via Romana XIX, over roman bridges, then a slog through industrial estates, a main road and crisscrossing a railway line. The next town was Redondela with the *Albergue de Mos* on the way, which we decided would be our destination. We arrived at Concello de Mos and thought we had found our Albergue. The *Albergue Peregrinos Santa Ana Veigadaña* looked new; it had been open for four months we heard later. The setting was lovely, quiet and peaceful, out in the country and edged with forest, so we stayed at 7 euro a bed. The dormitory was upstairs and downstairs were a bar and dining area, which turned out to be the local watering hole. The albergue was run by volunteers and it seemed to be quite a community effort with everyone rostered. They came for a drink during the afternoon and by evening, we met everyone. They served us a dinner of tuna salad and pasta at 7 euro. A great evening in good company, locals and pilgrims mixed up! This community enjoyed looking after their pilgrims. Language differences didn't matter.

Next morning they gave us breakfast for 2 euro. We set out in a very dull dark morning, threatening rain which never fell. About 3 kilometres we came across the village of Mos and the *Albergue de Mos*. I was pleased we had stayed in the wrong place. I was impressed by the pilgrim store. It announced its existence in nine languages written on a large stylised shell with nine fingers.

The climb out of Mos was steep, up the Rua dos Cabaleiros (Road of Knights) around Monte Cordedo. However, the reward was a view of the sea and the Rio de Vigo and a downhill run into Redondela. The *Albergue Xunta* was a well restored pilgrim hostel which looked inviting, but, as it was only midday and well before opening time, I continued through Redondela about three kilometres to the *Pensión Rustica Jumboli* where I met up with my Camino family — Michael, Laura, Angela and Courtney. Angela was having problems with her feet. I gave her my pain-relieving cream which seemed to help. The five of us dined together at the Jumboli Café about 100 metres up the road. Another night of conversation and conviviality, which made the pain of the day worthwhile. The Pensión was just off the main road which helped me to get a good night's sleep.

Saturday 1st August was a milestone. I had been away from home the whole of June and July and was nearing the end of my journey. God had been on my side all the way with only a few days now to Santiago. Persistence was paying off. First, a steep climb to the Alto da Lomba and back down to sea level at Arcade. The rewards were pleasant walking through forest and wonderful views of the Rio de Vigo. The road through Arcade was along a dangerous, narrow and noisy 700 metre stretch. Even the sign said this was *a tramo de concentración de accidentes* and to take *precaución*. Arcade could have been a pleasant seaside village with opportunities for a swim in the sea but I was keen to move on. The number of walkers had increased significantly and groups of cyclists passed me. I guessed that many started in Tui as Santiago was only 115 kilometres. Before long I crossed the Ponte Sampaio over the Rio Verdugo — an impressive long stone bridge with several arches. A memorial on the far side told its story. It was here in 1795 that local militia inflicted a significant route on Napoleon's troops during the War of Independence. The day was windless, the sea was calm, the sandy beaches were inviting me to rest and swim, but I decided to get a wriggle on and forged ahead up another steep incline off the main road.

The rest of the day was on ancient stone paths through quiet and peaceful countryside, offering a whisper of hope that all will be well. How delightful to be rid of the noisome traffic! I suppose He is there, but it's hard to feel God in the thunder of heavy trucks, much easier in quiet country lanes, woodlands, sandy beaches, calm seas and in the play of the sun on water and the light on the leaves. On the one hand, a crushing threat of danger and oppression, on the other, a sense of communion, allowing the spirit to soar far beyond oneself. The countryside and the forests gave off hints that I was not living my own life just by myself. Something Else was living in me and through me, I was part of a much bigger Mystery, I'm a mere drop in a much larger Ocean.

I stopped to rest by a wayside chapel in the midst of vineyards. The Capela de Santa Marta was built in 1817, according to a rough inscription on one of its heavy stones. Inside the furnishings were simple, but cared for with fresh flowers and electric candles. I would have lit a candle, but there were none. Instead, I thought about Maris, my wife, who decided to quit this earth ten years previously. Once, I could hear her voice quite firmly and often, gently encouraging me, but nowadays, her voice is softer and heard less often. I know that she is there, guiding me in partnership with God and helping me to overcome my many challenges. She continues to be part of my life. I continue to wear our wedding ring.

Sunday 2nd August turned out to be good steady walking. The steep climb depicted in my guidebook turned out to be a gentle incline. There were a few short stretches along a busy main road but for the most part the walking followed country lanes through forests and farm lands, at one time hugging the railway line. My back ached. I should have observed the Sabbath and taken a rest day, an internal voice complained, as I adjusted my backpack to find a more comfortable position and to ease the pain. I had been walking for eleven days since Porto. I'm only two days from Santiago. That's where I will take my rest.

I'd been following the yellow and blue arrows for thirty days. My destination was no longer distant, only 60 kilometres. Since leaving Fatima, I'd been saying the daily rosary, dedicating each decade to the welfare of family and friends and anyone else who needed help. However, each step of the Camino was a silent prayer of thanks and acceptance. The arrows were a source of comfort as I passed through towns and countryside, as I crossed bridges and hillsides. There were faithful companions, reassuring to find, and disquieting to miss. They encouraged me to keep moving forward and to leave the past behind.

The morning was misty and cool but I arrived in Caldas de Reis in fine clear weather. Just out of town I fell in with another pilgrim who told me the municipal albergue was full of school groups. I entered the town and saw the several storied *Hotel Lotus*. A large banner hung on the side of the building announced *Precio especial Peregrinos*. The rooms to the rear had balconies over-looking the river and the Ponte Romana. I enquired at the café Lotus opposite and paid 25 euro for a room, alas not overlooking the river. After a rest, I explored the town. Caldas de Reis nestles between the rios Umia and Bermaña. Its history is linked to its thermal springs that have been gushing from the grounds since pre-historic times. Celtic tribes were early inhabitants, followed by the Romans who established spas on the Via Romana XIX. In Christian times one of Spain's kings, Alfonso VII, was born here. Nowadays, Caldas de Reis is renowned as a major health spa. I passed the hot spring *Fonte Termal* where a number of pilgrims were resting their feet. I joined them. The water was hot but bearable like a warm bath. An impressive number of bars and restaurants lined the river banks. I entered one with a garden by the river and there I found Angela and Courtney. Angela was complimentary. She mentioned the times that they had to stop to rest because she was hot, tired or flustered or all three. I would turn up cool and collected. If only she knew!

If only she knew of the two inner voices I was always hearing. One was the voice of reason that told me not to listen to my tired body, that I had done this all before and succeeded, that what I worried about never happened, that I needed to live in the present, that the Camino (or Something Else or God) always looks after you, that the best and rewarding path was the one that offered challenges, that even when I had felt that I could not manage one more step, I'd gone about half the distance I was capable of. And yet, this other voice persisted, not to be conned by the voice of reason. The voice of doubt of my ability would not be silenced. It murmured to me sadly to accept the overwhelming evidence of my tired body and of my age and to act it, that I should take the easy and comfortable path. I didn't matter if I didn't finish. But the other voice jumped into the turmoil and exclaimed '*It does matter!*' Michael and Laura came by and so did Anthony and son Til. Our little Camino family was reunited, shared a meal, discussed our days and tomorrow's intentions and, before retiring to our beds, returned to the *Fonte Termal* and bathed our feet.

The walls of the *Hotel Lotus* were thin and somewhere I could hear a dripping tap. In the morning, they were setting up for a market by the Puente Romano and one of the stallholders insisted on giving me an apple, wishing me *Buen Camino!* The day was fine but by midday a misty rain settled on the pleasant countryside. Most of the walking was on pathways through forest and quiet country roads. The guidebook said there were few facilities on this stretch but I found a café for lunch. I'm not surprised that it was not on a formal list. It was under a lean-to off a private courtyard and full of junk — statues, barrels, tattered bunting, banners and flags. Everything was makeshift. The owner was eccentric but entertaining, full of knowledge about the next few kilometres to Santiago. So far, I hadn't stayed in a monastery. I had heard of the *Convento de Herbón*, a place for individual pilgrims seeking a more contemplative time under the care and hospitality of a Franciscan monastery. I enquired of the owner but he called it spartan and was not too flattering in his description. I heard the internal voice seeking comfort so I pushed on to Padrón.

The *Albergue Xunta* was full (a school group, again) but just down the road was a brand new private albergue. The dormitory and kitchen were shiny, the friendly owners reached out with a spontaneous welcome, not yet jaded by the constant flow of pilgrims. They did one's washing free. Angela, Courtney, Anthony and Til were in the dormitory, too. We went out to dinner at a pulperia and found Michael and Laura. The seven of us had dinner together. We joked about Michael and Laura's tastes. They tended to avoid the albergues and go up market, ensuring they had a room by ringing ahead. Our little Camino family dined together for the last time. How often had I shared a meal with people whom I'd known for a few days but felt they were old friends! We said goodbye to each other. The following evening we would be in Santiago, likely to be swallowed by the vast crowds. We exchanged emails and promised to keep in touch. The Camino is full of partings.

The final day to Santiago was varied. I valued the walking along natural paths through forests of oak, pine and eucalyptus but I had to face the inevitable pain of main roads that got busier the nearer to the city. I fell in with a big Italian in a bright yellow T-shirt. He asked me my age, and when I was told him I was eighty-two, he embraced me, took my photo and called me a hero. No doubt I'll feature in his reminiscences about his Camino, how he met this crazy ancient all the way from the antipodes. I met Anthony and Til on the outskirts of Santiago and together we walked through the tedious modern suburbs to the ancient quarter to the cathedral. It looked exactly the same as when I saw it four years previously, except that the front entrance was closed and blocked by scaffolding. As expected a large throng of people busied the narrow streets. To manage the crowds you had to enter the cathedral by the door to the left of the altar and exit by the right. Directly opposite was the *Seminario Mayor*, also known as *Hospederia San Martin Pinario*. Last time I stayed at the *Seminario Menor* about ten minutes away, but as I regarded the impressive building, I thought why not give it a go. They only had hotel rooms for that night, but I could change to a pilgrim room the following night. I was planning to stay two nights in Santiago. My body needed a rest after thirteen days walking from Porto and thirty-two days from Lisbon. The room was 47 euros, rather basic but I had a bed at a time of high demand.

After a rest, I ventured out into the packed streets and found my way to the pilgrim office behind the cathedral to collect my compostelle, my certificate of completion. When I passed the entrance to the courtyard earlier in the day, the queue stretched out into the street, but I was able to walk straight in into an office that reminded me of a bank with a row of tellers behind a counter. As he was not busy the young chap, himself a volunteer, who printed my compostelle had time for a chat. He asked how I found the Camino Portugués. Most pilgrims arrive via the Camino Francés. I told him that the route from Porto to Santiago was okay, the route from Lisbon had limited pilgrim infrastructure and far too much walking on busy dangerous roads. I would not recommend it. He replied that many had the same view. The situation is circular. There's limited infrastructure because fewer pilgrims walk; fewer pilgrims walk because of the limited infrastructure.

As I emerged into the busy laneway lined with bars and restaurants, I ran into Sue and Audrey, two Americans whom I had met at Rubiães. They invited me to join their friends, whom they only met that day. There were about ten of them, seated in one of the outdoor bars. They greeted me with enthusiasm and found me a seat. I sat down among them, clutching my compostelle carefully to avoid crushing or soiling it. One of them, Brendan, an Irishman, took an interest in me. He asked me my age and was intrigued. Then he dashed off and came back with a cylinder for my compostelle. I thanked him, tried to pay him but he refused. I settled down with this noisy boisterous group, enjoyed a few beers and a meal. I loved the spontaneity of this meeting, another Camino family coming together in support and congratulations. We would never see each other again, but while we shouted to each other above the din, we were bound by love and affection. How often had I witnessed this bonding! I was always in awe at the wonderful camaraderie among pilgrims. The spirit of God was busy.

22

*No one in the world can change truth. What we can do and should
do is to seek truth and to serve it when we have found it.*
—Maximillian Kolbe

F our years previously I visited Santiago. Physically, it was
the same. What was different was the mass of people
throng the streets. I was told that one thousand
pilgrims were arriving each day. The difference lay in the
increasing popularity of the Camino, particularly among the
Americans who told me they had been inspired by the film
'The Way'. The other factor lay in the timing of my visit. I had
arrived on 4th August, in the middle of the school holidays.
Four years ago, I turned up in September. Students were back
at school and university, and the walkers were mostly retirees.

I had reached my destination. My experience of previous
Camino walks taught me that the real Camino begins once
it is finished. The spiritual journey continues. My friends of
the previous night talked about a Mass in English in one of
the chapels of the cathedral. Although the door was opposite
the entrance to the Seminario, I had to go around the other
side to gain entry, which took about five minutes of jostling
through the throng. About twenty people attended the Mass,
including Brendan and his mates from the night before. We
received a welcome from Fr. Joe, an Irish priest and afterwards,
a nun invited everyone to a café around the corner for coffee.
Everyone has a sense of achievement that they had persisted
despite aching bodies, blisters and other ailments. Most people
had arrived by the Camino Francès, although no one started

back at St Jean Pied de Port back in France. They began at
Saria, a little over 100 kilometres. The minimum requirement
for receiving the compostelle was 100 kilometres of walking
or 200 kilometres of cycling.

The main event of the day was the Pilgrims' Mass at midday.
The Cathedral was packed; no chance of a seat. I enjoyed the
ritual, beginning with the spectacle of a procession of priests
in full regalia to the high altar. The countries of origin of the
day's pilgrims were read out. I heard Australia mentioned. I
looked around the congregation. I did not expect to see any
of my Camino friends; they were submerged in the multitude.
No one had a backpack. The bouncers at the door discouraged people bringing then in for both security and congestion
reasons, I guess. Yet, there were many pilgrims around me.
There were many tourists, too, people who, judging by their
physical shape, were unlikely to walk far. Yet, each had made
their own pilgrimage. I had long recognised that not everyone
walks the entire Camino carrying everything in their backpack. Many come to this shrine dedicated to St James to pray.
I found myself praying that I had arrived despite age, fatigue,
the hazard of mad drivers and other dangers. I felt a bond with
the people around me, in the same way I felt in communion
with those who had attended previous Masses right back to
the Middle Ages, with those who had walked to get here over
the last thousand years. Probably the ritual of this Mass was
not much different to the one celebrated one thousand years
ago. Pilgrims attend this Mass whether they are believers or
not. Many have never been even faintly religious. They enjoy
the ritual, the music and the unfolding of the drama. To the
believer, the Mass is far more, a celebration of the life, death
and resurrection of Jesus Christ. A catholic will recognise the
Mass no matter where or in what language. Here I heard a

mixture of Spanish and Latin but I knew exactly at what point we had arrived.

The people surged forward to receive Communion. Communion is the sharing of a meal, far more meaningful in this context. Everyone was respectful; the organ soared magnificently above our heads. A major spectacle lay in the botafumeira swinging along the nave. Every head was craned to catch a glimpse of the fuming essence and to admire the strength of six blokes working the rope. Its origin lay in the middle ages where its function was to suppress the body odour of a church full of unwashed pilgrims. Finally, the priests filed out in procession to the accompaniment of the organ at full throttle.

I endeavoured to open myself to the occasion but it did not have the same emotional experience as in 2011. On that first visit I sat in the cathedral and wept. I couldn't believe that I had completed the projects after so many years of planning. I felt the intensity of losing Maris as if it had just happened. I was in a mess and had to talk to someone, so I went to Confession. This time I was a veteran. I had walked four different routes of the Camino and had arrived at Santiago for the second time. I felt the same sense of achievement at having arrived; I felt the same hollowness of being without Maris. I was disappointed. The Camino Portugués didn't have the same sense of involvement as previous Caminos. Not until the latter stages did I meet other pilgrims with whom I could form a bond. Even then the relationships were superficial. I had no in-depth discussions. I did not speak to anyone about my motivation, why I was doing the Camino and no one shared with me. Dangerous traffic was never far away.

I could have spent the afternoon visiting the various museums and other monuments but I chose to return to the pilgrim office. I had read a notice at the *Seminario Mayor*. Using a quote from T.S.Eliot's Four Quartets *'We had the experience but missed the meaning'* the Camino Companions offered an opportunity for reflection, sharing in small groups, a quiet time to notice what was important and a debrief before returning home. I felt I had missed something, so I needed to talk to someone.

Marion was the facilitator and you met her at the pilgrim office. There was only one other, a Japanese lady, whose name, I'm sorry to say, I could not get my tongue around. Marion took us around the corner to the convent. She was an Irish nun with a lovely lilting accent. She settled us into a comfortable room, furnished for reflection with well-worn chairs and cushions. After welcome, she presented us with a series of questions and invited us to make some notes:

1. Why did you decide to walk the Camino?
2. What was the most significant for you as you walked the Camino? What did you learn from this?
3. What was the most difficult for you during this time? Did you learn anything about yourself as a result?
4. Identify any other insights about your own life, your spirituality, your friends and family, your life choices, culture and any other learning which you hope to remember for the future?
5. Are there any particular areas you want to explore further when you go home?

I tried not to dominate the discussion but I was more articulate than the Japanese lady who struggled to express in English her inner thoughts. I spoke about Maris' suicide as the emotional trigger for undertaking my first Camino and how my involvement grew from the lowest point in my life. There were two ways I could approach this tragedy in my life: as a victim or as a fighter. I was restless. I had lost my anchorage and was hoping the Camino might offer some structure. I became concerned with my Japanese friend. She was weeping and I was worried that my story may have traumatised her. I steered away from further talk of Maris and mentioned some of the significant elements of the Camino — a constant fear as to whether my body would fall apart and I would not make it, the opportunity to meet other people, how I valued the silence and the solitude. An ever-present challenge lay in the hills. The deadlier they were, the stronger the desire to quit, but I never did. I gave thanks every day. I mentioned how I tried to live every day and not be too concerned with what might happen. God seemed to look after me. What I worried about never happened. At one time, I was intolerant of pilgrims who had their baggage carried or arrived by vehicle. They were tourists in my view. I had learned not to be judgmental, to accept that there are many ways of being a pilgrim. The opportunity to meet so many people from different countries and cultures was wonderful. When I returned home I hoped that I would reach out to others and become more involved in the community.

I did not want to leave the Japanese lady in a distressed state. Having told my story, I felt a duty of care towards her. However, she seemed more relaxed. Marion reassured her as she told her story of family and marital problems. She seemed okay as we left. I thanked Marion for the opportunity to talk. The benefits of sharing can never be underestimated.

Every Spaniard, I am told, suffers distress if he doesn't have a favourite bar, and, while I was in Spain, I had one, too. It overlooks the pedestrian crossing opposite the Porto Camino leading up to the cathedral. I sat in the window and watched the people crossing. All faces were unfamiliar. I did not expect to see Angela or Courtney, Michael or Laura. Back at the *Seminario Mayor*, I changed to a pilgrim room at 23 euros, on the top floor, more austere but with the same facilities. I debated whether I would go out looking for my friends of the previous night and the morning's English Mass, but decided they probably had all gone their separate ways. Instead, I tried the set menu dinner in the Seminario's high vaulted dining room, which looked like the old rectory. There was even a pulpit where someone would have read the scriptures to the novices as they ate in silence.

The next morning Thursday 6th August I set out for the Atlantic coast. The start was misty but the day fined up. Shortly after commencing, I climbed a massive hill. If I had remembered that hill, I wonder if I would have bothered. I had already overcome its challenge, so why was I facing it again? However, I remembered the good bits — the extensive blue gum forests and the absence of heavy traffic. There was time even for silence and solitude. Last time, there were few walkers. Most people stopped at Santiago. Not this year! Walker after walker passed me, some in groups, others on their own. Several asked me my age and where I had started. Even a local inquired and described my effort as '*meritorio*'.

The nagging voice within was constant in its questioning why I was taking a route I had already covered. It complained it was sick of walking and wanted to go home. '*Get behind me, Satan*,' I muttered, but it wouldn't be silenced. The more walkers that passed me, the more anxious I was about a bed. My hope was to arrive at Vilaserio early. I had good memories of the *Albergue O Rueiro* so I inquired at the bar next door. I mentioned I had stayed there four years previously. The lady was pleased I had returned. I took a siesta and during the afternoon the pilgrims continued to arrive until there were only three beds left. Last time I looked out of the window and admired the line of tall blue gums on the ridge overlooking the village. This time they were missing, as if they had been blown down by a massive storm.

I had dinner in the bar with Vivienne who was a military policewoman in the British Army and stationed in Germany. I drank with two French guys, Oliver and Louis. They were dining at the bar and sleeping at the school house albergue, a very austere establishment with minimum facilities down the road. All three had started at Santiago and were intrigued that I was Australian and came from Lisbon.

The next morning at breakfast the lady thanked me for staying a second time and hoped to see me again. Shortly after leaving I came across a piece of pilgrim graffiti. I had read a lot in France but very little in Spain or Portugal. I enjoyed these more-or-less spontaneous reflections of previously passers-by. This one was written in English in large black letters on the trunk of a blue gum: *'Be the light of your soul. Shine!'*

The morning was cool with a strong wind. Galicia was living up to its reputation of being the windiest part of Europe. Most of the walking was through countryside. I was getting tired and that voice continued to berate me as to why I was covering the same ground. The monotony was relieved by my meeting an Italian girl who had started from home and had been walking for three months. I was impressed. I debated with myself whether I'd go to Finisterre or Muxia. I should go to Muxia because I'd been to Finisterre. However, Finisterre appealed to me as the 'real' final destination and there was more accommodation. There were many walkers so I guessed there'd be competition for a bed as it was the weekend. Another question: Do I need to walk from Finisterre to Muxia, or take a bus?

I arrived safely in Olveiroa, quite a delightful compact village, retaining much of its medieval ambience. All its detail came back to me as I walked through its narrow lanes. The municipal albergue where I stayed last time was full, so I retraced my steps back to the *Albergue Horreo* which was almost full, but they happened to have a bed in a corner of the dormitory. I was squeezed in, surrounded by a group of girls from Barcelona who were walking for five days. They seemed intrigued to, first, have a man in their midst and, secondly, that man was Australian and ancient. There was a lively bar and restaurant, full of people constantly coming and going. I quite liked being in the midst of the bustle even though I spoke to no one. I was content to be a silent observer for a change.

Sunday 9th August was fine and calm. The walking was through gentle blue gum country, mostly level with some tiresome climbs. My nagging voice continued to complain, but the other voice told me I was nearing the end of my walking. I came across more graffiti: *'Love is my religion'* in pink lettering complete with heart, a message to *'Max don't give up'* written on one of the way markers and on a rock painted in large purple letters *'Don't fuck up my zen space'* and on another rock in black letters *'Be aware of yourself.'* I was curious to know the circumstances that prompted the various authors to leave their messages behind.

The forests gave way to open fields before leaving the heights and descending to sea level. What a wonderful view to see the Atlantic! How many millions before me had been inspired and relieved to see that their destination was at hand, that they were nearing the end of the earth. I walked through the seaside villages to Cée where I stopped at the *Albergue Casa de Fonte*. It was clean and modern, looking as if it had just been opened this season. The couple running the albergue were outgoing, warm and responsive. The dormitory was large with plenty of space between the bunks. They could have fitted in twice as many bunks, such a contrast to other dormitories

I've slept in, crammed with bunks and barely enough room to deposit your pack. I introduced myself to a lady across from me. Herma was Dutch. She had begun walking at León. We explored the town together, found a bar for a coffee and returned later for a meal. We talked about motivation. She had three sons. Her greatest concern was her eldest son whom she rang every day. Nils was thirty-six and was unsuccessfully trying to rid himself of his addiction to drugs. I sensed her pain. My mind raced back to the many calls I had taken at Lifeline from young men who were despairing of ever overcoming their addiction. I saw them at risk just as I sensed Nils was. I said to Herma that parents felt the same anguish as their children, that it was normal for people with addictions to have relapses. It was important that they don't despair and never give up giving up (to use the slogan from the ad.) She asked me why I was walking. I told her of Maris, the first time I had mentioned her suicide to anyone on this Camino. This was the first time I felt it appropriate. Herma had opened up to me. Although we had known each other for an hour or so, we formed a bond that allowed us to trust each other.

We were warmly farewelled the following morning. The distance to Finisterre was short, only 13 kilometres but the walking was painful. My body was telling me it had had enough. I walked along the beach. The weather was fine enough for swimming and many walkers had taken advantage of the mild conditions to strip and enter the water. Someone was looking after me when I entered Finisterre. As I left the beach I paused to read a notice: *'Rooms with Breakfast and Shower'*. The message was repeated in German and French. I walked around to the *Pensión Lubina* and in the bar/reception I met Herma. She had booked ahead but the gentleman whose room she was going to take decided to stay another night. The owner, a big German lady who had little Spanish, had put her in a two-bedroom apartment up on the road away from the beach. I was told there was no room at the pensión, but Herma explained that she did not mind if I took the other room. So I found myself in this holiday apartment grateful to Herma for her intervention. I rested for the afternoon pleased that I was walking no longer. I had left myself three days to walk perhaps to Muxia and take a bus back. However, the trip would require two buses with an awkward connection requiring several hours of waiting. I decided to scrap Muxia and spend three nights in this very comfortable holiday apartment with Ikea furnishings and a great view along the beach and sea. I went out later to buy stuff for breakfast and visited the municipal albergue where I stayed last time to collect my compostelle for the 90 kilometres walk from Santiago. The lady got out of her seat, came around the desk and gave me a hug. Perhaps, that's something she keeps for the octogenarians plus because she mentioned she gave a ninety-year-old her compostelle earlier in the week. Herma and I had dinner together at a nearby restaurant. She had walked to the lighthouse and was disappointed because it was overrun by tourists all of whom had arrived by coach.

Next morning Herma moved back into a room at the Pensión, leaving me in the apartment. Nobody came to boot me out, so I stayed for two more nights. The German lady was rather lax in her registration routine. She hadn't taken any of my details. I had a genuine rest day. Rain kept me off the beach and inside. I dozed and mindlessly watched television, including an Italian movie dubbed in Spanish about the son of Spartacus. I mused over my achievement... I left Lisbon thirty-eight days ago. I passed thirty-two days walking and six rest days, three at Fatima and one each at Coimbra, Porto and Santiago. I had covered 705 kilometres, 95 by bus. Not a bad achievement for an octogenarian! I sent texts to the family in Australia and to Mat and Laura in Lisbon. I had made it.

In the afternoon when the rain had turned into a mist, I ventured out, collected five shells from the beach and bought enough items to cook my own dinner. How I enjoyed pottering about in the kitchen, using every utensil and enjoying a glass of red on the way. I felt rested and almost ready to start walking again, but my body reminded me to maintain my resolve to quit. Next morning the rain was heavy. I felt for the walkers in heavy wet weather gear passing below on the street but I was content that I'd finished walking and was not one of them. I was dry, warm and comfortable. I was lethargic and wasn't inclined to get wet if I could avoid it.

The family replied to my texts with congratulations. I felt proud of my family, of my daughters, Angela and Jacinta, and sons, Stephen and Tim. I was proud of my seven grandchildren and looked forward to seeing them again. I thought of my Maris and mused over the many happy times we had together as a family. I chose to reflect on her life rather than the circumstances of her death. I recalled a time we had a brief break from the kids, leaving Angela who was five years older to look after the family. Each evening, we rang to see how things were at home and spoke to each of the children. When we came to Tim who was the youngest, we would hear Angela in the background with: '*Be happy!*' Angela loved her role of being the little mother and the younger children respected her. They were not to worry mum and dad with minor complaints. Just a simple little memory, but part of the fabric of our family life.

After lunch I roused myself from my torpor and ventured out into the rain. I clad myself in my wet weather gear and walked the five kilometres to the lighthouse. The rain and wind had not kept away the tourists. They had arrived by car and coach, the comfort seekers had stayed in their vehicles but the venturesome were milling around the lighthouse and climbing down the exposed rocks tumbling down to the sea, little groups everywhere. The wind was cold and wet. I found a sheltered nook down near the sea and watched the waves of rainy mist sweeping past. The sea was barely visible. Today that mist looked as if it was always there but what a contrast to the last time when the sky was cloudless and I could see the vast Atlantic Ocean stretching to America. I sat in my shelter under a ledge facing the mist and the sea beyond. I could see no one else. I felt in solitude and stayed with the moment. I listened to the sounds of the restless sea, the waves breaking over the rocks below. I was humbled, immersed in a raw force, unfettered and unforgiving, capable of taking my breath away with both its magnificence and its ruthlessness. I was mesmerised, under the magic of this sacred place where pilgrims for the last thousand years have wrestled with the wonders of creation and of their achievement.

I felt the emotion swelling out of my gut. I shed a tear just as I wept four years ago. I thought of Maris and wished she was here with me, both our hearts full of gratitude as we stared out through the misty rain to the invisible Atlantic and the Americas beyond. She wrote journals and included useful quotes from her reading as part of her efforts to manage her depression. They are a record of her deeper thoughts. I've kept these journals, mostly in exercise books, in a cupboard on what was her side of our bed. I have glanced through them cursorily but, perhaps, I now have the strength, ten years after her death, to go through them in detail after I return home.

The spell was broken by a noisy family scrambling down the slippery rocks into my secret place. Time to move! I edged myself closer to the restless sea and threw the last two stones I had brought from my garden in Jindabyne, a symbol of leaving behind my past life and its erring ways.

I would have enjoyed a warm drink but the coffee shop was closed and looking forlorn, as if it hadn't traded for the season. I braced myself against the wind and heavy rain and walked downhill back to the town and to the comfort of my apartment. I was warm and cosy and enjoyed preparing my meal. I spent the evening watching Spanish television (Galician version) and listening to the steady rain lashing the windows, pleased that I wasn't out in it. I hoped and prayed that all my fellow pilgrims had found shelter, too. I was grateful I hadn't walked to Muxia. It would have been a soggy end to my pilgrimage.

I met Herma at the bus stop for Santiago and we sat together and shared our experience. She was returning to Holland and I was returning to Australia. I mentioned that I had thought a lot about her son Nils and had included him in my list of people needing prayer. She was gratified that I had taken the time to think of him. He was her greatest concern at the moment. We said goodbye ('*Buen Camino!*') at the bus station. She was taking a bus to the airport and I was returning to the *Seminario Mayor* for another two nights before taking the train to Madrid on Saturday. I made the midday pilgrim Mass and had lunch in my favourite bar watching the waves of pilgrims crossing the road. I did not expect to see any familiar faces. Everyone whom I had met would have been home by now.

That evening in the bar at *Seminario Mayor* I heard Aussie accents so I introduced myself to the group. They were four Australians, husbands and wives, who had arrived that day after walking from St Jean-Pied-de-Port. One of the men mentioned that he had heard me speak about my book on the Camino at a Probus Club at Newport on Sydney's northern beaches where I used to live. In fact, my talk had compelled him to find out more and to encourage his friend and wife to accompany them. And here they were! What a piece of feedback! To think that I had inspired someone!

The next morning, I attended the English Mass. Father Joe was the celebrant, the kindly old Irishman. He was a volunteer along with his helpers who spend their time ministering to the pilgrims as they arrive in Santiago. I recognised some of the helpers from the previous week. Among the familiar faces was Brendan, the Irishman who bought me a cylinder for my Compostelle. The theme of Fr. Joe's homily was: *'Everything is a gift from God'*. It's a familiar message but it needs repeating to remind us constantly of our dependence. If you think you're in control, you're dreaming. Often, on the Camino, when I wasn't sure of where my next bed was, I would think *'It's in God's hands.'* Others used to say *'The Camino will look after you'*, which is probably another way of saying the same thing.

Fr. Joe gave us a pilgrims' blessing, the message being: Now that you've finished your Camino, the real Camino begins.

'As you kept us safe on our Camino way, may you keep us safe on our journey home. And, inspired by our experience here, may we live out the values of the Gospel, as our pilgrimage through life continues.'

After Mass, everyone went for coffee in the nearby bar/café. It was a different group of people to the previous time but they had the same experience. We are many, but the Camino makes us one. Brendan came too. He asked how I found Finisterre. I said I was pleased to find him here. He was still hanging around, he replied, still finding himself. I wished him well in his search and commented we are all searching.

I attended my last midday Pilgrim Mass. Another massive crowd was in attendance. It was the feast day of Maximillian

Kolbe, a Polish priest most famous for volunteering to die in place of a stranger at Auschwitz concentration camp. His writings are often quoted, among the most famous is:

'No one in the world can change truth. What we can do and should do is to seek truth and to serve it when we have found it.'

A fitting message for a pilgrim Mass!

As I watched the drama of the Mass unfold, I reflected on what had been accomplished. The Camino presented many challenges. If I had walked a Camino without challenges, it would be useless, just another holiday, just a pleasant way to pass the time. The Camino presented many difficulties but they made me strong. It gave me problems to solve, dangers to overcome, people to help and encourage. The challenges and difficulties were opportunities for growth. The greater the struggle, the more enriching the experience. It enabled me to discover the true meaning of gratitude when I encountered the warm kindness of strangers. It gave me the opportunity to be humble, to accept that I was not in control, it gave me the realisation that God had given me everything I needed to reach my destination. I learned many lessons. I discovered many truths about myself, all relevant to my life beyond the Camino. I need to release myself from pre-occupations that blind me to all that is life-giving in the present. My life has the potential to unfold unlimitedly. Through the power of strong inner resolve, I have the potential to transform myself, those around me and the world in which I live.

The soaring organ music was like an epiphany as if I was hearing the voice of God. The real Camino begins once I leave this beautiful Santiago cathedral and return home. The floods have receded, the river has broadened and I'm sailing in calmer waters. The swirling waters have subsided but my personal journey will continue. My pilgrimage is far from over. I'll continue to grow. I'll continue my search for truth and meaning. I'll continue to seek answers to questions that may never be answered. I'll never stop puzzling over potential answers. Ambiguity is part of life. I'll never reach the heights of love of Maximillian Kolbe but I'll work on finding myself by losing myself in the service of others.

My pilgrimages have breathed a new zest to my octogenarian spirit. My whole life is a pilgrimage.

I guess I'll just keep on walking.

Acknowledgements

I wish to thank Mat Edmunds for permission to use his photographs on the front and back cover. Thanks, too, to the Camino Companions, Santiago, from whom I received a copy of the Beatitudes of the Pilgrim.

I am thankful for the following books which were the source of quotations used in this text; Janine Casevecchie: *Une idée par jour de spiritualité*. Editiones duChêne. 2009. Daisaku Ikeda : *Buddhism for You*. Determination. Middleway Press. 2006

The following are guide books I used along the way.

François Lepère et André Dehnel: *Sur le Chemin de Saint-Jacques-de-Compostelle (La via Tolosana, la voie de soleil...)* Lepère Editions.

Mireille Retail et Marie-Virginie Cambriels : *Miam Miam Do Do. Le Chemin de Saint Jacques de Compostelle. La Voie d'Arles/ Camino Aragonés*. Les Editions du Vieux Crayon 2010-2011.

John Brierley : *A Pilgrim's Guide to the Camino Portugés*. Camino Guides 2014.

André Dehnel, François Lepère et Céline Heckman : *Sur le Chemin de Saint-Jacques- de-Compostelle (Le Chemin portugais, la Via lusiitana...)* Lepère Editions 2011.

The following I found useful spiritual guides :

Jill Kimberly Hartwell Geoffrion : *Praying the Labyrinth. A Journey for Spiritual Exploration*. The Pilgrim Press. 1999.

Jill Kimberly Hartwwell Geoffrion: *Praying the Chartres Labyrinth. A Pilgrim's Guidebook*. The Pilgrim Press. 2006.

Gaële de la Brosse (ed.): *Guide Spirituel de Chemins de Saint-Jacques*. Presses de la Renaissance. 2010.

Guide Spirituel du Pèlerin en Chemin avec Saint-Jacques. Communauté des Prémontrés, Abbaye Sainte Foy, Conques. 2008.

Finally, thanks to my patient proof readers, friend Margaret and daughter Angela, both legends in their own way.

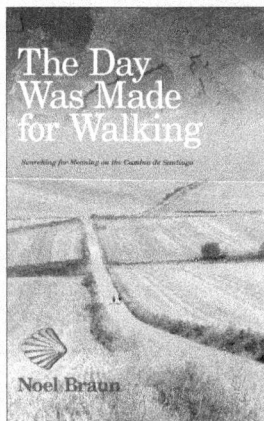

The Day
Was Made
for Walking

Searching for Meaning on the Camino de Santiago

Noel Braun

N oel Braun yearns to walk the Camino, the ancient pilgrimage route that leads across France and Spain to Santiago de Compostela. Since the suicide of Maris, his beloved wife of forty-two years, he has struggled to find himself. But is it pure madness? He's an old bloke. At seventy-seven-years, he should be sensible, act his age and relax in a rocking chair. Can his body and spirit withstand the demands? Can he leave family and friends behind? Noel believes this is a journey he MUST undertake. It's a compulsion, a spiritual quest of self-discovery, an urgent need to commune with the world around and beyond him.

When Noel begins his journey, he discovers it's not just the rigorous demands of the physical world he must answer. The territory of the heart and soul has its own challenges, which have him searching for spiritual and emotional insights. His travels are interwoven with accounts of the many engaging characters he meets. In time he realises he himself is one of the Camino's characters.

The Day Was Made for Walking merges the spiritual with the physical, the ancient with the contemporary. It is a memoir, but also a glimpse into history and a travel guide..

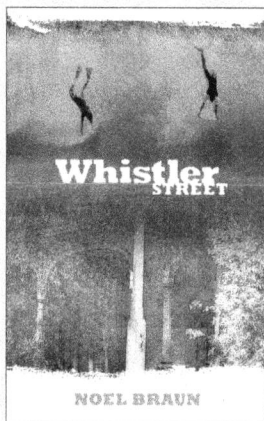

After a childhood in the Western Australian surf, Vince Kelly, burning with a desire to save mankind, enters the Catholic priesthood. In contrast, his beach mate, Jamie Griffiths, lacking any direction, drifts into a disastrous job and marriage.

Following his unwitting involvement in Jamie's mother's death, Vince suffers an emotional and spiritual crisis, shattering all his former rock solid beliefs. In desperation, he quits both Perth and the priesthood. He crosses the desert to Sydney and settles in Manly, hoping to find new meaning and purpose.

As soon as he sees the quaint Federation house in Whistler Street, he knows it's an ideal refuge for his recovery. He transforms the house into a home, makes new friends and begins to rebuild his life but is plagued with indecision and guilt.

Back in Perth the despairing Jamie cries for help. Already guilt-ridden at abandoning his lifelong mate, Vince leaves Manly, painfully aware that on his return he must make some vital decisions about his own direction.

Braun is a deft writer ... good storytelling ... with a revelation at the end that strengthens the work. A good read.'
—Wendy O'Hanlon, *Acres Australia*

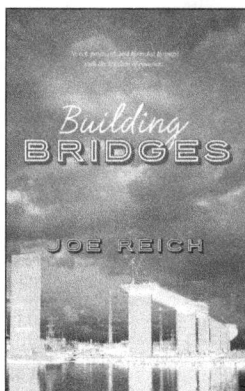

New Releases... also from Sid Harta Publishers

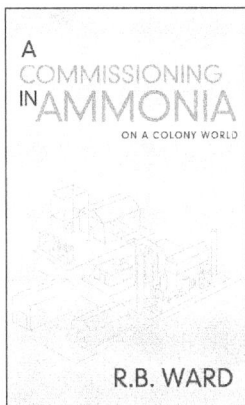

A COMMISSIONING IN AMMONIA
ON A COLONY WORLD
R.B. WARD

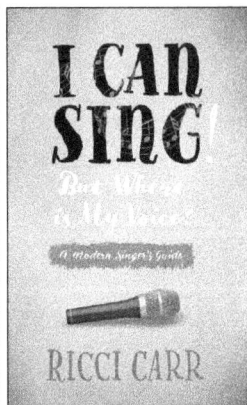

I CAN SING!
But Where is My Voice?
A Modern Singer's Guide
RICCI CARR

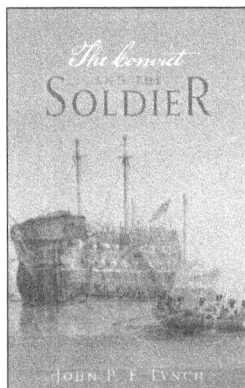

The Convict AND THE SOLDIER
JOHN P. F. LYNCH

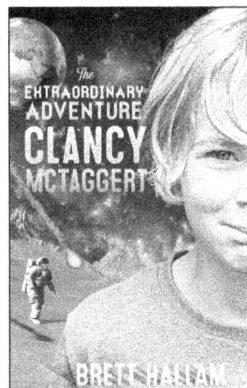

THE EXTRAORDINARY ADVENTURE CLANCY MCTAGGERT
BRETT HALLAM

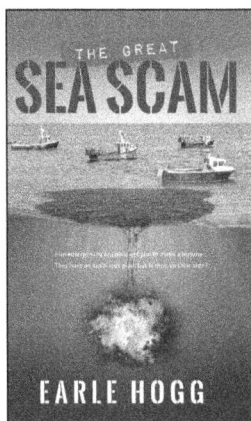

THE GREAT SEA SCAM
EARLE HOGG

Best-selling titles by Kerry B. Collison

New Releases... also from Sid Harta Publishers

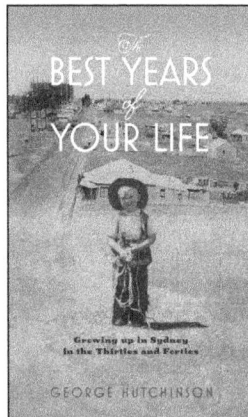

THE
THREADS
OF TIME

DAVE CRAWFORD

The Song of
MAWU

JEFF EDWARDS

Eliyahu's
MISTRESS

ROGER MENDELSON

TO HELL
AND BACK

A Policewoman's Story

CAROLYN PETHICK

The
BEST YEARS
of
YOUR LIFE

Growing up in Sydney
In the Thirties and Forties

GEORGE HUTCHINSON